F V

Illuminated Fantasy

Illuminated Fantasy

From Blake's Visions to Recent Graphic Fiction

James Whitlark

Rutherford ● *Madison* ● *Teaneck*
Fairleigh Dickinson University Press
London and Toronto: Associated University Presses

© 1988 by Associated University Presses, Inc.

Associated University Presses
440 Forsgate Drive
Cranbury, NJ 08512

Associated University Presses
25 Sicilian Avenue
London WC1A 2QH, England

Associated University Presses
P.O. Box 488, Port Credit
Mississauga, Ontario
Canada L5G 4M2

The paper used in this publication meets the requirements
of the American National Standard for Permanence of Paper
for Printed Library Materials Z39.48-1984.

Library of Congress Cataloging-in-Publication Data

Whitlark, James, 1948–
Illuminated fantasy.

Bibliography: p.
Includes index.
1. Fantastic fiction—Illustrations.   2. Science fic-
tion—Illustrations.   3. Visual perception.   I. Title.
PN3435.W49   1988   741.6′09   86-46326
ISBN 0-8386-3305-6 (alk. paper)

Printed in the United States of America

Contents

Acknowledgments

SINCE THE SPECIAL COLLECTIONS STAFF OF REGENSTEIN LIBRARY (AT THE UNI-versity of Chicago) found for me an unlisted cache of rare comic books—the day my research began—I have received varied assistance. First, I wish to express my gratitude to the pioneers of my discipline, notably the virtual founder of Religion in Literature, Dr. Nathan A. Scott, Jr., Chair of the Department of Religious Studies, University of Virginia. Next, I thank my colleagues for acts of kindness too numerous to detail. Also, I acknowledge my indebtedness to Dr. Harry Keyishian, the Chair of the Editorial Board of Fairleigh Dickinson University Press, and Dr. Bernard Levine, who care-fully read an earlier draft of my manuscript. In writing to copyright owners on three continents, I have received much help and encouragement, par-ticularly from those artists whom I reached personally, each invariably granting permission gratis, with Philippe Druillet even penning an original drawing on his response from France.

To the publishers and individuals listed below (in the order of their appearance), I am grateful for permission to reprint the following pictures:

Philippe Druillet, "Yragael," from *Heavy Metal,* July 1982. Text by Demuth, translated by Pauline Tennant. Reprinted by courtesy of Philippe Druillet, Colombes, France. All rights reserved.

Garry Trudeau, "Doonesbury" strip, *Tales from The Margaret Mead Taproom,* by Nicholas von Hoffman and Garry B. Trudeau. Kansas City: Sheed and Ward, 1976. Reprinted by permis-sion of Universal Press Syndicate, Kansas City. All rights reserved.

Dan Barry and Bob Fujitani, *The Amazing Adventures of Flash Gordon,* 16 March, 1977. © 1977 King Features Syndicate, Inc., New York. Reprinted by permission. All rights reserved.

Esteban Maroto, picture from *The Magic Goes Away* by Larry Niven, published by Grosset and Dunlap, New York, 1978. Copyright © by Larry Niven. Reprinted by permission of S. I. International, New York, All rights reserved.

Dave Morice, pictures for John Keats's "La Belle Dame Sans Merci" from David Morice's *Poetry Comics: A Cartooniverse of Poems* (1982), Simon and Schuster, New York. Courtesy of Dave Morice, St. Louis. All rights reserved.

Von, pictures from *Macbeth: The Folio Edition.* New York: Oval Projects/ Workman Publishing, © 1982. Reprinted by permission of the publisher. All rights reserved.

Dave Morice, pictures for Samuel Taylor Coleridge's "Kubla Khan" from David Morice's *Poetry Comics: A Cartooniverse of Poems,* Simon and Schuster (1982), New York. Courtesy of Dave Morice, St. Louis. All rights reserved.

Lewis Carroll's own drawing in "Alice's Adventures under Ground" from *The Complete Illustrated Works of Lewis Carroll,* edited by Edward Guiliano. Copyright © 1982, published by Crown Publishers, Inc., New York. Reprinted by permission of the publisher.

Sir John Tenniel's picture in "Alice's Adventures in Wonderland," from *The Complete Illustrated Works of Lewis Carroll,* edited by Edward Guiliano. Copyright © 1982, published by Crown Publishers, Inc., New York. Reprinted by permission of the publisher.

Eleven of the Major Arcana of the Swiss Marseille Tarot cards. Reproduced by courtesy of the Trustees of the British Museum, London, and the Robert Harding Picture Library Ltd., London, as agent for the Rainbird Publishing Group's photographic archive, London.

The remaining eleven of the Major Arcana of the Swiss Marseille Tarot cards. Reproduced by courtesy of the Trustees of the British Museum and the Robert Harding Picture Library Ltd., as agent for the Rainbird Publishing Group's photographic archive, London.

Mike Vosburg and Frank Chiarmonte, picture in *Isis,* Oct/Nov. 1977 issue. ISIS is a trademark of DC Comics Inc., New York, and is used by permission. Copyright © 1977 DC Comics Inc. All rights reserved.

Front cover of *The Mad Morality or the Ten Commandments Revisited* by Vernard Eller. Copyright © 1970 by Abingdon Press, Nashville, the publisher; Alfred E. Newman © 1986 by E. C. Publications, Inc., New York. Reprinted by permission of both publishers. All rights reserved.

Sir John Tenniel, picture from *Through the Looking-Glass.* Reprinted from *The Complete Illustrated Works of Lewis Carroll,* edited by Edward Guiliano. Copyright © 1982. Used by permission of Crown Publishers, Inc., New York.

Gene Day, picture from *Kung Fu,* November 1982. Copyright © 1982 by Marvel Comics Group, the publisher, New York. Reprinted by permission. All rights reserved.

Nancy Etheredge, jacket art of *The Tao of Pooh* by Benjamin Hoff. Copyright © 1982 by Benjamin Hoff. Reproduced by permission of the publisher, E. P. Dutton, New York, a division of New American Library, which holds the rights covering the United States, Canada, and the Open Market; and also by permission of Methuen Children's Books, of London, which holds the rights covering the British market. All rights reserved.

M. C. Escher, picture of "Drawing Hands," from Bruno Ernst, *The Magic Mirror of M. C. Escher* (1967), published by Ballantine Books, Inc., New York. Reprinted by permission of © M. C. Escher Heirs, c/o Cordon Art-Baarn-Holland. All rights reserved.

Ioanna Salajan, pictures from *Zen Comics.* Copyright by the publisher, Charles E. Tuttle Co., Inc., Tokyo, 1974. Reprinted by permission. All rights reserved.

Ioanna Salajan, pictures from *Zen Comics.* Copyright by the publisher, Charles E. Tuttle Co., Inc., Tokyo, 1974. Reprinted by permission. All rights reserved.

Frederick Franck, picture in *EveryOne, The Timeless Myth of Everyman Reborn,* published by Doubleday and Co., Inc., New York. © 1978 by Frederick Franck. By permission of Joan Daves, New York, the agent for Frederick Franck. All rights reserved.

Paul Reps, picture in *Zen Telegrams.* Copyright by the publisher, Charles E. Tuttle Co., Inc., Tokyo, 1959. Reprinted by permission. All rights reserved.

Introduction

THE CENTRAL AND LATER DECADES OF THE TWENTIETH CENTURY HAVE NOT only been marked by the popularity of fantasy in general but of fantastic graphics in particular. Thousands of specialty shops disseminate this visual vogue. In these odd amalgams of Arabian bazaar, spaceport emporium, and bargain basement, classic picture books by William Blake and Lewis Carroll sometimes vie for a place near graphics journals and diagrams of the starship *Enterprise*. The screening of major fantasy films, many of them inspired by comics, is typically coordinated with the appearance of comic-book versions. These continually join the garish heaps of other current comics. Older, more expensive issues occupy places of security, with a mint-condition copy of *Action Comics,* no. 1 (the 1938 premier of Superman) selling for $30,000 in 1986.[1] Collectors scrutinize finds from the "Golden Age" of comics—the period during World War II when total sales occasionally exceeded 40 million copies a month, more than any other kind of magazine at the time.[2] Connoisseurs of more recent art lounge against the nearest available wall and thumb through adult fantasy periodicals (e.g., *Epic and Heavy Metal*). These feature a wide variety of visual styles, including the almost photographic precision of Boris Vallejo, the grotesque cartoons of the French artist Moebius (Jean Giraud), and the virtually baroque ornateness of Philippe Druillet. In the general chaos, clerks seldom bother to separate science fiction from fantasy, often a difficult task because many books combine the two.

In their unmingled forms, though, a real difference divides these genres—a difference that helps define each. Science and traditional "hard" science fiction (based on disciplines closely related to mathematics) favor consistent, logical extrapolation from plausible premises. Illustrators of such science fiction should make certain that their drawings accurately and literally con-

11

Philippe Druillet, "Yragael," from Heavy Metal, *July 1982.* (Reprinted by courtesy of Philippe Druillet.)

form to the text. Because of its consistency, science fiction long ago acquired a modicum of respectability—not sufficient to satisfy its fans but enough so that bookstores often group both science fiction and fantasy under the former label. Being dreamlike, fantasy has less to do with logic and possibility; where, as often, there are pictures, their linkage to the words is ideally as complex as the structure of visions. This relationship may even be like that in elaborate medieval gospel books, where fantastic depictions of plants and animals ornament manuscript borders with little or no connection to the Holy Writ. In conventional terminology, such pictures illuminate—not illustrate—their script; by extension, the word "illumination" will be used throughout for pictures with a devious or dubious relationship to their texts, regardless of the pictures' styles.

As a genre relatively new to academic consideration, fantasy even lacks a universally accepted definition, and no one has adequately studied the general differences between the literalness of illustration and the paradoxes of illumination. Literary criticism needs this distinction; without it, confusions arise. In an article about George Cruikshank (Dicken's illuminator), J. Hillis Miller theorizes that in fictional works, the relationship of text and picture is "a complex and problematic reference between two radically different kinds of sign, the linguistic and the graphic."[3] Conversely, in his *Elements of Semiology,* Roland Barthes argues that "in . . . cinema, advertising, comic strips, press photography, etc. . . . at least a part of the iconic message is . . . either redundant or taken up by the linguistic system."[4] Miller's emphasis on complexity accords with illumination and Barthes's stress on a close link between visual and verbal imagery fits illustration, but neither definition describes as large a body of graphic literature as its author seems to intend.

The contrast may best be seen by scrutinizing samples from each genre, first a fantastic Doonesbury comic strip in which President Ford plans to attack American Samoa.[5] According to previous strips, Duke, the governor of that territory, has engaged in every conceivable form of corruption and barbarism, culminating in the seizure of an American cruise ship. Finally, his superiors contemplate action. In conflict with Barthes's generalization, the pictures duplicate none of the textual imagery, but maintain, at most, an analogy between the two, as when the golf flag collapses at the emotional climax of the conversation. The date, style, and content of the dialogue suggest that the speakers are Ford and Henry Kissinger, who are not shown. Instead, by drawing speech lines to the president's mansion, Garry Trudeau gives pictorial form to the common expression, "The White House says" (an expression, by the way, that he does *not* use in the text of the cartoon). Further complicating matters, in the second frame, two mountains appear behind the building, are replaced by a single one in the third, and by an eroded crag in the fourth, as if millions of years have elapsed. Although each

DOONESBURY

Garry Trudeau, "Doonesbury" strip, from Tales from the Margaret Mead Taproom, *1976. Copyright G. B. Trudeau.* (Reprinted with permission of Universal Press Syndicate. All rights reserved.)

panel looks relatively realistic taken by itself, the entire sequence so inexplicably violates time and space that it as well deserves to be called fantasy as Druillet's alien scenes. Trudeau earned a Pulitzer Prize for editorial art in White House strips marked by comparable inconsistencies. Political cartooning tends to mix real and impossible images (see chapter 4). As long as their *relationship* is paradoxical, the elements may be as prosaic as artist and author choose. Indeed, such verisimilitude heightens the fantastic effect (see chapter 11). Far from focusing on reassuring duplication between text and picture (as in Barthes's above-mentioned statement about comic strips), any valid approach to fantasy in comics must analyze what Miller calls the "complex and problematic reference between two radically different kinds of signs."

In science-fiction comic strips, though, Barthes's emphasis seems more suitable. Typically, a "Flash Gordon" strip dated 16 March (1977) shows figures watching the arrival of a futuristic vehicle. Combining the upper portion of a plane with the lower section of a hydrofoil, the craft descends straight down from the sky like a helicopter.[6] By the conventions of comic-strip art, the thick-necked character's crude grammar matches his squat form as neatly as the term "vertical-landing jet" does the aircraft. The artist has used some (but not much) imagination to extrapolate from present forms to the future ones mentioned in the text. Admittedly, visual and verbal images

Dan Barry and Bob Fujitani, The Amazing Adventures of
Flash Gordon, *16 March 1977. (© 1977 King Features
Syndicate, Inc. Reprinted by permission.)*

are always in a sense inherently different, but in this case speculations on that difference do not appreciably further interpretation of the story.

According to the Hugo Award-winning artist Vincent DiFate (speaking at a 1983 meeting of the Science Fiction Research Association in Midland, Michigan), illustration has sometimes fallen short of the ideal. In the 1940s, for example, publishers began hiring surrealists for book covers, perhaps merely because both stories and art seemed strange to them; but even relatively surreal science-fiction writing did not become common until the new wave of the 1950s. New-wave stories investigate complex and sometimes contradictory patterns of the mind, approaching fantasy.[7] Thus, artists might with almost equal reasonableness illuminate the fantasy elements or illustrate the science-fiction ones. This has been a common problem because the new wave merely made the mixing of fantasy and science fiction respectable. That combination of genres frequently occurred in the pulps, but was too often incompetent through confusion about what was scientifically possible. DiFate, however, accurately observed that illustration of science fiction has once again gained prominence.

As an example of modern science-fiction illustration at its best, consider *Empire: A Visual Novel* with pictures by Howard Chaykin and text by the multiple Hugo and Nebula Award winner Samuel Delany. In addition to the hardware so prominent in early science fiction (such as the futuristic aircraft in the "Flash Gordon" strip), Delany's work focuses on software and other information systems. A rebellion sweeps the Empire, but its object is not merely to overthrow oppressors and their intergalactic battle cruisers but to destroy the monopolistic control of information by a group called the Kunduke. Many of the people, though, are content in their ignorance, such as a miner of the hell city Malabolge, who rises momentarily to the bright surface only to retreat in terror to the "comforting darkness" below.[8] Just as Delany writes for a public sophisticated enough to expect more than the old shibboleths, Chaykin draws for connoisseurs, who appreciate (and are willing to pay for) expensive paper, careful reproduction, almost photographic realism, and even occasional trompe l'oeil. For instance, part of one picture (e.g., a face, a meteor, a splash of blood) may project beyond its border, giving an illusion of three-dimensionality, but also of a world where conventional boundaries are breaking down—precisely the kind of empire that Delany describes. Here the book has much in common with fantasy, which is also characterized by the violation of conventional expectations. Delany, though, does not plunge the reader into the chaos of pure fantasy, where scientific information would be meaningless, nor does Chaykin destroy science fiction's traditionally firm link between picture and word. As Delany explained to me in a January 1983 interview, Chaykin's illustrations revealed to Delany a new dimension in his own work. These paintings show that there is no direction in the weightless vastness of outer space, a theme that Delany subsequently elaborated on in his introduction to *Empire*. Thus, in the end, his skill at analysis translates even this aspect of the pictures into words, making the bond between word and picture even firmer. His concern to fit facts accurately into a theory is typical of good science fiction. As Kingsley Amis contends in his *New Maps of Hell,* "science fiction . . . maintains a respect for fact or presumptive fact[;] fantasy makes a point of flouting these. . . ."9

Just as science fiction has been coming closer to fantasy, so fantasy is approaching science fiction in "science fantasy," a subgenre called "rivets and sorcery" by Larry Niven (another Nebula and Hugo Award-winning author).10 In an essay appended to Niven's science-fantasy novel *The Magic Goes Away* (1978), Sandra Miesel describes works of this type as employing an "internally consistent" extrapolation from impossible premises. Science fantasy is written in such a way that "it must not be taken at face value."11 In other words, it has a tendency toward allegory. In Niven's *The Magic Goes Away,* for instance, the energy crisis of the late 1970s is allegorized into a predicament in 12,000 B.C. when, according to Niven, sorcerers depleted the natural resource of mana, a Melanesian word used by Niven to signify a preternatural energy that gives power to their enchantments. The reader's pleasure derives partly from seeing a familiar situation in new terms, not in supposing there ever was or will be precisely a "mana crisis." As Niven emphasizes consistency, so the pictures come very close to being illustrations, but as his text is not to "be taken at face value," so also with the art. The cover by Boris Vallejo shows a muscular barbarian leading a voluptuous sorceress through the clouds, while a skull larger than a man looms behind them. Although a normal-sized human skull plays a part in the story, this unnaturally enlarged one is Vallejo's own allegory of threatening death. Similarly, a number of the internal illustrations by Esteban Maroto depict incredibly large moons, varying from slightly above normal to gigantic proportions (even though Niven offers no such description). The moon, however, does figure prominently in the narrative as a contemplated mana source. The arabesquelike intricacy of Maroto's style, as well as the massive lunar shapes, adds a haunting alien quality to the scenes, suggesting dreamlike adventure. Because of some significant independence from the texts, the pictures are illuminations. (Comparably, medieval illuminations also make important figures larger than realism allows.)

While the above-mentioned "Doonesbury" episode represents an extreme of complexity and *The Magic Goes Away* constitutes greater—though not total—consistency between picture and text, the average falls somewhere in between, as in *New Tales of the Arabian Nights* by Richard Corben and Jan Strnad. Harlan Ellison's introduction to this adaptation sets the stage by

Esteban Maroto picture from The Magic Goes Away *by Larry Niven, 1978.* (Copyright © by Larry Niven. Reprinted by permission of S. I. International.)

wishing for the impossible—to voyage with Sinbad, even though Ellison realizes that "if [Sinbad] ever really lived, he was probably [just] some poor Middle Eastern fisherman with a gift for self-aggrandizement." Furthermore, even if such an adventure were possible, who would really want to confront the monsters that Sinbad described? There is generally as self-contradictory a quality to the wishes that fantasies vicariously grant as to the fantasies themselves. Appropriately, Corben's style is itself inconsistent, juxtaposing photographic realism in some scenes with childishly crude sketches of legendary creatures that look like mere blobs of paint—which, of course, they are.

The style of Shahrazad, the narrator, is sanctimonious as she attempts to discourage her sister from deserting the harem where Muslim law holds them. Corben's sensationalistic pictures, however, glorify adventure (the wild aspect of the work to which Ellison responds). These styles conflict throughout the book, particularly at the climax: in Shahrazad's tale to her sister, scarcely has a terrible but pious genie finished lecturing Sinbad on the evils of impetuous conduct when Sinbad suddenly seizes the heroine, leaps with her onto a flying carpet, throws their clothes overboard, and flies toward new discoveries. Shahrazad piously comments, "And so, through humility and service to Allah, Sinbad . . . found contentment and peace."[12] As Shahrazad concludes her sermon against adventure, the illumination shows her sister eloping with an African sailor. This contrast between unctious text and irreverent pictures belongs to a pattern common in fantasy: supernatural, often bizarrely religious ideas joined to antireligious sentiments. Similarly, in Niven's *The Magic Goes Away,* sorcerers rebel against the last deity in existence and, in previous episodes of the cited "Doonesbury" strip, a virgin angers a volcano deity by refusing to sacrifice herself. Why would anyone find strange gods, paradoxes, and picture/text discrepancies intriguing? Analyzing this problem of what makes illuminated fantasy marketable requires the use of such disciplines as psychology, including recent clinical research.

To some extent this is beginning to be done as in Martin Bridgstock's 1982 article entitled, "A Psychological Approach to 'Hard' Science Fiction." He hypothesizes that both fantasy and fantasy-tinged new-wave science fiction appeal to a different personality type than "hard" science fiction.[13] The hard variety (which particularly emphasizes consistency) is presumably more congenial to the kind of person the psychologist Liam Hudson calls a "converger." According to Hudson, a converger "thinks in an orderly, analytical way; he likes to be rule-bound; and is happiest dealing with the world of things."[14] Disliking the incoherence, frequently strong emotion, and irrationality of dreams and nightmares, convergers often manifest interest in science and technology.[15] The opposite personality type, "divergers" (identifiable because they do particularly well on creativity tests) have no hostility to the dreamlike; thus, according to Bridgstock, they are more likely to enjoy fantasy.

Bridgstock's hypothesis may not apply to all humanity since Hudson's investigation focused primarily on American males; the need to qualify Bridgstock's theory (by showing that it does not apply to all humanity), however, is far less than the need to show that his theory has the following wider implication. Hudson divides people according to whether the analytical or creative way of thought predominates. Ultimately, his findings will have to be related to other recent research, in particular, breakthroughs in studying the mind's contrasting modes:[16]

LITERAL MODE	VISUAL/POETIC MODE
language systems	visual imagery and space perception
sequence in time	simultaneousness
analysis	perception of patterns as a whole
routine processes	new information
literalness	interpreting analogy, metaphor and emotion
the body's right side	the body's left side

Effective thought requires use of both modes but there are at least two manners in which such use can occur: (1) the converger's way of subordinating visual/poetic to literal thinking (the approach of science fiction and, to a far greater extent, of traditional realism);[17] (2) the diverger's method of developing both modes with a playful relationship between them (the way of fantasy). Tension between the modes flourishes in even seemingly juvenile fantasy, such as a typical episode of Charles Schulz's comic strip "Peanuts" (10 Jan. [1981]). Its first panel shows Charlie Brown's younger sister, Sally, contemplating her Sunday School lesson, Matt. 6:3: "When thou doest alms, let not thy left hand know what thy right hand doeth." With a child's uncomprehending literalness, she interprets Christ's command as if it required her to cultivate a split personality. Subsequently, she writes with her right hand while her left one demands to know what she is doing. Finally, she abandons her homework and complains, "My hands hate each other." This embodies two related themes common in fantasy: (1) characters should progress beyond the childish literalness for which Sally is derided; and (2) eventually, more than one side of a character is likely to manifest itself. As usual, Sally gives up, eagerly seizing any pretext to avoid her homework.

The words of the strip are relatively fanciful, whimsically playing with Biblical interpretation, imaginatively employing metaphorical language (i.e., personifying the hands), and creatively adapting *psychomachy* (a venerable old variety of religious literature in which two sides of the human self divide in argument). Schulz's popularity may owe even more to his childlike drawings. After years of practice, he has developed a stylization as appealing as primitive art. The contrast between his seemingly crude sketches and his erudite allusions is obvious, particularly in strips about Lucy's psychiatric booth, where her jargon includes such polysyllables as "iatrophobia" (fear of doctors).[18]

Noting individual instances of picture/text discrepancy, however, is different from defining its overall significance. In the eighteenth century, Gotthold Lessing furnished a somewhat oversimplified theory that could, nonetheless, have furthered study of this relationship. In his book *Laocoön*, he argues that poetry and painting differ radically because poetry unfolds itself over a period of time, while painting is seen at a glance. Lessing, though, does not use his insight to examine the complexities of illuminated texts. Rather, in his neoclassical dislike of the fantastic and the self-contradictory, he advises against an art that tries to combine the visual and the literary, a conclusion anticipated by Jean Baptiste Du Bos's *Réflexions critique sur la póesie et la peinture* (1719).[19] Recently, more sympathetic theorists such as Roger Caillois, Eric S. Rabkin, and Tzvetan Todorov have attempted to define fantasy and the fantastic,[20] but none has faced the many problems of picture/text divergence and its pleasant yet often unsettling effect on the mind. Such a study should examine both mental modes that illuminated narratives employ so dramatically.

First, from the standpoint of the time-concerned mode, Part I of this volume will trace the relationship of fantasy to some long-lasting historical trends. What is characteristic of fantasy patterns is precisely their persistence as if, in the flux of wars, plagues, famines, and the sometimes equally upsetting turmoil of daily life, people needed to cling to enduring dreams. From Lovejoy's classic study of the great chain of being to more recent and controversial works by Gaston Bachelard and Michel Foucault, researches into intellectual history have revealed the surprising endurance of fantastic ideas.[21]

Next, from the viewpoint of the visual/poetic mode, Part II will focus more closely on this persistence by examining fantastic images' partial independence of their temporal contexts. Here, though, the texts, which must be read word by word (rather than surveyed at a glance like the pictures) reintroduce the issue of time, which fantasy never entirely escapes. Consequently, Part III will confront the problem of how illuminated fantasy brings time and seeming timelessness into a satisfying rapprochement.

As is perhaps implied by the subtitle of this volume *(From Blake's Visions to Recent Graphic Fiction)*, the focus will be on the stream of English-language nineteenth-and twentieth-century illuminated works, which flows from the same culture as Blake's prophetic books. This culture has spread around the globe, as one can begin to appreciate by noting the prominence of Mickey Mouse and Snoopy books and toys from Europe to Japan (where a disneyland has opened). Since fantasy in English has profited from other traditions, the most-relevant foreign influences will be noted. In particular, the last two chapters will attempt to investigate a tentative connection between some English-language illuminated fantasy and systems of thought deriving from the Far East.

Illuminated Fantasy

I
Themes in the History of Illuminated Fantasy

1

Around the Golden Calf: Sacred Word vs. Graven Image

PICTURE-TEXT DISCREPANCY IS BUT ONE OF THE MANY ANOMALIES COMMON to fantasy. The genre characteristically transgresses the norms of everyday experience (where creatures do not breathe fire, levitate, etc.) and combines images from mutually exclusive contexts (e.g., the traditional way of representing a unicorn by drawing a narwhal's horn on the forehead of a horse). Furthermore, because of its penchant for unconventionality, fantasy poses its own seemingly timeless images against another approach to eternity, that of orthodox religion. The confrontation of the two constitutes a long history.

At present, who is the god (or who are the gods) of fantasy? In the introduction to Charles Addams's compendium *Addams and Evil,* his long-time friend Wolcott Gibbs writes of "the misshapen, the moonstruck, and the damned" thronging the volume and of "whatever Thing [Addams] calls his God."[1] "Nothing sells like blasphemy!" laments a caricature of J. Edgar Hoover in Dan O'Neill's *The Collective Unconscience of Odd Bodkins.* On the next page, the one-time Catholic seminarian O'Neill, whose newspaper comic strip formerly reached 500 million readers, even goes so far as to travesty the Pentecostal coming of the Holy Spirit, perhaps because "The blasphemy against the Holy Ghost shall not be forgiven unto men" (Matt. 12:31).[2] While the cartoon's text alludes to the "Gift of Tongues" (the sudden ability to speak in a new language, a grace bestowed by the Holy Spirit), the

27

picture punningly represents a bird with many tongues protruding from its beak. In his beautifully illuminated novel *The Swords of Heaven, the Flowers of Hell* (1979), the popular fantasist Michael Moorcock tells of fiendish inhabitants of "Heaven," who send out "angels" to urinate acid on the dwellers of "Hell." In his introduction to the book, Moorcock explains that he "became . . . a thoroughgoing atheist" (as did each of his co-workers) while scripting the comic strip *Bible Story.*[3] In paintings for *The Swords of Heaven, the Flowers of Hell,* Howard Chaykin exhibits his unmistakable style (as in Delany's *Empire*), but with one significant difference. At its most extreme, Moorcock's fantasy virtually compels him to abandon clear illustration. On the second page, for example, a host of superimposed, partly transparent, mysterious forms constitutes his attempt to render Moorcock's idea that the protagonist is not one man but a multitude of heroes. Unlike Christian beliefs about the soul, even unlike reincarnation, the consciousness of Moorcock's hero shifts from one mature body to another—a concept so nebulous and unconventional that it could scarcely be literally illustrated.

So-called "comix" (underground comic books) are notorious for irreverence, e.g., *The New Adventures of Jesus* by "Foolbert Sturgeon" (Frank Stack) and the relatively pornographic *Tales from the Leather Nun* by Dave Sheridan et al.[4] Even the more respectable fantasy comic books sold to adolescents generally lack reverence. For instance, Stan Lee, former editor of the extremely popular Marvel Comics Group, begins his *Origins of Marvel Comics* with a parody of Genesis: "In the beginning Marvel created the Bullpen [the cubics of its artists and writers]."[5] The volume describes the invention of one semi-divine hero after another. For years, Lee sought some way to "present a strip featuring God" without shocking pious readers (*Origins,* p. 178). Finally, realizing that Norse mythology would adequately allay objections, he began the still-flourishing magazine *Thor.* It concerns a young divinity and world savior whose Father is "Odin . . . the all wise . . [sic] the Omnipotent" (*Origins,* p. 205). Then, presumably to give equal time to the demonic powers, Lee brought out the magazine *Dr. Strange, Master of Black Magic.* Its title character allegedly uses evil forces to good ends. In the August 1982 issue of Marvel's *Bizarre Adventures,* the devil literally boots "G-d" out of heaven and the Latter is treated rather shabbily on earth until He proves His skill at video games. Nonetheless, due to Marvel's brilliance in its field, the Catholic Church actively cooperated with that company in the publication of the comic books *Francis, Brother of the Universe* and *The Life of Pope John Paul II.*[6] Because of John Paul's modernism (shocking to Church conservatives) and St. Francis's defiance of the conventional wisdom of his day, both are depicted more as heroic individualists than as representatives of a dogmatic tradition. At Christian book stores, one can buy devout comic books by less inventive companies, but these do not reach as wide distribution; nor are they well-designed to excite the imagination, even if they contain fantasy.

Popular fantasy is frequently irreverent for a number of reasons, among them that parody or even defiance of religious tradition gives the works a marketable vividness. Naturally, religion is not the only subject parodied. Fantasy often combines with some other genre to play with the latter's conventions, as *Star Wars* mixes fantasy with sci-fi or as *The Lord of the Rings* mingles fantasy with the rambling pattern of Dickensian fiction (with special reference to *Pickwick Papers*). Nonetheless, religion typically appears as an underlying theme, e.g., the "Force" in the *Star Wars* sagas or the elaborate "Valar" mythology in Tolkien's *Lord of the Rings* (and more explicitly in his *Silmarillion*). Close as the "Force" is to the Chinese metaphysical concept *Ch'i* (Universal energy) and close as Tolkien's Valar are to Judeo-Christian angels, there are significant differences. (The Force comes only from life forms while *Ch'i* includes all energy, and the Valar have greater independence of action from God than do the angels of orthodox theology.) Subtly or dramatically, religions in fantasy tend to diverge from their models just as the preconceptions of normal consciousness are distorted in dreams. In the Occident, the Judeo-Christian tradition has usually served as the pattern for variation—one of many reasons for conflict between the secular arts and that tradition—a conflict as yet unended. Even today, Fundamentalists set fire to "Star Wars figurines" and fantasy books "ranging from 'The Omen' to 'Snow White,'"[7] as the monk Savonarola (A.D. 1452–98) did to the paintings of the Renaissance. A brief look at the history of opposition to fantasy and illumination may help to explain why their earlier development seems so different from the recent vogue. Religious antagonism to visual portrayal of the supramundane can be traced back to the Second Commandment, which has had a complex impact on the development of graphic fantasy.

Considering the transcendent nature of God, neither words nor pictures would seem capable of portraying His Being or works with satisfactory precision. The tradition of Biblical inerrancy, however, guarantees to Scriptural language an accuracy not claimed for visual art (which, as already noted, may often have a problematic relationship with words, particularly in depicting more than mundane scenes). Without much explanation, Exod. 20:4 decrees: "You shall not make for yourself a *pesel* (sculptured image) or any *temunah* (likeness) of what is in the heavens above or on the earth below, or in the waters below the earth."[8] At first glance, this prohibition might seem an inducement to fantastic art as a replacement for forbidden realism, but the commandment's historical function was to prohibit heathen idols, most of them phantasmagoric in form. The more bizarre the being depicted, the more likely people would believe that it existed somewhere as a god of heaven, water, or earth. Albeit unconsciously, idolators were fantasists because their imaginings were self-contradictory, their gods typically impossible amalgams of creatures.

In Judaic tradition, on the one hand, stands the Holy Word, a firm moral guide throughout the vicissitudes of human history. On the other hand appears visual art, associated with idolatry and thus with immorality, irreverence, sensuousness and even sensuality (adultery being one of the Bible's favorite metaphors for service to idols, e.g., Ezek. 23:19–20). Recall how strongly the Hebrews felt about idolatry. When Moses first returned from Mount Sinai with the Ten Commandments, he issued orders leading to the slaughter of about three thousand of his own people for dancing around the golden calf (Exod. 32:28). Having won the attention of his flock (i.e., of those still alive), Moses could call for radical purity. With the exception of the late Reverend Jim Jones, modern religious leaders have generally been reluctant to do away with their congregations, especially since declining church attendance in some denominations has long threatened to accomplish this anyway. Even in Biblical times, religion underwent changes. Solomon, for instance, commissioned a Temple of the Lord, including representational art such as the cherubim mentioned in 1 Kings 6:23–29. Having escaped censure for this, Solomon drifted into actual idolatry. Today, when so many people find it too troublesome to worship even one God, it may seem strange that idolators bothered to serve several. As the Victorian poet Arthur Hugh Clough once ironically proclaimed:

> Thou shalt have one God only; who
> Would be at the expense of two?
> No graven images may be
> Worshipped, except the currency.[9]

Nonetheless, the current fantasy vogue evidences the willingness of people to offer billions for merchandise, movie tickets, books, and so forth connected with heroes who save the world in some spectacular fashion. The craving for mythology never quite dies, but to what extent early Judaism gave visual form to supramundane concepts is a matter of controversy.

In *Jüdische Künstler,* the great Jewish theologian Martin Buber hypothesizes: "The Jew of antiquity was more of an aural *(Ohrenmensch)* than a visual being *(Augenmensch)* and felt more in terms of time than space."[10] As the art historian Joseph Gutmann has commented, Buber's generalization needs qualification. Art appears to have long existed in Judaism, though more tolerated than encouraged. Typically, in the thirteenth century, Rabbi Meir of Rothenburg ruled that the pictorial embellishment of prayer books *(mahzorim)* was not forbidden by the Second Commandment but was unsuitable because it might distract the reader from the contemplation of God

Himself.[11] Buber's generalization, nonetheless, suggests an essential truth, that Judaism emphasized a historical consciousness associated with written records (the Scriptures). It did not encourage visual fantasy associated with the doings of pagan gods at some unclear mythological time. Despite discouragement by pious prophets, large groups of Israelites sometimes switched from orthodoxy to idolatry with all its sensuous pomp and sensual pleasure, its shining icons and ritual orgies.

In his controversial work *The Origin of Consciousness in the Breakdown of the Bicameral Mind,* the psychologist Julian Jaynes argues that opposition in the Bible to idolatry helped to inaugurate a new more modern state of mind to written language. He hypothesizes that idols and icons once had commonly acted as triggers for the opposite, visionary mode, which could also be induced by poetry. Jaynes sees Biblical tradition as trying to bring imagination under the control of a consciousness dedicated to law and morality, while visionaries not subject to such control were "hunted down and exterminated like unwanted animals."[12] The Bible itself only includes those visions that the Jewish community found consistent with Judaic theology. Jaynes's theory implies that after the rise of the heightened, moral consciousness of Judaism, fantasy remained as a throwback to a visionary way of life increasingly at odds with a more-and-more rational culture.

Early Christianity heaped ridicule on the immoral gods and bizarre superstitions of the pagans (just as the scientific rationalism of the last few centuries has found difficulty in taking even Christianity seriously). In his pamphlet *De Idolatria,* the Christian apologist Tertullian (ca. 160–230) condemned pictures of the supramundane as preposterous and blasphemous, an opinion apparently shared by some other influential Christian writers such as Origen (ca. 185–254), Clement of Alexandria (ca. 150–215), Eusebius of Caesaria (ca. 265–340), Arnobius (ca. 255–327), and Lactantius (ca. 240–?). Convened in the Spanish city of Elvira, the first Christian council that has surviving documents (ca. 309) forbade pictures on walls of churches. Nonetheless, in a church at Aquileia constructed only a few years after the Council of Elvira, there are not only representational but freely imitated Judaic and even pagan motifs.[13] After all, an artist's province is the visual mode, which concerns itself with vivid images, not the literal consistency sought by writers of canons and creeds. In the Byzantine Empire, the eighth and ninth centuries witnessed intermittent mob violence, vandalized cathedrals, and even systematic persecution conducted by some Byzantines almost as antagonistic to representational art as their Islamic enemies. Although such hatred of images was uncommon in Europe, Rabanus Maurus, Archibishop of Mainz (d. 856), well-expressed the Roman Catholic mood: "writing is of more profit than the vain pictured form. . . . The Egyptians were the first to paint light and shade; but it was the Lord who graved letters on the rock."[14]

This distrust of illumination was not groundless. In her best-selling history of the fourteenth century, *A Distant Mirror,* Barbara Tuchman eloquently describes medieval books of devotion:

> In the margins brimming with burlesque, all the comic sense, fantasy, and satire of the Middle Ages let itself go. Buffoons and devils curl and twist through flowering vines . . . sacred texts trail off into fantastic creatures, bare-bottomed monks climb towers . . . imaginary beasts twine through the pages.[15]

Protestants have often advocated literal interpretation of the Bible and reacted against the imaginative, allegorical interpretation of medieval exegesis. Their fervent desire has been for consistency and literalness. Comparably, they have particularly objected to illuminations so different from the text. Understandably, in his poem *Don Juan* (1.46), George Gordon, Lord Byron, who was reared a strict Protestant, finds prayer and pornography irreconcilable:

> The Missal . . .
>   Was ornamented in a sort of way
> Which ancient mass-books are, and this all
>   Kinds of grotesques illumined; and how they,
> Who saw those figures on the margins kiss all,
>   Could turn their optics to the text and pray,
> Is more than I know. . . .[16]

Similarly, in *The Queen of the Air,* the art critic John Ruskin (another nineteenth-century Protestant) complains:

> In the Psalter of S. Louis itself, half of its letters are twisted snakes; . . . and there is rarely a piece of monkish decorated writing in the world, that is not tainted with some ill-meant vileness of grotesque . . . And truly, it seems to me, as I gather in my mind the evidences of insane religion [and] degraded art . . . as if the race itself were still half-serpent . . . and the track of it, on the leaf a glittering slime. . . .[17]

Actually, Protestantism in the nineteenth century was more tolerant than in earlier centuries when the wars of religion brought much smashing of church art. In 1592, the English Puritan preacher William Perkins went so far in his dislike of visual images as to condemn even the ancient Greek, Roman, and medieval art of employing *mental* images to help remember useful facts: "The animation of the images which is the key of memory is impious: because it calls up absurd thoughts, insolent, prodigious and the like which stimulate and light up depraved carnal affections."[18] Those forerunners of British Protestantism the Lollards (and, later, the Puritans as well) "declared that art should be true to earthly fact precisely because the human imagination was suspect."[19] In reference to idealized Greek gods and zoomorphic Asian deities, Wilbur Urban's book *Language and Reality* offers the following very un-Protestant theory:

> Since it is the excessive, the infinite, the *mysterium tremendum,* that is always symbolized, the consciousness that the symbol both is and is not a re-presentation of the thing for which it stands is the very essence of the religious consciousness. . . .[20]

To the literal-minded Protestants, though, deviation from realism does not suggest some profound psychological or spiritual perception; it merely prevaricates.

Religious opposition to the unbridled imagination has had some effect on past fantasy (in addition to probably suppressing it from time to time). Consider, Chaucer's fantastic *The House of Fame.* A dreamer finds himself in a temple where marvelous figures of ancient pagans and signs of the celestial gods (line 460) are "graven" (line 473) on the walls. Impressed by these "ymages" line 472), the dreamer (being more theologically naive than the author, Chaucer) begs Jupiter to save us just as, in Roman mythology, that god had answered the prayer of the goddess Venus (line 466).[21] The lines about images having been "graven" are reminiscent of Exod. 20:4, as in the translation in a sermon by John Wyclif (founder of the Lollards and client of Chaucer's patron): "Thou shalt none image have, graven with man's hand."[22] The temple looks out onto a desert, an unhallowed area from which the dreamer turns to Heaven for salvation from "Illusion" (line 493). Instead of being saved, he is carried aloft by Jupiter's bird. The abduction is compared to Jupiter's rape of the youth Ganymede, as, for centuries, Christian apologists have remarked such scandals to show the moral superiority of their God over the pagan one. Eventually, the dreamer arrives at the mad House of the goddess Fame, where people idolatrously beseech her for reputation—itself mere illusion because it seldom reflects a person's true worth. Chaucer is not inviting the reader to enjoy illusionary worlds (as in much modern fantasy) but to renounce them as delusive. Dreams themselves are the work of Morpheus, a god (or devil) "unmerrie" (line 74), dwelling by a river of hell (line 72). Similarly, in Chaucer's poem *Book of the Duchess,* Morpheus sleeps in a cave "as derk / as helle pit" (lines 170–71). This poem concerns a knight who plays chess with the goddess Fortune, an idol ("ydole") who brings death as part of her game, suggesting that the knight should not have concerned himself with this image but devoted himself to God. Even the pagan poet and musician Orpheus and the pagan artist and inventor Daedalus, both great mythical figures, cannot aid the knight (lines 569–70). At the end of his mythological poem *Troilus and Criseyde,* the narrator denounces all the pagan gods and their rites.

Picture from Ovide moralisé, *in Roger Loomis,* A Mirror of Chaucer's World, *1965.* (Reprinted by permission of Bibliothèque nationale, Paris.)

As to the illumination of Chaucer's fantasy, evidence is lacking. No pictures incontestably completed under his supervision survive. The most famous illustrations of his work belong to the Ellesmere manuscript (dating from about ten years after his death). These paintings (except for a few minor divergences) literally follow his realistic descriptions of the Canterbury pilgrims rather than illuminating his fantasy. In seeking medieval pictures for his book *A Mirror of Chaucer's World,* Roger Loomis frequently finds himself obliged to turn to non-Chaucerian manuscripts. For instance, to accompany the rape of Ganymede mentioned in Chaucer's *The House of Fame,* Loomis adds a painting from the *Ovide moralisé.* Jupiter appears twice in the same scene, once as an eagle carrying Ganymede and again as a king, who drops fire from one hand and holds a feather in the other. In contrast, the text of the *Ovide moralisé* describes his hurling a thunderbolt ("fulmine") and clasping a scepter ("sceptrumque").[23] The illuminators' substitutions make Jupiter less majestic. In particular, the feather seems to be a comic reminder that he demeaned himself in the form of a bird to pursue a pretty boy. Probably the graphic artist here mocks the pagan god—one of the many ways in which medievals portrayed (and thereby perpetuated) mythology while themselves remaining within the Christian fold—an enemy of pagan fantasy.

Quite naturally, medievals tended to justify their works in Christian terms, not all precisely in the manner of Chaucer but with one technique or another. It is evidence of fantasy's enduring quality that it survived at all. Probably one of the many reasons that fantasy currently flourishes is that it encounters no such clear-cut limitations as in the Age of Faith.

Another difference between modern and previous illuminated fantasy lies in the changed attitude toward graphic literature. In 1658, the Protestant Bishop Johann Amos Comenius published *Orbis sensualium pictus,* the first illustrated primer. Since then, illustration has become the norm, illumination the anomaly. From *Orbis sensualium pictus* also descends the tradition of presuming that picture books are in some sense for children because, in the Middle Ages, illumination had connoted culture and wealth.

Modern attitudes toward fantasy come from at least three sources: (1) the present decreased need to worry about Christian authorities; (2) the public association now of fantasy with the childlike; and (3) the growing understanding that fantasy is literally untrue, not a depiction of real demons ready to lead the unwary into idolatry. Concerning this third source, André Malraux goes so far as to say, "To medieval thinking the imaginary was never something that could not exist," since so much of the earth was then unexplored that monsters might still be lurking in the uncharted darkness.[24]

In her study *Fantasy: The Literature of Subversion,* Rosemary Jackson suggests that even present

[l]iterary fantasies . . . have a function corresponding to the mythical

and magical products of other cultures. They return us to what Freud identifies as an animistic mode of perception. . . .[25]

Jackson makes modern fantasy readers seem as rustic as Malraux's medievals. (Even medievals may not have been quite so credulous.) Certainly today, one can enjoy ingenious lies while knowing them to be fabrications. Part of the technique of modern fantasy is its implicit or explicit contrast of its strange worlds with mundane existence. The modern reader does not necessarily "return" to the pre-conscious but may view its strange procession of images from the sidelines as if watching a parade.

Jackson, though, well suggests that fantasy has a connection with religious imagery, yet is psychologically subversive, an overturning of order and of what seems to be reality. In ages of faith, subversiveness was not particularly encouraged, and even today, the characteristic irreverence of fantasy provokes criticism. As science fiction constitutes a speculative science transcending (or transgressing) the orthodox discipline, so fantasy is frequently a speculative theology at odds with religious orthodoxy. Today, however, religion is not all conservative. The previously mentioned *Collective Unconscience of Odd Bodkins,* which seems so preoccupied with blasphemy, is published by Glide Memorial Methodist Church in San Francisco, known for sometimes projecting slides of "Peanuts" cartoons during the church service.[26] Fantasy's free exploration of timeless concerns is not inimical to all modern religious thinkers, nor is religious thought as limited as some may think. The metaphysician Humphrey Palmer well remarks:

> Everyone engages in theology. For everyone—including philosophers who call theology nonsense and preachers who reject "propositional" theology—everyone holds some beliefs about the ultimate nature of the universe, and makes some inferences from those beliefs.[27]

One may add to Palmer's observation that these inferences do not always follow the dogma of any systematic religion but may range beyond consistent thought into the paradoxes of fantasy.

According to Jean Hagstrum's classic study *The Sister Arts,* when painters and poets tried to imitate the external world, critics have generally stipulated that poetry should resemble painting and depict a common reality.[28] When, however, for religious, philosophical, or other reasons, poets and painters have attempted to portray a heavenly realm or primarily psychological experience, poems and paintings often have become fantasies and significantly diverged from one another.[29] In *Blake's Composite Art,* W. J. T. Mitchell demonstrates that the visionary poet William Blake radically rejected the traditional belief that there is a common reality that poets and painters could and should imitate.[30] Generally considered one of the first Romantic rebels, Blake makes a convenient representative of another major theme in the history of modern fantasy: artists' battling bourgeois conventionality (nowadays supported by the bourgeoisie, but in Blake's time, with far more resistance than help).

2

Blake: Visionary against the Commonplace

AN ENEMY OF SLAVERY, COLONIALISM, TYRANNY, ORGANIZED RELIGION, AND sexual continence, William Blake generally opposed restraint. His illuminated books not merely present events impossible in the mundane world, but rise to fantastic flights of imagination difficult for most readers to envision without frequent rereading. His rebellion against eighteenth-century poetic conventions gives an eccentricity and vividness, even to such relatively simple poems as "London":

> I wander thro' each charter'd street,
> Near where the charter'd Thames does flow
> And mark in every face I meet
> Marks of weakness, marks of woe.
>
> In every cry of every Man,
> In every Infants cry of fear,
> In every voice; in every ban,
> The mind-forg'd manacles I hear
>
> How the Chimney-sweepers cry
> Every blackning Church appalls,
> And the hapless Soldiers sigh
> Runs in blood down Palace walls

But most thro' midnight streets I hear
How the youthful Harlots curse
Blasts the new-born Infants tear
And blights with plagues the Marriage hearse.[1]

Thus, in one of his *Songs of Experience,* Blake bemoans the oppressiveness of that city into which he was born in 1757. His childhood was largely unremarkable aside from several visions of God and His angels.[2] Such experiences continued throughout his life and provided much of the imagery for his works. He did not, however, merely record hallucinatory voices and visions word by word and image by image. His frequent revisions (of "London" and virtually all his poems) constitute enough proof that he was a conscious writer. Of his pencil drawings, Mitchell concludes that they "grope through numerous erasures and trial alternatives before focusing themselves clearly."[3] Blake also learned from writings of previous mystics, people described by Abraham Hammacher as "Illuminists . . . who . . . undermined the basic values of rational thought through Orientalism" and occult studies.[4]

In 1808, Blake sought fame and fortune (unsuccessfully) by exhibiting sixteen of his paintings. Instead of adopting a popular style that would attract crowds, Blake furnished the few visitors with his *Descriptive Catalogue* designed to introduce them to his fantastic world. In an 1810 edition of this brochure, Blake explains that his works are inspired by "Visionary Fancy or Imagination," but he deems this more real than everyday life (p. 555). Nevertheless, although the "Eternal Forms" perceived with the "imaginative eye" are changeless, they may be represented in countless manners, as in his using pictures of Moses and Abraham not to depict those historical individuals "but the States Signified by those Names" (p. 556). He further explains that each of these psychological states has "multitudes" of examples. With such a flexible system, Blake often employs strikingly contrasting images, as in "The Death of the Good Old Man," where the spirit is a literal double of the deceased; and in "The Reunion of the Soul and the Body," where the spirit is of the opposite sex. Blake not only represents "Eternal Forms" or "States" differently from one book to another but, even on a single page, text and picture maintain considerable independence. In his study *Symbol and Image in William Blake,* George Wingfield Digby summarizes:

> Sometimes [in Blake's work] the pictorial symbol parallels or amplifies the written one; sometimes it gives the contrasting aspect, or opposite and contrary point of view.[5]

Digby's term "parallels" sounds too much like illustration, ignoring subtle

William Blake, "The Death of the Good Old Man," from

William Blake, "The Reunion of the Soul and the Body,"
from The Grave Etching, *1813.* (The Metropolitan Museum of Art, New York, Harris Brisbane Dick Fund, 1917. Reprinted by permission.)

but significant differences, and he does not include all of the various ways that Blake's drawings relate to his words. In particular, Digby ignores the common phenomenon of a picture's amplifying a metaphor or poetic ambiguity in the text, while simultaneously contrasting with the literal meaning.[6] Nonetheless, he well theorizes that Blake's art is a complex (sometimes even contradictory) representative of patterns of the imagination. In his *Blake's Composite Art,* Mitchell admirably contends:

> The aesthetic and iconographic independence of Blake's designs from their texts. . . . reflects Blake's vision of the fallen world as a place of apparent separation between temporal [i.e., written] and spatial [i.e., visual] . . . phenomena. . . . [and] entices the reader to supply the missing connections.[7]

Blake calls the phenomena of our world "Minute Particulars" and reveres them as "Holy" representatives of the "Eternal Forms" contained within God.[8] In his cherishing the individuality of each being, he accords with what C. N. Manlove terms "a central and recurrent theme [of all fantasy]. . . . its insistence on and celebration of the separate identities of created things."[9] Opposed to the depersonalization and utilitarianism of mass society, modern fantasists feature anomalous beings (e.g., fire-breathing dragons) or present the details of existence in such a contradictory manner (as with picture/text discrepancy) that each facet assumes a lustrous, separate life. As fantasist, Blake employs conflict, contrast, and contradiction to isolate, highlight, and illuminate his imagery and to suggest a world beyond the staid limits of normality.

Blake's first great work of illuminated fantasy was *Songs of Innocence* (1789) and *Songs of Experience* (1794)—published as separate books but so integrally connected that they constitute a single opus. Not only did the unconventionality and difficulty of the *Songs* (his simplest major works) drastically limit sales in his time but such problems as picture/text divergence still hamper some scholars. In "The Little Boy Found," for example, the prints show a woman leading a child, while the text reads:

> . . . God ever nigh
> Appeared like his father in white.

In his commentary, Geoffrey Keynes admits that the pictured adult is "Ostensibly female," but speculates that Blake must have intended her to be "androgynous" (p. 137). In the most comprehensive, generally available study of Blake's pictures, *The Illuminated Blake,* David Erdman completely ignores the feminity of the apparition, speaking of the figure as "him."[10]

The Little Boy Found

The little boy lost in the lonely fen,
Led by the wandring light,
Began to cry, but God ever nigh,
Appeard like his father in white.

He kissed the child & by the hand led
And to his mother brought,
Who in sorrow pale, thro' the lonely dale
Her little boy weeping sought.

William Blake, "The Little Boy Found," from Songs of
Innocence *and* of Experience. (Reproduced by courtesy
of the Trustees of the British Museum.)

Because that poem mentions a "father" who "by the hand led" the child, Harold Bloom inexplicably ignores the picture of the haloed woman and simply writes of the child's being "Led by this ghostly father."[11] There is the slight possibility that the woman pictured is the mother, but her halo (not visible in all prints) and her leading the child as God does in the poem render the relationship of picture and text ambiguous. For Blake, both verbal "father" and visual mother equally well (or inadequately) could represent God, who is the Human Imagination ultimately eternal and beyond sexual distinction. How better could Blake call attention to his nonliteralistic interpretation of God, the Father, than through this picture/text discrepancy.

Basic to the *Songs* is a contrast between Imagination, the relatively timeless poetic and visual mode, and Reason, the time-concerned literal one. As a number of critics have pointed out in commentaries on these *Songs,* Blake once wrote of the ethical philosopher Lavater as being "offended with the innocence of a child . . . because it reproaches him with . . . acquired folly."[12] Vehicles of vision to the childlike, the poems are also a reproach to adult logic, and this reproach is integrally connected to the fantasy of Blake's works. One may see an obvious instance of this in "The Ecchoing Green" (p. 6), where, surrounding the text, a network of branches too thin to support their own extended length impossibly holds large boys. While they harvest grapes beyond the sight of Old John, he is engrossed in ordering the children home for the night. Behind his back, one of the boys passes grapes to a girl, whose hat resembles a halo. Placing a text in the middle of the picture inevitably prevents the latter from being completely realistic. Here the boys' gravity-defying perch on the text's viny border provides a fantastic counterpoint to the adult prudence of Old John, who abandons his seat beneath the sheltering oak only to head homeward. While the picture gives the children's point of view—their reluctance to leave and the boys' surreptitious pleasure in evading adult authority—the poem merely states:

> . . . the little ones weary
> No more can be merry.
>
> (p. 7)

Similarly, the poem "Nurses Song" contains the debate between nurse and children, the former arguing that the sun has set, the latter that it has not. The illumination shows the sun bisected by the horizon, yet the children's shadows lie directly under them as if at noon. As is typical of Blake, the fantastic contradiction in the drawing stems obliquely from the text. The nurse remarks that while the children play,

> My heart is at rest within my breast

And everything else is still.
(p. 24)

The drawing exaggerates this stillness into a miraculous suspension of time; as long as the children play, they are in the high noon of Eternity.

In *Songs of Innocence,* poems that devote approximately equal space to picture and text (e.g., "The Lamb") tend to be somewhat more happy than those with very sparse illuminations (e.g., "The Chimney Sweeper," a vivid condemnation of child labor; "Holy Thursday," a portrait of children herded to church; "A Dream," the story of an ant "troubled wilderd and forlorn," and "On Another's Sorrow," a consideration of grief and its consolation). Furthermore, the miniscule illumination of "The Chimney Sweeper" (p. 12) represents the distant hope within the poem that someday God will free the children from their coffinlike chimneys. In the painted heaven accompanying the text, children truly dance for joy, but throughout the poem, the sprightly meter forms an ironic contrast to the tale of oppression. According to Blake, "Unorganized Innocence" cannot exist[13] (i.e., both the systematic skills of Reason and the vision of Imagination are necessary, though for Blake this does *not* mean the domination of the latter by the former). Throughout most of the *Songs of Innocence,* the organization is external to the children and is supplied by guardians who are not always well-meaning. Despite its winged cherubs, angels, spirits, and diminutive fairies, the fantasy of *Innocence* seldom flies far from restraint. The title character of "The Little Black Boy," for example, can imagine no better fate than stroking the hair of a white child at the knee of a paternal God. For Blake, original innocence is too vulnerable; he expresses desire for a higher innocence, the condition of those who have passed through and transcended the grim state of Experience.

The title page of *Songs of Experience* shows children beside their dead parents (p. 29). Its "Introduction" has, as an illumination, a figure hovering in the sky on a scroll-shaped couch, the scroll associating him with writing (p. 30). The couch floats in the clouds, perhaps to signify that he is lost in abstraction, the state that Blake satirizes in *Experience.* The figure "sees" the "Present, Past, & Future," but to him the "Holy Word" is a being he "heard" long ago among trees now "ancient"—a longer time dividing him from verbal inspiration than in the previous "Introduction" (p. 30). The discrepancy between picture and poem, extant in *Songs of Innocence,* takes on a new form. In *Innocence,* the texts seem to favor adult caution and the pictures glorify the fantastic defiance of it. However, in *Experience,* the texts frequently reflect a fantastic terror (e.g., "Tyger tyger, burning bright") but the illuminations are only closer to the Eternal perspective in their freedom from such hysteria. Considered as a whole, *Songs of Innocence* has more simple lyrics and striking illuminations than *Songs of Experience.* In the latter, the verbal art frequently outshines the visual—appropriately so since Blake's state of Experience is characterized by desire to describe and control oppressive systems that seem more fearful the longer one contemplates them. The illumination of "The Lamb" (p. 18) is far more symmetrical than that of "The Tyger" (p. 42), yet the speaker of the latter poem is so sensitized to the negative qualities of organization and order that he describes not the claws and teeth of the tyger as terrifying but its "symmetry." In the poem entitled "London" (p. 46), the "weakness" and "woe" are associated with the streets' and river's being "charter'd," controlled by written regulation. The speaker hears "in every ban, / The mind-forg'd manacles." The critic Keynes well identifies the old man in the illumination of "London" as "Urizen [reason personified], himself crippled by the conditions he has created" (p. 151). In *Songs of Experience,* "The School Boy" treats the sorrows of organized learning, "The Garden of Love" laments organized morality, and "The Chimney Sweeper" (counterpart of the identically named poem in *Songs of Innocence*) criticizes the whole religio-political order ("God & his Priest & King"). The most pervasive image is being confined within ordering restraints. Even the baby of "Infant Sorrow" speaks of himself

> Struggling in my fathers hands:
> Striving against my swadling bands.
>
> (p. 48)

Since the manacles of Experience are merely "Mind-forg'd," however, some poems in that section, while recognizing the sad facts of mundane existence, can break sufficiently free from limitation to predict a time when "clouds of reason" will flee ("The Voice of the Ancient Bard," p. 54). Among the most interesting of these poems are "The Little Girl Lost" and "The Little Girl Found." The first of these begins with a prophecy that the earth shall awake, seek God, and transform the earth's wasteland into a garden. Next comes the story of the wanderings of Lyca, who like the earth achieves a paradisiacal condition. Lyca is "[s]even summers old" (p. 34). However, in her timeless land, "summers prime, / Never fades away" (p. 34), complicating the question of her age. (Recall that from the Blakean perspective the timeless and the childlike have much in common.) The illumination takes advantage of the verbal ambiguity to depict Lyca as a young woman, first seen embracing a nude lover, then reclining nervously in the forest, and finally sleeping peacefully while naked children play with lions. Thus the illuminations develop another ambiguity of the text, for in Blake's time the word "lost," when applied to a girl, usually referred to her having been banished from her home for fornication or adultery. Lyca's having "wandered long, / Hearing wild birds song" may describe her morals as well as her travels. She is called a "virgin," but perhaps ironically. (Similarly, Blake interpreted the Biblical term "virgin" when applied to Christ's mother to mean merely a young woman, for Blake often wrote approvingly of what he considered Mary's promiscuity.)[14] "The Little Girl Found" tells of her parents' search for her. Instead of bringing her back, as the mother of "The Little Boy Lost" tries to do with her child in *Songs of Innocence,* the girl's parents live with her in the wild, which has now become an apocalyptic paradise regained. While the children of *Songs of Innocence* naïvely follow their guardians, in "The Little Girl Found" (p. 36), the adults must follow the child to regain a new Eden. As is typical of *Songs of Experience,* though, the illuminations are less exotic than the poem. In the poetry, the lion reveals itself to be a crowned spirit. More prosaic but equally symbolic, the last illumination (p. 36) adds children not mentioned in the text and changes the "tygers" surrounding Lyca to lions to make the final scene recall paintings of the Biblical peaceful kingdom. Behind them intertwine the Tree of Life (an emblem used throughout *Songs of Innocence*) and the Tree of the Knowledge of Good and Evil. (The latter appears in such *Songs of Experience* as "The Poison Tree," where the deadly apple grows from constrained wrath, and "The Human Abstract," where the evil tree springs from "The Human Brain.") Only with the two sides of the mind joined, as with the two trees in this illumination, can "organized" innocence flourish.

During the period of the composition of *Songs of Innocence and of Experience,* Blake produced another masterpiece on the theme of mental division *The Marriage of Heaven and Hell* (1793). The poem begins with the "just man" exiled and raging in the wilderness; the illumination portrays nubile maidens, some picking fruit, some reclining while birds fly in the background. The "just man" of the text, obsessed with his own undeserved exile, sees lions, wilderness, and reason to rage, while the picture shows maidens, birds, and fruit trees, the paradise he could enter if he changed his state of mind. Similarly in a later section labeled "A Memorable Fancy," an angel's moralizing convinces an artist that he is damned until the angel departs and the artist finds himself in a paradise. Then the artist, by means of his own "phantasy," makes the angel see the Bible as a hell. The difference between heaven and hell is merely one of perception and "firm perswasion that a thing is so, make[s] it so." At dinner with Blake, the Prophet Isaiah explains, however, that it was "in ages of imagination this firm perswasion moved mountains" (*Marriage,* p. 38). Blake unfortunately lives in an age of "systematic reason," so it is difficult for him to change the world through his "phantasy."

The Marriage of Heaven and Hell ends with a prophecy of the destruction of the British Empire, but another of Blake's poems composed that year,

Appear to the Americans upon the cloudy night.

Solemn heave the Atlantic waves between the gloomy nation,
Swelling, belching from its deeps red clouds & raging fires
Albion is sick. America faints! enrag'd the Zenith grew.
As human blood shooting its veins all round the orbed heaven
Red rose the clouds from the Atlantic in vast wheels of blood
And in the red clouds rose a Wonder o'er the Atlantic sea;
Intense! naked! a Human fire fierce glowing, as the wedge
Of iron heated in the furnace; his terrible limbs were fire
With myriads of cloudy terrors banners dark & towers
Surrounded; heat but not light went thro' the murky atmos

The King of England looking westward trembles at the

William Blake, picture from "America: A Prophecy" and
"Europe: A Prophecy." *1983.* (By permission from
Dover Publications, Inc.)

America: A Prophecy, gives him more room for political satire in this epic of Britain's lost colony. On the fourth page, in the upper right corner, the King of England, Defender of the Faith, even appears as a dragonlike Anti-Christ. On the upper left, the monarch is shown again, this time transformed to a sinister angel. With book of law in hand and robes forming a serpentine tail behind, he descends to address Parliament. At the bottom right, he becomes a naked figure clutching his head in agony. Ironically, the same person serves as elevated sovereign, fallen angel, and condemned soul. At the bottom of the same page, one reads, "The King of England looking westward trembles at the . . . vision." Although in Blake's engraving the elevation of the word "vision" is necessary to keep it from being engulfed by the darkness of the infernal hill pictured beneath it, the placement also gives a special emphasis to this important word in Blake's vocabulary. As one learns in line 61, the King, as guardian of the Law, is dominated by Urizen (tyrannous rationality personified). Confronted with the nonrationality of vision, the British monarch holds his head as if war waged within. At a time when the rulers of France had so recently been guillotined (January 1793), the King of England should have reconciled the visionary and rational side of human experience or else the revolution that divided his mind and empire might destroy him. The Blakean scholar David Erdman comments, "kings if they correct their vision in time, i.e., if they keep their heads, can—keep their heads."[15] Unfortunately, for Blake's king, the next page shows him apparently decapitated and damned.

Quite obviously, given the state of censorship in eighteenth-century Britain, Blake could not make a living from such political satire. Indeed, in 1803, the accusation that, in a moment of anger, Blake "damned the King" was enough to bring him to trial in 1804, charged with sedition.[16] The accuser, a British soldier, failed to prove the charge—something he could have done easily if he had heard of Blake's *America* (or any of a number of his other poems), but Blake's works were virtually unknown to the public.

Thus, Blake had to earn a living largely by illuminating other writers' books. Consequently, in 1791, Blake made six engravings for a book by Mary Wollstonecraft entitled, *Original Stories from Real Life; with Conversation, Calculated to Regulate the Affections, and Form the Mind to Truth and Goodness.* The title well reflects a text that now seems rather prudish. For the eighteenth century, however, such an effort to reason children into virtue (instead of thrashing them into it) was commendably progressive, a part of the liberal movement that slowly transformed British politics and society. The book make Wollstonecraft's reputation, preparing the way for her justly famous *A Vindication of the Rights of Woman* (1792). Blake, nonetheless, was neither an advocate of reason nor virtue. Understandably, his illuminations blandly undercut the work. Despite being constantly told to rejoice in doing good, the pictured children do not look very joyous. At the words "Indeed we are very happy!" the two girls lower their heads.[17] The strangest of the engravings shows a dog licking a man who exults, "Thou wilt not leave me!" This much of the picture mirrors the story. The peculiarity is that the pictured man is looking not at the dog, whom he addresses in the narrative, but at the two sleeping children, who lie stiff as corpses on a tiny bed. He clenches his fists as if to compel them to obey his words and remain his possessions. Having Blake as one's artist was indeed a mixed blessing.

So different from the text are Blake's twenty-two engravings for the Book of Job that the prolific Blakean scholar S. Foster Damon has even theorized that they are meant to represent the psychological states depicted on the twenty-two Major Arcana of the Tarot, a deck of cards long used in divination.[18] For instance, the sixteenth Major Arcanum of the Tarot depicts inverted figures falling, condemned by God for their pride, also the subject of Blake's sixteenth picture in this series, though Blake's engravings are very far from slavish copies of the allegedly corresponding Tarot cards.

Despite the obvious uniqueness of Blake's visionary works, they share common features with other illuminated fantasy, even with such popular members of that genre as modern comic books. Comparable to Damon's *Blake Dictionary,* with explanation of strange terms from Abarim to Zion, is the twelve-part *Official Handbook of the Marvel Universe* describing mythological personages with such names as Arnim Zola and Dormammu, as bizarre as those of Blake. Mystical themes appear in comics as in Blake's poems, and sometimes readers respond as enthusiastically as Raymond Orkwis, who wrote to *Master of Kung Fu Comics* (no. 81) to praise the magazine's exploration of the "spiritual" quest. He lauded it for helping him attain "a union with yin [the universal feminine principle in Chinese metaphysics]— my anima, to use the word now in the Jungian sense [image of a man's unconscious as a feminine soul]." This talk of Jungian archetypes (cf. Blake's "Eternal Forms") and of union with the feminine side of one's nature seems more what one would expect to hear from a Blakean enthusiast describing men's uniting with their feminine counterparts (called "Emanations") than from a comic-book reader. Occasionally, comics refer to Blake's better-known works (e.g., the allusion to "The Tyger" in *Conan the Barbarian,* no. 135, entitled "The Forest of the Night," concerning the fierce beasts created by a savage god). In general, though, similarities stem from the common nature of fantasy, not from specific borrowings.

Blake's mastery of illuminated fantasy makes him a convenient starting point for the study of that genre. The peculiarities of illuminated fantasy, as well as his own idiosyncrasies, hindered his popularity during his lifetime. As his reputation has grown, the acceptability of that genre has also increased. Today fantasy is on a crest of popularity and, typical of current adulation, a recent general bibliography entitled *The List of Books* (1981) describes Blake as "the greatest English poet after Shakespeare."[19]

William Blake, "Thou hast fulfilled the Judgment of the Wicked" from The Book of Job. *(By permission of The Fitzwilliam Museum, Cambridge, England.)*

3

Picture Books for the Eternal Child: An Enticement for Young Minds

*F*ROM SLIGHTLY BEFORE BLAKE'S TIME TO THE PRESENT, ONE THEME UNITES MOST graphic fiction—the notion that the reader is a child or at least childlike. Attitudes toward juvenility, however, have differed widely. From the printing of Bishop Commenius's *Orbis sensualium pictus* (1658) to the beginning of Romanticism, picture books primarily fell into the pedagogical tradition: volumes designed to appeal to the rationality of the young and lead them away from childishness. Blake and his fellow Romantics had the opposite intention—to postpone adulthood, permanently if possible. Romantic reverence for innocence merged with a comparable yearning for the alleged simplicity of the Middle Ages, e.g., in Germany, the pioneering folksong anthology *Des Knaben Wunderhorn* (The Boy's Magic Horn, 1805–1808), the folktale collection of Jacob (1785–1863) and Wilhelm (1786–1859) Grimm, and the rise of *Kunstmärchen* (literary fairy tales). In Britain, Wordsworth's Immortality Ode epitomizes the Romantic attitude:

> The youth, who daily farther from the east
> > Must travel, still is Nature's priest,
> > And by the vision splendid
> > Is on his way attended;
> At length the man perceives it die away,
> And fade into the light of common day.[1]

Among the major Romantics, only Blake turned such nostalgia into illuminated fantasy, as in his *For Children: The Gates of Paradise,* where pictures include "Aged Ignorance" cutting the wings from an angelic boy and a robed child in fetal position addressing a giant worm as "my mother and my sister" (an echo of Job 17:14). While pedagogical literature is characterized by simplified, conventional ideas, fantasy "is ultimately the most philosophical form of fiction." It appeals to the young, not because it is "simplistic, but because children, until they are educated out of it, are interested in everything."[2]

Children enjoy pure fantasy, sometimes much more than they relish condescending pedagogical fiction (which is tailored to their vocabularies and supposedly little minds). The latter is literature for children in the same way that medicine is for a diseased patient. Maria Montessori, a reputedly progressive educator, denounced fantasy as "a pathological tendency of early childhood."[3] Similarly, despite sometimes using imagination to sugar-coat teaching morality, pedagogical fictionalists tend to belong to that strand in our culture that sees fantasy as a weakness to be outgrown. In her essay, "Why are Americans Afraid of Dragons?" (1974), Ursula Le Guin tells of a friend of hers who, ten years previously, had visited the children's section of a city library to ask for Tolkien's *The Hobbit.* "The librarian told [her], 'Oh, we keep that only in the adult collection; we don't feel that escapism is good for children.' "[4] According to Brian Attebery's study of fantasy in the United States, it is "a tradition . . . counter to the main force of American belief."[5] Nonetheless, as the following historical survey suggests, illuminated fantasy has generally defended one or another childlike view of the world.

VICTORIAN FANTASY

Edward Lear and Nonsense

Rather than confront social conventions, nonsense sidesteps them (probably one reason for its Victorian popularity), making it less threatening to adult interests than even more rebellious varieties of fantasy. There is, though, enough unconventionality in it to challenge modern critics, among them Thomas Byrom, author of *Nonsense and Wonder,* the best study of Edward Lear. It devotes thirty pages to "Picture and Poem Discrepancy" because, as Byrom remarks, "in each [poem], this discrepancy is the key" to the works.[6] Unfortunately, he somewhat exaggerates the relevance of Lear's epilepsy, which, according to Byrom, made the former undergo anxiety and alienation, manifest in picture/poem discrepancy. Incongruity, however, is too common in fantasy to be dismissed as the result of one writer's illness.

THE COMPLETE NONSENSE BOOK

There was an old man who screamed out
Whenever they knocked him about:
So they took off his boots, and fed him with fruits,
And continued to knock him about.

Edward Lear, picture from The Complete Nonsense Book.
(By permission of Dodd, Mead and Company, Inc.)

Lear, an artist whose paintings are photographically realistic, chose for his nonsense a childlike crudeness—a common style in cartoons. Like much fantasy, Lear's limericks usually express youthful derision of the old, as in the following:

> There was an old man who screamed out
> Whenever they knocked him about;

There was an Old Person of Tring,
Who embellished his nose with a ring;
He gazed at the moon every evening in June,
That ecstatic Old Person of Tring.

Edward Lear, picture from The Complete Nonsense Book.
(By permission of Dodd, Mead and Company, Inc.)

So they took off his boots, and fed him with fruits,
And continued to knock him about.

The words sound as if a helpless person quite normally screams his protest against violent treatment by a band of lunatics. The cartoon, though, shows a smiling reveler treated like a piñata. In terms of fantasy, the cartoon presents the familiar theme that pleasure and pain depend less on external circumstances than on mental attitude.

One anti-authoritarian convention of comic cartooning employed by Lear is his making the heads so large that even adults appear childlike. Further stripped of dignity is an "Old Person" who dangles an incredibly large nose ring. If, as the picture implies, the object of his gaze is the sun, not (as the text avers, the moon), he is likely to go blind soon. Byrom observes that "the sun-moon face is about the same size as the ring in the Old Man's nose; so that, if the Old Man's face—especially his nose and his smiling mouth—are put inside the ring, the sun-moon and the Old Man become one and the same" (p. 135). The two faces do look a bit alike, particularly the noses. Conceivably, though, Lear may have intended no more than to balance his composition. What Byrom needs to support his view (that the Old Person ecstatically contemplates himself) is reference to fantasy in general, i.e., the virtual universality of narcissism in that genre.

Religious ecstasy actually fascinated Lear, yet his interest is characteristically hedged with a defensive humor. Typically, upon reading Sir Edwin Arnold's poem *The Light of Asia* (the life of the Buddha), Lear wrote: "If ever I meet with this Edwin Arnold, I shall go down plump on my knees. As it is, I am about to turn Buddhist as fast as possible, if not sooner."[7] Lear's attitude toward ecstasy is ambiguous. The Old Person is obviously foolish. One wonders, however, if Lear at least partly sympathizes with the blissfulness of the character's ignorance. According to Byrom, the cartoons express both Lear's childlike "sense of the strangeness and grossness of the grown-up world" and his "spiritual yearning" (pp. 15 and 150). Only a subtle (perhaps even far-fetched) reading can detect such a yearning in the slapstick of Lear's nonsense, but in Lewis Carroll's fairy stories, yearning and nostalgia form the most evident ingredients.

Lewis Carroll and the Fairy Tale

Notable for his parodies of pedagogical verse, Carroll, at least in his best work, eschewed didacticism, choosing instead a form of "fairy-tale"—a name he applied to *Through the Looking-Glass* in its prefatory poem.[8] Fairy-tale-like characters, e.g., a gryphon, a duchess, and members of royalty, throng *Alice in Wonderland,* while *Through the Looking-Glass* includes knights, kings, queens, and a unicorn. Like his Pre-Raphaelite friends, he idealizes youth and the past. This nostalgia is particularly evident in *Three Sunsets and Other Poems* (composed 1853–1891). It even contains one lyric ("After these Days") dedicated to the Pre-Raphaelite painter Holman Hunt (Carroll, p. 827). "Stolen Waters," another of these poems, derives from "La Belle Dame Sans Merci" by John Keats, a poetic precursor of Pre-Raphaelite romanticized medievalism. Carroll's poem concerns a knight who, in a dream, encounters a queenly fairy. She seduces him with the words, "Youth is the season to rejoice." Then, suddenly, she ages, causing him to flee. Finally, he hears a "clear voice" singing of an "angel child" and counseling him:

> Be as a child—
> So shalt thou sing for very joy of breath—
> So shalt thou wait thy dying,
> In holy transport lying—

> So pass rejoicing through the gate of death,
>   In garment undefiled.

(Carroll, p. 846)

He realizes that the voice may be "madness," but he decides to follow it anyway and only laments that he even once slipped from purity in a sensual dream. E. Gertrude Thomson's picture accompanying the poem shows two butterfly-winged, naked girls approximately the same size as a nearby squirrel. The connection between verses and drawing is that they both evoke "a fairy dream of youth" (Carroll, p. 840)—a theme emphasized by the fact that it is the only one shared by the two. Despite being twenty-one—an odd age to be so nostalgic—Carroll, in his poem "In Solitude," apostrophizes:

> I'd give all wealth that years have piled,
>   The slow result of Life's decay,
> To be once more a little child
>   For one bright summer-day.

(Carroll, p. 840)

In a different way, the illumination also appreciates childhood: one naked little girl sleeps, while another lazily leans next to her (even though the poem recounts the joys of sleeping alone.)

In the article "Toward a Definition of *Alice*'s Genre: The Folktale and Fairy-Tale Connections," Nina Demurova demonstrates that Carroll's *Alice* books contain ironic play with the pattern of the fairy tale. In this irony, they resemble such other mid-Victorian children's books as John Ruskin's *King of the Golden River* (composed 1841), Thackeray's *The Rose and the Ring* (1855), Charles Kingsley's *Water Babies* (1863), and Charles Dickens's "The Magic Fish-Bone" (*Holiday Romance,* 1868) [9] The structure of fairy tales is fairly loose, a series of episodes usually of a quest with an even greater variety of possible variations than those described by Vladimir Propp in his *Morphology of the Folktale.*[10] Victorian irony and parody make the structure even looser and less predictable. Despite being classics, Carroll's best works (like most fantasy) lack the logical unity conventional in realistic fiction.

One might presume that since Carroll in some sense wrote the *Alice* books for and about Alice Liddel, they could be a *roman à clef,* their unity and realistic content easily established in a foundation of biography. The continuing study of Carroll's works, however, fails (except in a few details) to provide such an explanation. Instead, the opposite is more and more revealed as in Jeffrey Stern's article, "Lewis Carroll the Pre-Raphaelite." It demonstrates that Carroll's own drawings of Alice derive from Dante Gabriel Rosetti's portraits of the young model Annie Miller, particularly one painting depicting her as the eternally youthful Helen of Troy.[11] Just as the Alice of Carroll's works is not precisely the real little girl Alice Liddel for whom he wrote them, so his drawings are not (as was previously thought) inept attempts to portray her, but fairly good likenesses of the idealized young woman in Rosetti's painting. Carroll's books belong to the Romantic and Pre-Raphaelite tradition of devotion to eternal youth and should not be seen as arising completely from personal idiosyncrasies.

In her perceptive article "'To See Clearly': Perspective in Pre-Raphaelite Poetry and Painting," Julia Whitsitt shows that both the verbal and visual arts of the Pre-Raphaelites differ in the treatment of details from those of the eighteenth century. In literature during the earlier period, the tendency of the so-called Age of Reason was toward generalization rather than detail, and in art it was toward subordination of detail to total effect, particularly by perspective, which requires background figures to be small and dim. Harkening back to the naïveté of the Middle Ages, the Pre-Raphaelites drew foreground and background details with equal clarity, giving a characteristic flatness to their works. In literature, they pursued detail virtually for its own sake.[12] Although Whitsitt does not refer to Carroll, his writings carry to extremes this anti-rational tendency toward separate, barely related images. His view is like a child's lucid perception of the parts of the world but without comprehension of their integration. In a famous example from *The Hunting of the Snark,* Carroll repeats the following quatrain six times:

> They sought it with thimbles, they sought it with care
> They pursued it with forks and hope;
> They threatened its life with a railway share;
> They charmed it with smiles and soap.
>
> (Carroll, p. 196)

The parallel syntax imposes a kind of order on these miscellaneous items, which makes their disparity all the more obvious. In Henry Holiday's accompanying picture, "care" and "hope" are two beautiful young women, the former in a shroud, the latter with an anchor—a continuation of medieval Christian iconography; but the poem gives no clue that they are pictured thus. Just as the verses throng with separate images, so the illumination is a crowd scene with even more details than are mentioned in the poem. "Rendering objects in more precise details than that with which they are normally perceived can produce an hallucinatory effect, for such precision changes our relations to our world."[13]

Carroll's Preface to the second part of his novel *Sylvie and Bruno* praises its principal artist, Harry Furniss, for his "artistic ingenuity" in depicting the "most minute details" of the writer's work (Carroll, p. 659). Carroll's own drawings have notable simplicity, presumably because as an artistic amateur he was unable to achieve the complex detail that he creates in his writings. Some of his sketches have a certain charm and power, but if he were satisfied with them, he would not have paid for the detailed work of professionals. Their illuminations maintain a typically playful relationship to the texts. In *The Hunting of the Snark,* one drawing has the caption, "He had wholly forgotten his name." Actual illustration of this negative and abstract concept is virtually impossible; Holiday simply shows seven people engaged in disparate occupations (Carroll, p. 183). The last picture stands above the equally unpromising text, "Then, silence." The drawing shows spectral faces, one of them presumably that of the Baker who has vanished (vanishing being another difficult concept to convey in an etching). Outlines of the faces intermingle with foliage and shadow, while a hand and bell appear in the upper left corner. Just as the method of the text is to bring details together in a far-fetched manner, so the pictures juxtapose barely connected images from the text and elsewhere to create a hodgepodge.

Once again comparable to children's spontaneous approach to life, Carroll awaited individual moments of inspiration for each segment of his writings rather than laboriously proceeding from a general plan. In the Preface to the first part of *Sylvie and Bruno,* he explains the composition of that book:

> As the years went on, I jotted down, at odd moments, all sorts of odd ideas, and fragments of dialogue, that occurred to me—who knows how?—with a transitory suddenness that left me no choice but either to record them then and there, or to abandon them to oblivion. (Carroll, p. 494)

He continues that he has never written a book sequentially and some of his inspirations have come to him "in dreams." (Inexhaustibly rich in such details, the *Alice* books will be examined in my chapters 7 and 9 respectively, because the contexts permit fuller treatment there.) From the Pre-Raphaelites descends a tradition of elaborate, idealized art much seen today, particularly on the covers of most fairy-tale-like books of fantasy.

Charles Dickens and Caricatures

Victorians also employed other varieties of illuminated fantasy, including an expressionistic style that caricatured people and created emotional atmosphere through exaggerated attention to shadow. In his *Autobiography,* Henry James provides a childhood memory of George Cruikshank's style:

> [*Oliver Twist*] perhaps even seemed to me more Cruikshank's than

Dickens's; it was a thing of such vividly terrible images, and all marked with that peculiarity of Cruikshank that the offered flowers of good-nesses, the scenes and figures intended to comfort and cheer, present themselves under his hand as but more subtley sinister, or more sug-gestively queer, than the frank badnesses and horrors.[14]

Such also is generally the style of John Leech's pictures for Charles Dickens's most famous fantasy, *A Christmas Carol* (1843). As has often been noted, Dickens viewed the world with a caricaturist's eye, a habit owing much to his familiarity with the tradition of British cartooning, particularly the satiric prints of William Hogarth (1697–1764). Nonetheless, with the important exception of shared fondness for exaggeration, Dickens's own style differs from pictorial caricature as in his description of the Spirit of Christmas Past in *A Christmas Carol:*

> It was a strange figure—like a child: yet not so like a child as like an old man, viewed through some supernatural medium, which gave him the appearance of having receded from the view, and being diminished to a child's proportions. Its hair, which hung about its neck and down its back, was white as if with age; and yet the face had not a wrinkle in it, and the tenderest bloom was on the skin. . . . But the strangest thing about it was, that from the crown of its head there sprung a bright clear jet of light, by which all this was visible; and which was doubtless the occasion of its using, in its duller moments, a great extinguisher for a cap, which it now held under its arm.
>
> Even this, though, when Scrooge looked at it with increasing stead-iness, was *not* its strangest quality. For as its belt sparkled and glittered now in one part and now in another, and what was light one instant, at another time was dark, so the figure itself fluctuated in its distinctness: being now a thing with one arm, now with twenty legs, now a pair of legs without a head, now a head without a body: of which dissolving parts, no outline would be visible in the dense gloom wherein they melted away. And in the very wonder of this, it would be itself again; distinct and clear as ever.[15]

Obviously, no etching in a book can illustrate this imaginative flux, yet the element of fantasy largely resides in the metamorphoses and alternations that Dickens describes. In other parts of the book, a door knocker becomes a spectral head, ghosts fade in and out of the mist, and scenes magically dissolve as Scrooge travels through time and space. Confronted with a kind of cinema of his life filled with short, dramatic cuts and lavish special effects, Scrooge constantly vacillates, slipping from emotion to emotion. When the visions have passed, he exclaims, "I am as happy as an angel, I am as merry as a school boy" (Dickens, p. 127). Like the Spirit of Christmas Past, Scrooge is now both old man and child. At the end, the narrator comments that Scrooge's conversion is permanent (Dickens, p. 133). Recalling the constant shifting of Scrooge's mind and the frequent vicissitudes of his dreams, the reader may have difficulty believing in this permanence. In his classic article "Dickens: The Two Scrooges," the critic Edmund Wilson considers Scrooge a manic-depressive and deems the ending implausible, perhaps partly because, as is common with critics, he ignores the pictures.[16] While Dickens's prose skillfully exploits the temporal nature of writing to provide a motion picture ceaselessly changing, Leech contributes a kind of slide show summarizing the stages in Scrooge's progress. First, amid Leech's mass of Gothic shadows, the ghost of Jacob Marley confronts Scrooge, whose nightcap points straight up like hair standing on end or like a dunce's cap, both appropriate images for his stupefying terror. Next appear ghosts beside an impoverished woman (Dickens's scene of the relative powerlessness of the dead to help the living). In Leech's drawing, these images are simply night terrors, which is what is most important to the plot: Scrooge must be frightened into virtue. Leech attempts no figural representation of the Spirit of Christmas Past. Dickens's above-quoted description of that being is significant: it serves as a foreshadowing of Scrooge's conversion to childlike man, but the Spirit transcends static visual depiction. It is alternately man and boy as well as a many-legged creature and a Wordsworthian, mystical "light" of childhood. Leech comes closest to the last by depicting the luster that mysteriously remains after Scrooge extinguishes the Spirit by pressing its cap down upon its head. This luminance shines from beneath his feet, flooding him with its brilliance (a reminder of the Spirit's effect on him) but also casting grim shadows, an evocation of the mood of his nightmare. Next comes Leech's Spirit of Christmas Present, an adult giant surrounded by all manner of food. He represents the joys that Scrooge may have if he repents. In the subsequent scene, the bearded, robed figure fades to a Christlike outline, its boundary lines behind or encompassing two ragged children. Dickens is richly psychological while Leech boldly depicts the horrors that modify Scrooge's behavior. As in *Hard Times,* where Dickens satirizes utilitarian pedagogy and champions fantasy, so in *A Christmas Carol* (with the help of Leech), Dickens caricatures the evils of rational self-interest and shows the need for humane fantasy to give life meaning.

Kipling and Victorian Pedagogy

In addition to nonsense and tales of fairies and spirits, readers also perused didactic fiction such as Rudyard Kipling's *Just So Stories* (composed 1897–1902). The pictures that he drew for this volume are charming, the fables amusing, but these attractions do not adequately compensate for the faults that the work shares with much pedagogical fiction. Kipling's condescension manifests itself in baby talk gone mad. It includes not merely such conventional nursery words as "Mummy" and "Daddy" but numerous previously unperpetrated diminutives and words with syllables lopped off. There are even terms deliberately misused as a practical joke on the young. (It may seem strange that abuse of language should be pedagogical, but examples of less extreme verbal shoddiness are now common in educational TV for children, e.g., "Schoolhouse Rock.")

One of the unifying motifs of *Just So Stories* is corporal punishment. In the chapter "How the Camel Got his Hump," for instance, the title animal dreamily stares at his own reflection instead of working. Even in the midst of this iniquity, he looks unhappy, and punishment follows swiftly. A Djinn permanently affixes an "ugly lump" to the camel's back. In some thoroughly dreadful verses, Kipling makes the moral explicit: if children are lazy and speak in a "snarly-yarly voice," then their parents like the "nicest of the Djinns" will put them in a corner and raise on their backs "The horrible hump— / The hump that is black and blue!"[17] Although, of all the chapters, "The Elephant Child" best deserves a Marquis de Sade award for its frequent beatings and other descriptions of physical torment, the story entitled, "How the First Letter Was Written" even has a character named "Small-person-without-any-manners-who-ought-to-be-spanked" (Kipling, p. 115). Since this child lives before the invention of writing, she sends a message in pictures, which are misunderstood, causing someone else to be beaten. The story concludes: "very few little girls have ever liked learning to read or write. Most of them prefer to draw pictures and play." Since, however, pictures are ambiguous, the children must become literate. In the subsequent chapter, the little girl and her father discover writing. The story ends with his leaving her a clear, written message to do her chores.

The book's pictures look at first glance like illuminations, for they abound with evocative images—an Egyptian god complete with hieroglyphics and other motifs, both secular and religious, especially a reoccuring Noah's ark and Kipling's favorite symbol, the swastika (which in 1902 still carried exotic religious connotations). His stories make little obvious use of the religious ambience of the sacred images. Therefore, their relationship to the text would be richly problematic except that, for each large picture, he appends a page explaining how every figure relates to the narrative. These interpretations are often whimsical, but they do establish a fairly clear tie between picture and text. Like most didacticists, instead of opening the text to multiple interpretations, he authoritatively stresses his own (even when playing tricks on young readers). Although some of Kipling's writings deserve the status of classics, this book shows him at his most homiletic, eager to teach the young how to be members of the British Empire. In this work, such membership means being subservient to authority figures and calling people with skins darker than his own "Sambo" (Kipling, p. 52). *Just So Stories* is not a book for adults—would that it had never been given to children.

FIN DE SIÈCLE FANTASY

Although one might easily see elements of turn-of-the-century decadence even in *Just So Stories,* the literature of pure decadence is not really pedagogical, except in teaching ways of vice. Its quintessence is the uncensored manuscript of Aubrey Beardsley's unfinished fantasy *The Story of Venus and Tannhäuser.* Implicit behind its eroticism rests that guiding principle that Aldous Huxley later enunciated as a law of his *Brave New World,* that sex should be infantile, experimentation freed from procreation or even any deep emotion.[18] Crowds of usually naked and always perverse boys sport through Beardsley's text, among a range of other sexual partners including satyrs, a unicorn, and the goddess Venus. Practically every conceivable relationship appears except for mature, human love. Elaborations, sensual and otherwise, smother the prose, while the illuminations also turn detail into fetishes but in a different manner. The drawing "Venus between Terminal Gods," for instance, parodies medieval tapestries, its mythical figures separated with mazes of clinging vine. Venus's crown lies not on her head but on these sinewy arabesques. Like the other pictures, it is no realistic illustration of a moment in the story but a visual decoration added to the intricate decorativeness of the text itself.

Not so touched with lavender as Beardsley's work, but still within a similar "art for art's sake" atmosphere are the heroic fantasies of William Morris. They are often called the parents of modern, adult fantasy, but they do not sound very modern (nor, for that matter, very adult). Imitating every quaintness even to the prolixity of medieval prose, Morris creates pastorals of innocence in *The Glittering Plain* (1891), and his "W" books, *The Wood Beyond the World* (1895), *The Water of the Wondrous Isles* (1895), and *The Well at the World's End* (1896). An artist himself, Morris was fascinated by fifteenth-century wood-block illuminations, but he never presented a fully illuminated fantasy. The closest he came was his collaboration with the painter Sir Edward Burne-Jones for *The Earthly Paradise.* This "Big Story Book" (as Morris's friend William Allingham called it) finally saw print but without the hundreds of woodcuts, only a few of which were engraved. Where these were intended to be placed in the text is uncertain.[19] On a small scale, though, one may glimpse the kind of work intended by examining the poem *Love is Enough* (1871), with borders and text by Morris and other art by

Love is Enough.

THE MUSIC.

LOVE is enough: though the world
    be a-waning,
And the woods have no voice but
    the voice of complaining;
Though the sky be too dark for
    dim eyes to discover
The gold - cups and daisies fair
    blooming thereunder,
Though the hill be held shadows,
    and the sea a dark wonder,
And this day draw a veil over all deeds passed over,
Yet their hands shall not tremble, their feet shall not falter;
The void shall not weary, the fear shall not alter
  These lips and these eyes of the loved and the lover.

THE EMPEROR.

The spears flashed by me, and the spears swept round,
And in war's hopeless tangle was I bound,
But straw and stubble were the cold points found,
For still thy hands led down the weary way.

THE EMPRESS.

Through hall and street they led me as a queen,
They looked to see me proud and cold of mien,
I heeded not though all my tears were seen,
For still I dreamed of thee throughout the day.

THE EMPEROR.

Wild over bow and bulwark swept the sea
Unto the iron coast upon our lee,
Like painted cloth its fury was to me,
For still thy hands led down the weary way.

Sir Edward Coley Burne-Jones, trial first page for an edition of William Morris's Love is Enough, *ca. 1871.* (By permission of The William Morris Gallery, Walthamstow, London.)

Burne-Jones. Its juxtaposition of love with children and a garden reveals a thread that runs through so much of Morris's work, for, despite his socialism, his fantasies are not engagé by modern standards, but nostalgic, longing for the alleged purity of some golden age.

TWENTIETH-CENTURY FANTASY

Lord Dunsany and "Adult" Sword and Sorcery

Much of what happened to fantasy after the *fin de siècle* can be traced back to the Decadence; this is certainly true of Lord Dunsany's fairy tales with their Oscar Wilde-like cynicism and their illuminations in the Beardleyesque style of Sidney Sime. Dunsany's works are far closer to modern "adult" fantasy than Morris's, though, down to the present, one should not take the word "adult" too seriously when combined with "fantasy." There is usually a self-conscious relationship of fantasy to children's literature. "How Nuth would have Practiced his Art upon the Gnoles" (from Dunsany's and Sime's *The Book of Wonder,* 1912), for example, explores a common theme of juvenile fiction—a boy learning a trade—except in Dunsany's version the "likely lad" studies burglary from the villainous Nuth and is carried off by monsters. The tale ends:

> "And did they catch Nuth?" you ask me, gentle reader.
> "Oh, no, my child" (for such a question is childish).
> "Nobody ever catches Nuth."[20]

The lines imply that the reader is not a juvenile but may harbor the jejune notion that evil is always punished. Criticizing childish naïveté, Dunsany, nonetheless, encourages childlike wonder (the emotion after which his volume is named). The illumination shows three simian creatures near a house with a cross on it. To their right lies a mine with a lantern casting light in physically impossible patterns. The drawing of the picture preceded the composition of the story, and in accordance with Dunsany's instructions, Sime did not tell the former what the visual image meant. The latter wished to use it merely for inspiration. Thus Dunsany ignored details that did not inspire him, e.g., the cross, lantern, mine, and gorilla-like appearance of the "gnole" monsters.

Similarly, after seeing Sime's picture of a centaur holding the almost-Gorgon-like head of a snarling female creature, Dunsany wrote a tale of a young "man-horse," who leaves home and mother to capture this divinely begotten creature whose "beauty was as a dream"—surely an ironic description. In six other books (including *The Gods of Pegana,* 1905) Dunsany's stories inspired Sime's drawings rather than the other way around, yet the two still maintain considerable independence. Concerning their *Gods of Pegana,* Dunsany wrote:

> Of course, the gods and their heavens that he drew for me were totally

Sidney Sime, "The Bride of the Man-Horse," from Lord Dunsany's The Book of Wonder, *1912.* (By permission of Thames and Hudson, Ltd.; William Heinemann and Heinemann Publishing Co.; The Worplesdon Memorial Trustees for the Sidney Sime Memorial Museum, Old Rickford, Worplesdon, England; and the Curtis Brown Group Ltd., of London, which acts for the Estate of Lord Dunsany.)

different from anything that I had imagined, but I knew that it would be impossible to catch Sime's Pegasus and drive it exactly along the same track that I had traveled myself, and that if it were possible, it could only be done by clipping its wings.[21]

James Barrie and Eternal Youth

One of the qualities that allows Dunsany's tales to be called "adult" is his recognition of evil, as with the just-mentioned young protagonists who are dedicated to burglary and rape, respectively. Distinction between adult and juvenile fiction is not always clear-cut, and both are far more likely to accept children's foibles than before the Decadence. Carroll idolized youth, yet hated boyish pranks. Victorian adventure books fantasized about the rugged side of boyhood; nonetheless, the true breakthrough of unscrupulous children's fantasy occurs in Sir James Barrie's play *Peter Pan* (1904), on which his book *Peter and Wendy* (1911) is based. They explore the old theme of the eternal child but with a new amorality appropriate to the time of *The Picture of Dorian Gray* (1891) and thereafter. In that relatively modern world, people who believed less fervently in heavenly immortality perhaps fantasized more heartily about an endless, irresponsible youth here on earth. At any rate, *Peter and Wendy* envisions eternal childhood as "gay and innocent and heartless," a refrain throughout the volume.[22] When the lost boys go adventuring, they frequently find the bodies of the people whom Peter has slain (in fair fights, one presumes), but Carroll's Alice was never so violent. The last battle between the boys and the pirates costs fifteen of those buccaneers their lives. More disturbing is the flight from London to Never Land, during which Peter waits until the last second to save John, Wendy, and Michael each time they start to fall (and Peter grows tired of saving them at all). His rule over the lost boys does not bring security:

> The boys on the island vary, of course in number, according as they get killed and so on; and when they seem to be growing up, which is against the rules, Peter thins them out. (*Peter and Wendy*, p. 63)

Barrie never discloses what "thins them out" means. He does, though, describe Peter's character flaws from cockiness to thoughtlessness. Nonetheless, near the end of the narrative, Mrs. Darling gives Peter "the kiss that had been for no one else"—not even her husband and children. Peter is dearer to her, being part of the dream life she had in childhood, i.e., part of herself (*Peter and Wendy*, p. 210). In this world of the imagination, very little separates hero and villain, i.e., Peter and the pirate Captain Hook. At one point (the rescue of Tiger Lily, p. 111), the latter temporarily doubts his own

identity and thinks that Peter is Hook himself. Conversely, after feeding the
captain to the crocodile, Peter dons the buccaneer's robes:

> It was afterwards whispered among [the lost boys] that on the first
> night he wore his suit he sat long in the cabin with Hook's cigar-holder
> in his mouth and one hand clenched, all but the forefinger, which he
> bent and held threateningly aloft like a hook. (Peter and Wendy, p. 193)

Throughout much of the book, Captain Hook suffers from the realization
that his own self-consciousness keeps him from achieving "good form"—a
quality he recognizes in Peter (*Peter and Wendy*, p. 188). In an early version of
the play, Hook was a schoolmaster, a professional threat to children's (presumed) lack of self-consciousness.[23]

The whole book favors the latter and their world of play, as in F. D.
Bedford's illuminations for *Peter and Wendy,* which crowd more adventure
within each scene than is realistically possible, e.g., six wolves, six Indians,
eight pirates, Peter Pan, an Indian village, Wendy's house, a mermaid
lagoon, four flamingoes, the lost boys, a crocodile, Captain Hook, and a
pirate ship—all in one engraving. Although the galleon in the text is big
enough to hold a crew of seventeen and all the lost boys, Bedford's vessel
seems scarcely larger than a toy because of the gigantic scale he gives to
Hook. Due to the crowding and violations of perspective, the drawing
appropriately presents the characters like an array of images in the mind,
their exact relationship to one another as confused as in Carroll's childlike
view of the world.

Youths simultaneously adorable and horrible have become almost a modern cliché. Their exploits appear in such fantasies as Michael DeLarrabeiti's
Borribles series (1978–) where, if children go wild, steal, kill, and live for
adventure, their ears grow pointed and they remain immortally young.[24]
Similarly, the elves of Wendy and Richard Pini's *ElfQuest* series (1978–)
resemble children with pointed ears and also may become savagely violent.
To some extent, adolescent wildness and craving for adventure are virtually
inevitable in the genre, though more moralistic fantasists express them with
qualifications and restraints as in the fictions of J. R. R. Tolkien and C. S.
Lewis. Using imagination with moderation, these two have given fantasy a
new consistency (and consequent popularity) that make reference to them
inevitable in surveying the genre.

Neo-Christian Illumination: Tolkien and Lewis

Tolkien piously describes fantasy writing as the "sub-creation" of a "Sec-
ondary World," consistently obeying its own laws (only God being able to

ElfQuest Book I

by Wendy and Richard Pini

Since its first appearance in 1978, **Elfquest** has won every major award in its field including **Best Story** and **Best Artist**. It has become the best-selling independent comic publication in the United States with an international following that numbers in the hundreds of thousands, and grows with every issue.

Elfquest Book I compiles the first five issues of the black and white series into one complete **Full-Color** volume.

Elfquest is an intricate blend of art and story filled with action, humor and romance. This epic adventure of Cutter and the elves of Sorrow's End is destined to become a fantasy favorite for persons aged three to one hundred and three!

Wendy Pini, back cover of ElfQuest: Book 1, *1981.* (By permission of The Donning Company, Norfolk, England.)

create a real cosmos). Such subcreation evokes the universe of *"Faerie,"* by which he means exalted visionary experience, "indescribable though not imperceptible."[25] This is mysticism, but not traditional Christian mysticism, in which the word "faerie," if used at all, tends to involve the demonic (or at least daemonic) rather than a numinous state, which Tolkien thinks a Christian writer should contemplate.

Despite his love of consistency, Tolkien achieved this numinous feeling through such subtle inconsistencies of mood and presentation as are customary in fantasy. In *The Hobbit,* for example, only three of the eight pictures he drew include people. The majority seem like scenes from an eerie, uninhabited past. Even the three pictures of people show no action, a far cry from the busy sketches typical in children's books and also a contrast to Tolkien's own action-filled text. With Celtic-like complexity of design, all eight drawings image a remote and alien antiquity. The narrative, though, gives the adventures a homely cast by focusing on Bilbo Baggins's longing for creature comforts. A perfect example of how children's and adults' fantasy cannot be completely separated, *The Hobbit* is the prologue to the "adult" saga, *The Lord of the Rings.* The latter gives free play to religious themes, e.g., the angelic Istari's incarnation into such wizards as Gandalf and Saruman—a notion absent from Christian dogmatics.

Lewis's greatest children's fantasy, the Narnia series, also involves a novel incarnation: that of God into the body of the lion Aslan. In a 1958 letter, Lewis explained that "Aslan represented the immaterial Deity. . . . [as] an imaginary answer to the question, 'What might Christ become like, if there really were a world like Narnia and He chose to be incarnate . . . in that world as he actually has done in ours?' "[26] In that letter, he held that Aslan was not an allegory of Christ but a separate (albeit imaginary) Being. This idea, unfortunately, led him into another theological problem. In 1955, the mother of the nine-year-old boy Laurence Krieg wrote Lewis to say that her son worried that he was committing idolatry by loving Aslan more than Christ. Lewis replied, "The things he loves Aslan for doing and saying are simply the things Jesus really did and said."[27] This is not literally true, since Jesus was not a lion living in Narnia. Here Lewis seems to interpret Aslan figuratively, i.e., allegorically as a metaphor for Jesus rather than as a somewhat different being who was incarnate as an animal. In the adaptation of dogma into children's fantasy, consistency is virtually impossible.

Since both Tolkien and Lewis tried for a consistency comparable to "science fantasy," they were well-served by the relatively illustrative art of Pauline Baynes, the artist they employed most often. Baynes's works, nonetheless, also have an illuminative quality, a childish flatness that makes them like mythical icons. By a comparable but different method—by (as he explains) describing characters "more briefly than [in adult] novelization"—

Lewis seeks to reach children's imagination.[28] Thus, like Tolkien, he is paradoxically committed to combining solid and consistent fiction with its exact opposite, the sketchy and numinous.

Neo-Paganism and Fantasy

Most of the innovations in twentieth-century illuminated fantasy derive directly or indirectly from the passing away of Christian hegemony and of its concomitant insistence on clear, traditional moral edification. Even in the Victorian period, fantasists were aware of non-Christian religions, but few writers took them very seriously. Typically, in the preface to the second part of *Sylvie and Bruno,* Lewis Carroll compared the system of his work to that of *Esoteric Buddhism* (a book by A. P. Sinnett combining Buddhism, Hinduism, and western occultism). A Christian deacon himself and son of an archdeacon, Carroll makes this comparison as a joke, not a declaration of sympathy for neo-paganism. Modern fantasists often go further toward ecumenicism, e.g., Marion Zimmer Bradley, author of the best-selling *Mists of Avalon,* and Andre Norton, winner of the Grand Master Nebula Award. In conversation (January 1983), Bradley told me that she permitted the use of her back yard to a local witches' coven so that they could worship in peace. Similarly, in a March 1982 interview with Charles Platt, Norton mentioned her friendship with "practitioners of Wicca," the religion of the witches (where magic and sexual energy are considered, in some respect, interdependent). She continued that in her writings she sometimes employed authentic spells and ceremonies, but in altered form because "This is necessary." Her friends had advised her against the sacrilege of revealing the mysteries.[29] A former children's librarian, Norton has published about a hundred books, mostly juvenile and adolescent fiction, notably her very popular Witch World series. Also a prolific author, Bradley gained her reputation through her Darkover books. Both series focus on heroic adventurers (particularly women) gifted with paranormal abilities directly or indirectly connected with their sexuality. Consequently, they often must choose to give their libidinous energies either to magic or to physical intimacies. Partly because of the readers for whom she writes, Norton's lovers seldom sexually consummate their relationships. Furthermore, in her interview with Platt, she disclosed that she found the sensual freedom in modern fantasy "evil and dangerous," on one occasion leaving her "physically ill" (p. 99). On Bradley's Darkover, paranormal powers cannot normally be practiced by the sexually active. There exists, however, a drug that permits ESP workers to copulate without ceasing their psychic labors, and Bradley does not shrink from sexual description.

Most of these authors' works lack internal illustrations or illuminations (indeed, Bradley told me of her dislike for her one book thus embellished), but Norton has been enjoying some recent success from her novel *Voorloper,* with pictures by Alicia Austin, a Hugo and World Fantasy Award winner. The story concerns a platonic friendship between an attractive young man and woman. The latter, Illo, is gifted with the power of healing, making her one of a group who do not marry until "their powers beg[i]n to wane."[30] The illuminations proceed in an odd manner, reminiscent of Wagnerian leitmotifs. When Norton first mentions Illo (as a girl sitting by a fire), Austin surprisingly shows her in a garden with flowers beside her. Precisely the same picture occurs again when the young man Bart finally meets her, but it does not illustrate the text there either, for Austin seems concerned with evocation of mood, not literal faithfulness to the words. As one might expect from the nebulous connection of Norton's fictional magic to Wicca, the book ends with hints that mysterious forces shape enchantment and life itself—a patterned existence in keeping with Austin's hauntingly evocative, repeated images.

Kahlil Gibran and Spiritual Fantasy

Yet another innovation of modern fantasy has been the rise of unorthodox "inspirational" books such as those of Kahlil Gibran, reputedly called "the Blake of the twentieth century" by the great sculptor Auguste Rodin.[31] Gibran's volumes substitute a nebulous, metaphorical religiosity for dogma. Romanticism pervades Gibran's writings, as in his chapter on "Children" in *The Prophet* (1923). It argues that parents should imitate children rather than the other way around because life must proceed ever forward. It likens parents to mere "bows," remaining behind while the children, the "living arrows" speed into the future. Gibran's picture (as with all of his illuminations regardless of subjects) shows nude bodies. Here an unclothed giant (perhaps God) holds a bow consisting of intertwined, naked forms.[32] Condemned for heresy, his first book, *Spirits Rebellious* (1903), was burned in the Beirut marketplace prefatory to his being exiled from his native Lebanon and excommunicated from the Maronite Catholic Church for writing a work deemed "dangerous, revolutionary, and poisonous to youth."[33] In the West, however, his volumes have enjoyed a persisting vogue, which has finally spread to Lebanon. The traditions (or anti-traditions) of inspirational fantasy continue in bestsellers such as Richard Bach's *Jonathan Livingston Seagull* (used in some Sunday Schools), which combines photographs of real gulls with the story of a talking bird whose skill at flight becomes a religious metaphor (though not really a Christian one). Bach's later work *Illusions: The Adventures of a Reluctant Messiah* ran for a time in the comic pages of newspapers.[34]

Parody: Gorey, Theroux, and Froud

Tolkien's and Lewis's writings owe a debt to, yet are less sermonizing than, Victorian religious literature for children, which was by authors not all that traditional themselves. These influences include the Congregationalist minister George MacDonald, who left his pulpit under charges of heresy, and the Reverend Charles Kingsley, who tried to combine Christianity with biological evolution in his published works (and whose unpublished ones are so unconventional that they even include a picture of him and his wife making love on a floating cross).[35] Norton and Bradley both employ the conventional patterns of juvenile fiction but with significant variations (as in the latter's *Heritage of Hastur,* where one of the boy-heroes falls in love with the other one). Gibran's and Bach's fantasies evidence some influence from pious children's literature, yet certainly do not belong to that genre. In summary, a tendency throughout the history of modern fantasy has been to play with the traditions of juvenile literature. Tension between stereotype and innovation particularly characterizes the subgenre of parody. Among the most effective recent examples of such works are Edward Gorey's little volumes, which look like turn-of-the-century picture books designed for a child's small hands. For centuries, authors have composed rhyming alphabets, e.g., *The New England Primer* (1691), which commences, "In Adam's fall / We sinned all."[36] Gorey's versions of the ABCs are less edifying. His book *The Gashlycrumb Tinies* shows a group of stiffly posed infants beneath the umbrella of a skull-faced nurse. The verses begin, "A is for Amy who fell down the stairs / B is for Basil assaulted by bears."[37] Thus, throughout the alphabet, child after child perishes of everything from "ennui" to devouring mice. No nurses literally have any part in the sequence, but the skeleton nanny pictured on the front suggests a malevolent fate to which the toddlers must passively submit. Another of these rhyming alphabets, "The Fatal Lozenge," has a cast including a possessed nun, a mad hermit, a religious fetishist, and a child molester (*Amphigorey* [pp. 67–76]). Any parent who actually gave one of these books to a child would have to be as heartless as "Lord Stipple" in one of Gorey's limericks. This peer informs his crippled son that the boy's deformity was heavenly vengeance because the mother's conduct "Gave pain to our Savior" (*Amphigorey* [p. 37]). In Gorey's *The Insect God,* a dumpy little Edwardian lass sits eating grass until giant praying mantises carry her off in a roadster. Six pages of childish verse and drab etchings in the style of an entomological journal lead to a human sacrifice. Gorey's booklets combine a celebration of dying young with an attack on rationality, which seems to have no place in his cruel, insane world. His humor, nonetheless, has a certain appeal to childlike irreverence. Indeed, the very similar macabre comedy of Charles Addams, originally aimed at the sophisticated audience of the *New Yorker,* spawned *The Addams Family,* a children's television program still rerun in various parts of the country.

I once found misshelved in the children's section of a bookstore the even-more peculiar fantasy *Master Snickup's Cloak,* "chronicled by Alexander Theroux [and] illuminated by Brian Froud." The latter (better known for his work for the best-selling volume *Fairies* and for the movie *The Dark Crystal*) is skilled at visual whimsy; *Master Snickup's Cloak* has an appealing juvenile format: a large, thin book, quaint elfin figures on the shiny cover, and large print within. Perhaps some mothers have bought it for bedtime reading and delighted their offspring with its vivid style, e.g., "Men castrated themselves and flung their severed genitals into the hopeless sky to placate an angry God."[38] The narrative begins almost like a fairy tale: the words "One morning it was . . . the Middle Ages" appear in archaic lettering next to a crippled court jester and a castle that looks as if it were built by Hieronymus Bosch. An orphan boy named "Snickup" falls in love with the little girl "Superfecta." In the drawing, she is either being supported by or crushing cupids under her wooden shoe—an appropriate ambiguity, considering what follows. For years, she persuades Snickup to do her chores, finally promises to wed him, and then marries a rich mill owner. Disconsolate, Snickup becomes a hermit. After overcoming demonic tempters, he dies in indescribable sanctity and filth. From his cloak crawls the flea that begins the fourteenth-century bubonic plague. Theroux writes that it flew to Kaffa (a port city in the Crimea) "as if carried along by destiny" ([p. 23]). Froud creatively interprets this simile as a winged skeleton transporting, not a real flea, but one painted on a wooden placard like the sign of an inn. This foreshadows the last scene where, behind a conspicuous wooden sign, the orphanage has become a brothel with Superfecta as the madam. The fable ends with her epidemic-ridden body dying in agonizing convulsions.

Blake Revisited: Sendak and Willard

Unlike these parodies, real children's books seldom plunge into such an abyss of despair and madness, but they are more daring than their Victorian counterparts. Recent picture books have almost equaled the boldness of Blake, occasionally quite explicitly. The controversial Maurice Sendak, who has brought a new wildness to juvenile fiction, has remarked, "I always go to Blake when I'm desperate—there's always something more to steal from him."[39] A few years ago, the Caldecott and Newbery awards for children's literature went to Nancy Willard for her book *A Visit to William Blake's Inn: Poems for Innocent and Experienced Travellers* (1981). Typical of its verses is her parody of a familiar children's prayer, where she has significantly added the name of Blake substituted for "the Lord":

Now I lay me down to sleep
with bear and rabbit, bird and sheep.
If I should dream before I wake,
may I dream of William Blake.[40]

The Comics: McCay, et al.

The greatest innovation in illuminated fantasy began near the end of the nineteenth century and seems coincidentally connected with the decline of Christian control over society. Despite protests from a few church groups, American newspapers began publishing Sunday editions with full-color comics to offer an amusing alternative to Sabbath-day Bible reading. Although black and white cartoons have appeared in Europe from at least the seventeenth century, the new "polychromatic effulgence," as an 1896 advertisement called it, achieved great popular success.[41] From 1904 to 1911, the *New York Herald* and *Evening Telegram* printed a number of colorful comic strips evidencing the influence of Edward Lear and Lewis Carroll.[42] Of these newspaper fantasists, Windsor McCay remains memorable for his *Dreams of the Rarebit Fiend* and *Little Nemo in Slumberland;* nonetheless, his style was rather primerlike. The same blemish marred many other comic strips and continued into the comic books when companies published strips in that form.

Fortunately, some writers and artists, while still basing their works on conventions of juvenile literature, managed to transcend the stereotypes. Their playfulness predominates in the "adult" comic books and appears from time to time even in children's. Typical of this wider range of reference is "Through a Glass Permanently," the first story in the February 1982 issue of *Flash,* a comic book censored for children, though the cover of this issue punningly addresses the readers as "whiz-kids". The basic structure of the story is that of most adventure comics for children: hero pursuing villain— except, as with better comics, there is some intellectual exploration of the themes. In a psychological allegory, the villain, a master of mirrors, falls in love with the allusively named woman Narcissa, whom he finds trapped within a looking glass. Far from what one would expect in juvenile fiction (if one were not familiar with the characteristic allusiveness of it), the story ends with the following lines from *Tethys Festivall* (1610), a poetic drama by the relatively obscure Jacobean author Samuel Daniel:

> Are they shadows that we see?
> And can shadows pleasure give?
> Pleasures only shadows be
> Cast by bodies we conceive,

And are made the things we deem
In those figures which they seem.
(*Flash* 34 (February 1982): 18)[43]

Daniel recalls Plato's myth of the cave, according to which mankind is like a prisoner raised in a cavern, where he mistakes the shadows on the wall (the changing events of this world) for the timeless reality beyond. Similarly, the villain has devoted his life to the mere reflections in his mirrors rather than to society, which he scorns. Particularly considering that most children nowadays are not familiar with seventeenth-century poetry and Platonic philosophy, picture-text relationshp here is difficult. Above pictures of the villain's weeping inconsolably, the magazine places Daniel's lines counseling acceptance, a marked contrast. By introducing the poet's description of the world as mere appearance, the comic suggests that the villainess was all the time no more than a narcissistic projection from the Mirror Master's mind. He is the only one who has ever noticed her. At the end, the hero seems puzzled, unable to discover what the villain sees. Denunciation of narcissism is extremely common in pedagogical children's literature, but here there is more than simplistic and unfeeling condemnation. In the last frame, the hero places a hand on the Mirror Master's shoulder in a gesture both of comfort and arrest; for at that moment the hero seems to be involuntarily empathizing with his enemy.

As the directly preceding example suggests, comic books, like most fantasy, manifest a great propensity for the bizarre. In 1947 William Gaines inherited Educational Comics (publisher of *Picture Stories from the Bible*); by December 1949, he had changed the name to Entertaining Comics and was publishing tales of horror. They were the comic books' culmination of a long exploration of the grotesque and unnerving world of childhood nightmares. Today, they still assert an influence on such illuminated fantasies as Steven King's *Creepshow,* but, except for the humor magazine *Mad,* the EC line perished when a reaction against comic books occurred.[44] In his work *The Seduction of the Innocent* (1954), the psychologist Frederic Wertham, the instigator of this reaction, charges the comics with damaging children's minds.[45] Ironically, one of his chief targets was *Wonder Woman,* written under the pseudonym Charles Moulton by another psychologist (William Moulton Marston) specifically to improve children's mental health. Unfortunately, Marston's image of a dynamic woman provided as a cure for sexism seemed to Wertham to be an incitement to lesbianism. Terrified by Wertham's nationwide campaign, comic-book companies either discontinued publication or self-censored their products through the Comics Code Authority (established October 1954). Consequently, comics became even more primerlike, only recently emerging in a new efflorescence. Now with the baby boom having come to an end, publishers generally realize that they must either attract adults or cut back production to virtual oblivion.

In the last decade, self-censorship has been losing ground, partly because of the May 1970 issue (no. 96) of *Amazing Spiderman,* which depicted a child on drugs, a previously forbidden subject. The Comics Code Authority immediately took action, only to find that Marvel Comics had published the issue at the specific request of the National Institute of Mental Health. Thereafter, the Code has generally been interpreted in a more liberal way. Even as recently as 1980, however, a story about "angel dust" in a *Daredevil* magazine (planned at the request of the Phoenix House rehabilitation center) was "shelved" because of pressure from the Comics Code Authority.[46]

Despite minor persecutions, fantasy has generally been permitted to develop over the last two hundred years in Britain and America. Other regions of the world have not always offered as receptive an environment. In Chile, during the early 1970s, some supporters of the socialist Popular Unity regime issued denunciations of the fascism and imperialism of Disney comics, e.g., Ariel Dorfman and Armand Mattelart's *Para leer al Pato Donald.*[47] Presuming that the English-speaking world will remain much as it is (a rather large assumption), fantasy will probably hold its own against didacticism. Picture books for the eternal child are not precisely what a conservative PTA would have children read, nor are they conventional fare for adults. Illuminated fantasy is anomalous, yet echoes certain basic patterns to be explored in subsequent chapters.

II

Persisting Images

4

Enduring Elements of Political Fantasy

PLACED ON EDITORIAL PAGES LIKE AN ANALYSIS OF CONTEMPORARY ISSUES, POLITI-cal cartoons are quite different—a fusion of timely reality with timeless images often drawn from legend and myth. Indeed, the British political satirist Michael ffolkes once confessed to harboring the superstition that his particularly savage caricature of the actor Jeff Chandler had acted like a voodoo doll, causing the latter's hospitalization.[1] Even though fantasy's connection with such prerational notions makes it not entirely desirable in rational decision making, according to Northrop Frye's *Anatomy of Criticism,* "Satire demands a token fantasy."[2] Cartooning, however, is particularly appropriate in modern politics, which has less to do with reason than with the illusionary techniques of advertising.

According to Bevis Hillier's history of visual satire, "the earliest true caricature" was a thirteenth-century Christian drawing of a Jewish financier shown with three heads, a pattern probably traceable to Asian idols.[3] Both Dagon (a god of the Israelites' Philistine enemies) and a stereotypical Satan accompany the financier. The anti-Semitism derives not merely from the scurrilous caricature but also from telescoping together Judaism, gentile gods, and medieval devils. This drawing of the despised Hebrew contains a discrepancy of picture and text found in most political cartoons. By the very nature of caricatures, they vary from the physical appearance of the person or persons ridiculed. Thus, labeling such a sketch with the name of its victim is literally a misrepresentation. Artists typically make some effort to convey the personality of the caricatured, but in this medieval example, one suspects the anonymous satirist saw only his own prejudices. In his study *Political Graphics: Art as a Weapon*, Robert Philippe argues, "Political iconography had traditional stereotypes, a kind of motionlessness, a repertoire of eternally true images," but despite being timeless, the types are not always true.[4] They are merely fantastic.

Judaism has not been the only faith weirdly caricatured. Scarcely a single group has escaped vilification. For example, Jesuits allegedly worshiping Mahomet, Masons supposedly conducting obscene pseudo-Egyptian rites, and Protestants purportedly driven to convulsions by Jesuitism masquerading as Methodism figure among the grotesque imagery of later cartoons.[5] In an interview in *Crimer's Journal,* the caricaturist David Levine mentions the following instance of cartoons' alleged power in political debate. The *New York Times* once decided that his picture of Nixon's undergoing a lie-detector test was too overpowering to be printed. Levine commented:

> When you read [a text], you have a different time element [than viewing a picture]; you may agree [with the text or] . . . disagree and push things aside mentally. But when you look at that drawing, you take it all in at once. And I think they were afraid of that.[6]

Aside from self-restraint by the media, the growth of democracy has made other censorship difficult. Among the principal test cases of governmental control of the press, number the three trials and acquittals of William Hone (all in 1817). He was accused of parodying the church Litany and Athanasian Creed while attacking the government and crown. His legal victories helped to ensure that tyranny would be opposed not merely with guns but in Hone's fantastic manner. For an example of his complex use of ancient religious imagery, consider his satires, "The Joss and His Folly" and "A Peep at the P★V★★★★N . . . the Temple of Joss" (1820), both with illuminations by George Cruikshank.[7] The latter begins:

> Fo's Chinese Temple is the haunt of sin,
> And all must w[hore] and drink who walk therein!

"Fo" is a Chinese name for Buddha, which in this context is also the meaning of the Pidgin English word "Joss." These terms commonly appeared in contemporary political controversy, where satirists applied them to monarchs' trying to assume the absolutism of Asian god-kings. Here the words indict King George IV, whose vastly expensive "Temple," Brighton Pavilion, formed the apotheosis (or, if one prefers, nadir) of Chinoiserie (a kind of architecture mixing Chinese and other styles). In this pamphlet, Hone predicts King George's "extinction," seemingly a pun on the Buddhist nirvana (usually mistranslated "extinction" or "annihilation").

The epithet "Fo" was oddly appropriate. At least by title, the British King served as Defender of the Christian Faith and Governor of the Church of England; but to gain Ceylon in 1815, the crown acquired by a fantastic treaty an additional responsibility, the protection of Sinhalese Buddhism. Neither George III (legally insane at that time) nor his son and regent, the future George IV, noticeably demurred. Evangelicals, however, cautiously protested British officials' participating in Buddhist ceremonies—a controversy that Hone may have recalled.[8] Inspired by Hone's reference to George IV as "Fo," Cruikshank portrays the king as a porcelain Buddha forming the lid of a teapot.

Even relatively crude satires may be problematic, for instance, Benjamin Franklin's woodcut in the *Pennsylvania Gazette* of 9 May 1754 (usually considered the first American political cartoon).[9] It consists simply of a roughly drawn serpent cut in eight sections, each labeled with the initial or initials of one of the American Colonies. Beneath the sketch, bold letters demand, "Join, or Die." In the Albany Convention of 1754, Franklin was frustrated by fellow delegates' resistance to his scheme of forming a council representing the Colonies to coordinate defense against assaults by the French and Indians. Colonial governments refused to approve this plan. Long afterward, Franklin believed that his proposal would have made the American Revolution unnecessary by allowing the Colonies to speak to Parliament with a united voice. In opposition to the Stamp Act of 1765, Paul Revere re-drew Franklin's cartoon, adding another link to stand for Georgia. One usually thinks of political cartoons' having a clear topical reference to one event, but over the years the same images often repeat, because the essence of any given satire is a timeless fantasy that can be applied to many situations. In Franklin's and Revere's versions, the words, "Join, or Die" suggest that union is still possible. Despite the recuperative powers of serpents, celebrated in old folk tales, the snake of the drawing divided into eight (or in Revere's sketch nine) parts hardly looks capable of recovery.[10] One wonders if the Colonies are satirized for their never being able to unite or if they are urged to join as a realistic possibility.

Although cartoons certainly played a role in the partisan struggles of British politics, the mass democracy of America offered even greater scope. The satirist who best realized this potential was Thomas Nast. Children's fantasy owes him a debt for his establishing the pictorial image of Santa Claus (while the subtly different written legend derives largely from "The Night Before Christmas," usually attributed to Clement Moore). Historians

George Cruikshank, picture from William Hone's "The Joss and His Folly," 1820. (Chinoiserie: The Vision of Cathay © 1961 by Hugh Honour. By permission of Harper and Row.)

of the political cartoon, however, recall Nast as the great opponent of Boss Tweed.

In 1871, under a death threat from the Tweed Gang (which had stolen between $45 million and $200 million from New York City), Nast moved his family out of that area. Otherwise ignoring warnings and turning down a half-million-dollar bribe (one hundred times his annual salary), he continued to attack corruption through devastating caricatures. William Tweed once bellowed, "My constituents can't read; but, damn it, they can see pictures!"[11] In a time much like our own, a leader of opinion needed to appeal even to the not very literate—a task for which Nast was eminently prepared. As a child, he had so little academic success that his parents switched him from school to school until a frustrated teacher finally told the boy: "Go finish your picture. You will never learn to read or figure."[12] Probably he suffered from a now-known learning disability resulting from a slowly developing verbal hemisphere of the brain. Some victims of this have pronounced creative abilities, such as Robert Shields, formerly of the Shields and Yarnell mime team. As in such cases, Nast later became capable of learning and began to teach himself, pouring over newspapers and making copious notes. When he had the money, he even paid university students "a dollar an hour" for reading to him while he caricatured government officials (Vinson, p. 13).

His work became an admirable blend of writing and visual art. His cartooning grew simpler, more modern. Lacking irrelevant distracting details, his caricatures better served as imaginative accompaniments for each written caption, which itself was frequently a simple slogan. Nonetheless, like most of his contemporary cartoonists, his works are sometimes more elaborate and wordy than is common in political caricatures today. His biographer, J. Chal Vinson, generalizes: "It really seemed that Americans still did not 'trust' pictures by themselves and felt at home with them only when introduced by the more familiar art form of the written word" (Vinson, p. 11). Nast's anti-Tweed cartoons have become classics, imitated by later practitioners of his art. One of his most famous shows the obese, immaculately suited torso of Tweed with a money bag instead of a head. During a 1978 political scandal, the modern cartoonist Paul Conrad copied this drawing and signed it, "Th. Nast and Conrad."[13] Another of Nast's creations depicts Tweed and fellow-gang members as vultures. In a 1972 sketch, David Levine copied it except for the heads, which became those of Nixon and friends. Yet another of Nast's cartoons shows Tweed and associates in a circle, each pointing to his neighbor as the guilty party. In 1973, Levine imitated this with alleged Watergate conspirators.[14] In some cases, modern caricaturists feel obliged to credit Nast for their borrowings from him; in others, his images are simply part of the general culture they use without mention. Indeed, once created, a fantasy image begins to slip into being a timeless property of all.

Historians generally credit Nast with Tweed's transfer from power to prison. Before his final fall, Tweed called Nast "vulgar and blasphemous" (Vinson, p. 18), a charge that could be leveled against many satirists because, in bringing down those in high positions, satire frequently chooses religion as its target. This is partly because religion often reinforces the social struc-

Thomas Nast, "The American River Ganges." (By permission of Dover Publications, Inc.)

ture. Although Nast was raised a Roman Catholic, he is often anticlerical as in his cartoon entitled "The American River Ganges": a papal crown resembling a crocodile's jaws threatens children, while across the river rises the Vatican linked to "Tammany Hall."[15] Nast implies that an alliance between Boss Tweed's Tammany Hall and the Roman Catholic church schools could imperil pupils' futures as drastically as if they became Hindus, believing their salvation was in the Holy Ganges.

Not only are political cartoons themselves brief graphic narratives but they are also relevant to this study because they are similar to satiric drawings in longer fantasies. Lewis Carroll hired political cartoonists for his books to utilize their skill at comedy and satire, but even more to the point is Mark Twain's last major work, *A Connecticut Yankee in King Arthur's Court.* It actually includes political cartoons within its pages. After finishing it, Twain sent word to his cartoonist, "tell [Dan] Beard to obey his *own* inspiration, and when he sees a picture in his mind, put *that* picture on paper, be it humorous or be it serious."[16] Beard took full advantage of this latitude. In the text, for example, to build up his reputation as a magician, Twain's protagonist pretends to exorcise a spirit from a holy well, but no such spirit actually exists. Beard, nevertheless, portrays this non-existent spirit as a skeleton dressed in Papal regalia with "church/state" marked on the tiara, "policy" on a dagger, and "slavery/superstition/ignorance" on the ecclesiastical robes. A cartoon hardly specific to Twain's work, it could be placed at any time on a socialist editorial page. Despite or because of the picture/text disparity, Twain lauded Beard's work as being better than his own.[17] Even a number of first reviewers of *Connecticut Yankee* devoted lengthy and detailed praise to Beard's drawings.[18] Evidently, for a book that fantastic, people accepted pictures that did not literally illustrate the text. Furthermore, Beard did catch some of his vitriolic spirit from *Yankee* itself.

The imagery of satire maintains appreciable continuity. Despite reflecting changes in mores and religious attitudes, twentieth-century political cartoons employ some images persisting from antiquity, particularly those of the Judeo-Christian tradition. The Nixon era, in particular, inspired enough religiously allusive visual satire to paper a fairly large church. It is doubtful, though, that anyone would want to pray to the deity pictured in them. Devotion and emotional involvement require the kind of God that Michelangelo painted on the Sistine ceiling, a Being who gently stretches out His finger to man. In contrast, in a 1970 parody of Michelangelo's fresco, the eminent humorist Edward Sorel draws the face of Billy Graham on the Divine Creator. A profound disparity of tone divides the cautiously speculative accompanying paragraph of small print from the blatant sadism of the massive picture, but this disparity contributes to the cartoon's atmosphere of incongruity and absurdity. Comparably, in another Sorel parody of Michelangelo's creation fresco, God, instead of bringing light and life, turns off a gigantic electric switch implausibly suspended in mid sky. The accompanying blurb, however, prosaically explains that all that is meant is that one Con Edison spokesman blamed a blackout on an "act of God."[19]

The remarkable caricaturist Paul Conrad has done at least four parodies of the above-mentioned painting of the creation. In one, God with the face of Uncle Sam descends in a cloaking cloud from the upper-right corner to point a gun toward the lower left.[20] The implication of its caption, that mortals should not arrogate to themselves divine prerogatives, could well be intoned from any pulpit. In the visual image, though, creation is merely God's "cover," His real occupation being spy and murderer—a not very pious image. To say the least, the divine Uncle and His C.I.A. seraphim do not look as if they are playing. A second Conrad cartoon shows God unable to create the world because He has not yet received "the environmental impact report," a bureaucratic phrase in ironic counterpoint to the grandiose vista of the drawing.[21] In a third cartoon, the deity extends His finger to point to a planet exploding with mushroom clouds labeled with names referring to

Michelangelo Buonarrotti, "Creation of Adam," detail from the Sistine Chapel ceiling. (Photograph reprinted by permission of Art Resource, New York.)

"Catholic vs. Protestant" in Ireland, "Arab vs. Jew" in the Holy Land, and "Hindu vs. Moslem" in the Indian subcontinent.[22] Again, the monumental drawing contrasts with the legalistic words: "The opinions expressed do not necessarily represent those of the sponsor or of management!" A fourth parody depicts a Nixon-faced divinity creating a so-called "independent prosecutor" for the Watergate investigation.[23] Since Nixon's face also appears on the prosecutor, the relationship between the picture and the phrase

Edward Sorel, "Lord and Order," from Making the World Safe for Hypocrisy, *1972.* (Courtesy of Edward Sorel, New York.)

"independent prosecutor" is ironic. We learn not to trust words issuing from Washington. This cartoon also carries to an extreme two other tendencies in these parodies. First, all these cartoon gods regard man from a higher elevation than did Michelangelo's. In this fourth Conrad cartoon, the two are bizarrely tipped a full 45 degrees from the horizontal. While Michelangelo's spatial arrangement suggests almost an equality between God and man, the greater height of the cartoon gods accentuates their look of pride.[24] This brings one to the second obvious tendency in these drawings—caricature. Richard Nixon suffered at the artists' hands a noticeable exaggeration of the Pinocchio nose, whose length in caricatures increased as his credibility

Paul Conrad, "The Men Who Played God," from Pro *and* Conrad, *1979.* (Courtesy of Paul Conrad, Los Angeles.)

declined until his features were fantastically distorted. None of the cartoon gods is an exemplar of divine beauty, for they are parodies of the creation of man in God's image, and caricaturists by profession seem to have reservations about anyone whom they depict.

They portray the fall of all beings, sometimes quite explicitly. In one Conrad cartoon, a robot on the moon hands an apple with noticeable bite marks to another robot, as if man's technology will transport original sin to any world visited.[25] The *American Cartoon Album* notes that the Garden of

*Paul Conrad, "The creation of an 'independent prosecutor,' "
from* The King and Us, *1974. (Courtesy of Paul Conrad,
Los Angeles.)*

Eden theme occurs in hundreds of cartoons.[26] In a Whitney Daron sketch,
for instance, an American astronaut tries to stop an antennaed, nude female
alien from eating a fruit on her world because, carrying odd cultural prejudices from his own, he confuses her with Eve.[27] Nixon also finds his way to
Eden. In an uncaptioned cartoon, Mike Peters shows a naked Nixon tossing

away a tape behind his wife in answer to a divine finger of accusation.[28]

Moving from Genesis to Exodus, the cartoons provide a variety of depictions of Moses' story. In commemoration of his parting of what the King James's version calls the "Red Sea," Mike Peters draws Nixon doing the same for his swimming pool. As he strides through the miraculously divided waves and smiles as if to an admiring throng, Pat admits, "Confidentially, it hasn't been easy living with him since the election."[29] Comparably, in a cartoon by Tony Auth, the notorious golden calf of Exodus becomes Henry Kissinger surrounded by prostrate congressmen. Although the original 1974 cartoon was captionless, Auth added four lines of explanation when he published it in a collection of his works. These lines describe Kissinger's anger at accusations of wiretapping and then mentions Congress's praise of him as a peace seeker, none of this precisely shown in the drawing.[30] Like most cartoons, this one is not a detailed allegory closely corresponding to the news item. Despite being occasioned by topical events (usually clearest in accompanying texts), political cartoons draw the power of their satire from fantastic presentation of timeless human concerns, making their relatively frequent use of Biblical allusions quite appropriate, even though the allusions are not always employed in a way that fundamentalists would appreciate. Consider, for instance, Pat Oliphant's sketch of a tablet-carrying, robed Nixon returning from the storm-capped summit of a holy mountain (in this case standing for his summit talks on nuclear-arms control with the Soviets). Unimpressed by the lightning-illuminated scene, a gentleman in modern dress remarks: "That's all very fine [but] do you have any word on food prices?"[31] Since Nixon appears rather out-of-sorts and out-of-date in his dragging robe, the reader identifies with the blasé speaker. In contrast, the Biblical story takes the side of Moses and God against the worldly cravings of the Israelites. In a 1971 painting for *National Lampoon,* Edward Sorel parodies Michelangelo's statue of Moses, furnishing it with Nixon's physiognomy, though (appropriately) retaining the horns.[32] The caricatured face and the two words on the magazine that he carries eloquently deflate the monumentality of his body. By implication, his "law and order" amount to no more than simplistic bromides like those of the famous *Digest.* The deliberately childlike crudity of caricatures puts the reader in a momentary childish mood that may make him feel at least a mild antipathy to law and order. A cartoon by Mike Peters even goes so far as to equate the Commandments with the Nixon tapes.[33] The chief joy of satiric fantasy is to show authority figures' being guilty of breaking the laws they make and enforce.

As Old Testament allusions frequently concern commandments, law, and order, New Testament ones often recall Christ's teachings about love and charity. For example, another Peters cartoon transforms Nixon into one of the Magi, tightly gripping a cup marked "Aid to Dependent Children."

Edward Sorel, painting of Nixon/Moses from Making the World Safe for Hypocrisy, *1972, from the* National Lampoon. (Courtesy of Edward Sorel, New York.)

Before dispensing funds to the Virgin Mary, however, he inquires suspiciously: "But does the mother have a job?"[34] The Christmas-card serenity of Bethlehem under the portentous star contrasts with his uncharitable words. In support of the need for Christian love to be sincere, there is a parody of the countless pictures of Christ as the Good Shepherd. In this cartoon, Sorel sketches a bucolic scene with a herdsman, crook in hand, walking down the narrow path. The discordant elements are a nuclear bomb in the figure's other hand and the face of Secretary of Defense Melvin Laird in place of Christ's. The caption reads, "The Laird is my Shepherd" and appends a news item describing how our war secretary told five hundred Presbyterians to follow Christ's advice to "love thy neighbor as thyself."[35]

Most often, though, satiric allusions to the New Testament concern Christ's miracles. A 1972 Nixon cartoon by Herbert Block has the caption, "Miraculous—he can walk on mud."[36] The picture contradicts the caption, but only to show that the President is even worse than the words suggest. With shady eyes upturned toward heaven, and hands folded in prayer, Nixon unctiously plods forward not on the mud itself but on the hands of those he tramples down farther into the mire. In a Conrad cartoon entitled "Father John McLaughlin, exorcist," when the readers see the priest holding a crucifix with Nixon dangling from it, some might object to playful reference to the cross, the sign of Christ's sacrificial death and miraculous resurrection.[37]

Although exorcism certainly existed in Biblical times, this cartoon alludes more specifically to the next age in ecclesiastical history, that of the Church. The friendship of churchmen with Nixon provided ministers with a kind of guilt by association, as in a Sorel cartoon entitled: "Pietà with Norman Vincent Peale and Billy Graham" (showing the corpse of Nixon in their laps).[38] As one might expect, Sorel's drawing of the Pietà is in no wise pious, for even in death, Nixon manages to have his hand on a pile of money. In a more satisfying discrepancy between caption and picture, an unnamed monk stands in the shadow beside Peale and Graham, perhaps to hint at a Vatican connection. In another cartoon, this one by Conrad, a sign reads, "Billy Graham Revival," while the caption presents the alleged words of that evangelist: "All those wishing to make a 'decision for Nixon' will please come forward."[39] The picture shows a vast, tented amphitheatre with no one in the audience but Nixon himself. The inclusion of Graham in these cartoons is partly explained by a Sorel caricature drawn shortly after the Nixon presidency. At the bottom of the sketch, the topical reference is established by the following devout words of Graham: "Perhaps we as Christians failed to pray enough for Richard Nixon. Let us not make the same mistake in failing to pray for President Ford."[40] Above this, Graham is shown allegedly thinking, "And dear God, if I get in trouble with Internal

Revenue again, please inspire President Ford with the same compassion you gave to Mr. Nixon. Amen." A cartoon by Block summarizes the mood of these satires of Nixon's ecclesiastical companions. In it, Nixon gleefully sledge-hammers a wall marked, "Separation of Church and State," while he chortles, "Who says I'm not trying to bring people together?"[41] Indeed, Kurt Vonnegut even published an article alleging that in a worship service before the GOP Convention, the Quaker theologian Dr. Elton Trueblood preached a sermon on the "Divine Right of Presidents."[42] One must recall that before Watergate, there was some widespread faith in the close connection between God and Country. All these satirists helped to lay that faith to rest.

Allusions to the Judeo-Christian heritage have been particularly effective because they emphasize religious dimensions of the moral tradition that political hypocrisy jeopardizes. Nonetheless, by the very nature of visual satire, it can only show such religion in caricatured form. In cartoons, the typical depiction of the clergy might best be called stained-glass-windshield humor after a common stereotype: a smiling minister, regardless of anyone's safety, drives with a multicolored church window above the dashboard.[43] The politically active but naïve campus chaplain in "Doonesbury" and countless other cartoon ministers awkwardly try to fit into a society they perceive as through a glass darkly. What is society truly like? Cartoons show only distortion and fantasy—but, perhaps, society also manifests these characteristics.

5

Illuminating the Classics

*F*ROM MEDIEVAL TIMES TO THE PRESENT, SOME PAINTERS AND CARTOONISTS HAVE had the audacity to add their art to texts that were venerable before their births. In the twentieth century, Classics Illustrated Comics massively engaged in this pursuit, but against considerable opposition. Educators feared the vulgarization of culture. Parents organized against the corruption of their offspring. In response to the former objections, the company tried to be faithful to the original. This, however, did not assuage the contempt of the literate at seeing the great books transformed into garishly colored cartoons. Later, because of the parents' groups, the company revised its comic books to conform to stereotypical notions of what children's literature should be like. Characteristically, a second edition of the comic-book version of Victor Hugo's *The Hunchback of Notre Dame* gained a happy ending and depicted violence less vividly than did Hugo. These alterations intensified the scorn of literary purists. At the beginning of the 1960s in a surrender to public pressure, the company ceased printing.[1]

In addition to such opposition (and all the other objections that people have raised to fantastic art), illuminators of classic fantasy encounter difficulties inherent in the activity. Authors of classics drew on the cultural context of their own periods and on the resources of language (verb tense, etc.) to structure their works. Living at later periods and functioning within the very different resources of the visual arts, subsequent illuminators almost inevitably reinterpret the classics in an anachronistic way, while fantastic imagery itself frequently mixes ordinary time with the unreal "once upon a time" sense of temporality found in fairy tales and myths. Since originally most of the classics had no pictures, each work had a purely textual structure that must be recognized before considering how the addition of pictures changed it. Being in essence temporal, texts are characteristically organized in terms of time. In his definitive study *Time and English Fiction,* David Leon Higdon states that each narrative text belongs to one of the following four basic patterns: (1) processed time (arranged in chronological order); (2) retrospective time (recalling the past); (3) barrier time (movement toward an announced or foreshadowed result); or (4) polytemporal time (movement between many time periods).[2] Adding drawings to any of these textual patterns produces a new, more complex arrangement, as can be seen in a few instances from recently illuminated classics.

Examples of chronological order, two of Franz Kafka's most famous parables, "Before the Law" (*Vor dem Gesetz,* 1919) and "An Imperial Message" (*Eine Kaiserliche Botschaft,* 1919), appear in the April 1982 issue of *Epic Illustrated* with pictures by Leo Duranona. A Bohemian Jewish lawyer, Kafka had at his disposal certain personal and traditional associations of law, e.g., his own legal experience, the age-old notion of interminable legal delay, the Jewish history of fruitlessly seeking justice from anti-Semitic lands, and the image of God as revealed through the principal Jewish scripture, the Torah (variously translated as God's law of instructions). With a Job-like craving to justify himself and a naïve, pre-Holocaust assumption that the law is "accessible to everyone," Kafka's protagonist in the first parable seeks out the "Law," only to be halted by a doorkeeper. This guard is no Nazi monster; he even provides the protagonist with a stool to sit on. The seeker waits for years, growing old and finally dying (the process of his aging shaping the narrative). As he lies in his death agony, the guard closes the door, explaining that it was designed for the seeker alone. One never learns if he had access to food. Time passes in a simple, chronological manner, but actions lack credibility. They transpire in a vague, mythlike world. In Kafka's posthumously published *The Trial* (*Der Prozess,* 1925)—but not in Duranona's version—the parable is followed by a parody of rabbinical commentary, a dialogue between "K." and a priest or holy man (*Geistliche*). It stresses the need to continue contemplating the story. Duranona uses instead the earlier, shorter version, which suits the need of graphic fiction to reduce narrative to a few dramatic scenes. At first, the monstrous doorkeeper is three times the size of the seeker, but after age withers the latter, the doorkeeper holds the dying man in one hand close to his enormous mouth as if to devour him. In contrast, the unemotional text flows on, conveying a sense of the man's boredom, frustration, and growing senility. When the seeker's eyes fail, he begins to see (or imagine) a light shining "immortality" *(unverlöschlich)* from the portal of the "Law." Duranona shows a luminous opening streaming radiance from beneath the rose window of a Gothic cathedral. Instead of Kafka's ambiguous mystery, Duranona provides a spectacular Christian miracle. Rose windows are sacred to the Virgin Mary, symbolic of mercy, not "Law." Where Kafka is tentative, Duranona's rose window strongly suggests that a merciful Christian God waits within and that only the evil doorkeeper prevents the seeker's entry.

Kafka, in his diaries, drew figures that the critic Daryl Sharp calls "airy" or "windy" because they lack substance.[3] Admittedly, Duranona has a similar quality to his art. In "Before the Law," Kafka writes of the flowing robes of the doorkeeper, and Duranona well inflates the characters' clothing, making it balloonlike, a quality particularly obvious when the body of the aging seeker decreases like a deflating dirigible. To readers of recent illuminated fantasy, though, Duranona's figures with pointed cowls suggest the style of the controversial French cartoonist Moebius and his imitators; thus the graphics connote boldly anti-authoritarian cartooning of the 1970s or 1980s, not Kafka's ambiguous attitude toward the hollowness of all men.

Duranona's "An Imperial Message" (the part of Kafka's "Building of the Great Wall of China" published during his lifetime) presents comparable but slightly different discrepancies between picture and words. According to the text, a dying sunlike emperor of a populous country "has sent a message to you [presumably the reader]." The story follows the process of passing through the territory that the messenger is traversing, then speculates about the future difficulties of passage. After demonstrating the impossibility of the messenger's ever arriving, Kafka concludes that "you" sit at the window dreaming the message. One way of interpreting this parable is as the state of modern man, who dreams that God has disappeared from his life. In this dream, God sends a messenger, a Messiah, who is only a superior human being, not omnipotent. (In Jewish tradition, God is One, His Messiah a lesser being.) According to Jewish reckoning, the Messiah has never arrived. Such a great difference and distance divides the earth and the heavenly realm that a modern may wonder if salvation ever will come. In the absence of revelation, all one can do is dream.

With the exception of the emperor, all of Duranona's figures wear robes with pointed cowls, as in the other parable. These costumes have more of a Tibetan than a Chinese look to them. The pictured emperor, however, has guards on his long fingernails, typical of the Chinese upper-class, and a Far Eastern stone dragon towers above the imperial courtyard. Kafka does not actually describe China as it ever existed, yet such is the nature of his words that one may envision any mythical Cathay that one chooses. Furthermore, the text with the word "you" presumably designates the reader, but unable to do this, Duranona substitutes a male figure, an obvious picture/text discrepancy, particularly if the reader is feminine.

In "Radicalization of Space in Kafka's Stories," the critic Kimberly Sparks remarks that in one of Kafka's characteristic treatments of time, objects "proceed from a state of differentiation and organization to a state of randomness," while energy spreads out, becoming proportionately weaker.[4] This process (called entropy by physicists) characterizes Kafka's "An Imperial Message." The messenger moves from the order of the royal bedchamber to the throngs in the palaces. Beyond them lies the near chaos of the capital. Despite being unusually strong, he finds as he elbows his way past millions of bodies that his energy is draining away. Years later, exhaustion and age cost him his life before he accomplishes his mission. Duranona's pictures give an opposite impression of time. First, in an enormous bed reposes an old man. After the messenger leaves him, subsequent scenes add more and more people, crowding the panels with tiny figures. By the last page, the citizens have shrunk to teeming dots within the confines of the symmetrical layout of the city. This drawing suggests both order and the energy of masses crammed within a small space. Kafka's treatment of entropy emphasizes the weakness of man, easily exhausted and destroyed in his struggle. Duranona, however, progressively reveals how overpopulation produces energetic mob scenes, reducing people to the condition of busy insects. In the last panel, a stream of ants (resembling the previously pictured citizens) scurries across the window sill.[5]

As a result of the subtle difference between illuminations and words, the reader/viewer almost simultaneously encounters two very similar stories that do not convey quite the same impression. Furthermore, Kafka's parables are self-contradictory from the start. In "Before the Law," the door that the seeker could not enter is one meant only for him. In "An Imperial Message," "you" know that the emperor has sent a message, even though there seems to be no way that news could come. Illuminating these works, however, makes the very method of their presentation paradoxical, so that one is constantly reminded of their fantasmagoric nature.

An example of Higdon's next pattern of time, the recollection of the past, Keats's "La Belle Dame Sans Merci" is strangely illuminated in Dave Morice's *Poetry Comics* in what Morice calls "a diabolical plot to overthrow the Foundations of Poetry."[6] This book is a collection of famous poems set in cartoons that deliberately transgress the spirit of the original. Where even Duranona's serious approach to Kafka yields discrepancies, Morice's comic treatment of Keats does so more obviously.

As Higdon observes, retrospective fiction tends to contrast the narrator's present condition with the past one that he recalls. At the opening of "La

AN IMPERIAL MESSAGE

by Franz Kafka
adaptation by Leopoldo Duranona

Leopoldo Duranona, pictures for Franz Kafka's "An Imperial Message" from Epic Illustrated, *April 1982. (Artwork: Copyright © 1982 by Leo Duranona. By permission of Marvel Comics Group.)*

Belle Dame Sans Merci," a knight is pale, "haggard," "woe begone," and wet with a cold sweat from "anguish moist and fever dew." Semblances of a formerly white brow and rosy cheeks are quickly withering. Presumably, he recently was young and, as he recalls, in love. According to the knight, the experience distinguishing his present and past states occurred in a nightmare. He dreamed of his beloved's former lovers and awoke to find himself no longer in the "elfin grot" but "On the cold hill side." In addition to all the problems of illuminating chronological fiction, retrospection adds the difficulty of portraying a movement from present to past. Graphic art possesses no tenses. If Morice wished to be faithful to the original, about the best he could do to distinguish the knight's past from his present would be to draw a youth for the former, an elder for the latter and hope the viewers would accurately connect the two. Furthermore, the text is unclear as to whether the knight has really made love to a fairy maiden or dreamed the experience. Even if Morice wished, such an ambiguity would be difficult to show. Perversely, Morice eliminates ambiguity and transformation. From the first moment of the poem to the last, the knight and all the other characters have "happy faces." To indicate further mockery, Morice inscribes "cutism" in his first panel. Modern literature no longer approves Keats's archaic diction and pretty imagery. In particular, his bemoaning loss of innocence after sexual intercourse sounds quaint. Morice sees Keats's Romanticism as a cartoonlike view of life. In the pictured version, it is a childishly sketched rabbit that inquires, "O what can ail thee, knight-at-arms, alone and palely loitering?" Then a bird comments, "The sedge has withered from the lake, and no birds sing" (p. 86). The grinning animals listen as he reveals his woe, though after a frame they vanish, with the scene shifting to a flashback. Anachronistically, the "Elfin Grot" displays a neon sign. Since the knight bestows "kisses four" on the fairy maiden's eyes, Morice depicts her with four eyes and, of course, a moronic "happy face" smile. Even the "starved lips" of the phantoms "with horrid warning gaped wide" appear as imbecilic grins. At the end, the bird, again announcing that "no birds sing," has its wing partly over its smirking mouth to stifle its amusement (p. 89).

Retrospective texts combine two stories: the narrator's present history and the (often suspect) tale that he tells of the past. Since by definition illumination diverges from a text, it adds at least one more narrative to the new version (though not necessarily a story as different from the original as Morice's "La Belle Dame Sans Merci").

An example of barrier time or foreshadowing as a structural technique is Shakespeare's *Macbeth*. It was probably composed in 1606, a few years after the accession of James I to the English throne. His coronation gave topical

Dave Morice, pictures for John Keats's "La Belle Dame Sans Merci" from Poetry Comics: A Cartooniverse of Poems, *1982. (Courtesy of Dave Morice, St. Louis.)*

interest to a tale about his Scottish heritage. Playgoers may well have known from Holinshead and other historians the general drift of the story. Within the play, the witches repeatedly foreshadow the future. They are cryptic enough to confuse Macbeth, but a Jacobean audience, familiar with the conventions, would rightly foresee the destruction of anyone in league with the powers of darkness. Nowadays, though (long after Goethe wrote of Faust's salvation) deviltry and damnation are no longer synonymous. In popular culture, a number of comic-book heroes such as Ghost Rider derive powers from the devil, which they use for meritorious acts. Thus the basic structure of the play is not necessarily obvious to unscholarly moderns— precisely the readership for which a thirty-year-old Brazilian artist (hiding behind the pseudonym "Von") prepared his illuminated version.[7] It constitutes the first comic-book rendition of the complete script of a Shakespeare play (since Classics Illustrated always abbreviated their editions). However experimental, modern directors of Shakespeare's plays do not typically use pseudonyms (although their reviews may sometimes make them wish they had). Writers and artists of comic books, however, have often resorted to pen names, since the genre flourishes just at the border of the disreputable, like the drama in Shakespeare's time.

While most editions of Shakespeare have tasteful covers, Von's has a garish one. Typical of comic books, warm colors there predominate in a scene of sanguine mayhem. Blood-dripping sword in hand, Macbeth stands poised above a throng of attackers. This part of the composition is reminiscent of the children's game called "king of the hill"—an apt analogue for the play itself, much of which concerns struggle for high place. Macbeth's helmet and gory weapon protrude from the clear line demarcating the picture from the title. A common device in comic books, this makes the scene more three dimensional and also suggests the character's breaking through restrictions— again an appropriate association for a man who spends most of the play piercing all boundaries of law, loyalty, friendship, and human decency. Behind him the sun sets, a proper introduction to a drama located so much in darkness. The bottom of the picture exhibits an image that may surprise viewers unfamiliar with the conventions of comics. Macbeth appears again but in a new pose, his sword having completed the arc it began at the top of the illumination as if he had won his way through his foes so quickly that he could be seen in two positions at once. In doing so, though, he has abandoned the hill. In comics, the most completely clothed or securely armored combatant is generally the villain—in this case Macbeth. Since comic-book villains traditionally lose, his defeat is perhaps, in that sense, foreshadowed, but not for any supernatural reason.

Unlike any scholarly edition of the work, Von's page 1 establishes the tone for the rest of the pages by being devoid of notes or even line numbers. In the

Von [*pseud.*], *picture for* Macbeth: The Folio Edition, *1982.* (Oval Projects/Workman Publishing, © 1982. Reprinted by permission of the publisher.)

illuminations, to which far more space is devoted than to text, the witches' faces protrude from small squares—again a conventional indication that the figures break through natural boundaries. Both the cartoon witches and their doggerel are crude yet evocative. Even wearing macabre makeup, actors or actresses bring to witches' roles an underlying humanity, while Von's witches are mere caricatures. Indeed, his art carries the dehumanizing aspect of *Macbeth* far beyond the original, for he stylizes the whole into a cartoon, a pure creation of the imagination—and more a modern than a Renaissance imagination at that. A significant difference between present and Renaissance attitudes arises from a recent greater distrust of authority. Unlike scholarly editions, Von's does very little to reveal the political and religious order underlying the work. Indeed, as will be seen, Von undercuts it from time to time. Nonetheless, understanding Shakespeare's foreshadowings requires some familiarity with the Jacobean assumptions that God will destroy the devil's allies, particularly those who betray legitimate kings.

Nowadays, as Von seems to realize, we sympathize more with characters if they seem less monarchic. In the illuminations of *Macbeth* 1:2, the sympathetic character King Duncan sits crownless and appareled in a kind of tartan bathrobe. Even while arriving at Macbeth's castle—a moment when, for Jacobeans, his royalty should be most evident to accentuate the evil of Macbeth's killing an anointed king—Von's Duncan covers his white hairs with only a thin tiara. In contrast, when the villainous Macbeth becomes king, he is frequently pictured wearing a large, many-spired crown, and even his battle helmet has a crownlike golden emblem upon it. Von shows the English monarch Edward the Confessor not merely crowned but vested in a combination of royal and priestly robes. This occurs as part of one of Von's ironies. All downcast, one of them apparently weeping, cripples on crutches are depicted limping away from the king. Although the text testifies to cures, the illumination displays the opposite—the disappointing failure of an allegedly saintly king to perform anticipated miracles. If the English King (the play's chief exemplar of good rulership) is a disappointment and if Malcolm, the next successor to the throne of Scotland, should be doubted in his tale of these healings, Von presents a very dark, bleak, and modern view of politics. The drawings are also modern in their concern for unpretentious, everyday detail. Conspicuous in the central foreground of the picture portraying Edward's attempts at healing, a lop-eared dog, oblivious to majesty, sniffs the ground. Similarly, in the first picture of Duncan, a panting hound looks away from the enthroned king. So also does one of his councilors, who even has his back to the monarch, while a partly bent figure has his buttocks (albeit nobly cloaked ones) pointed more or less in the royal direction. Such subtle touches conflict with the assumption that a king should be the center of power and respectful attention—perhaps not an assumption made by all

Jacobeans, but one that Shakespeare and his patron James I presumably shared.

The closest the pictures come to approving royal charisma appears at the very end. With hands slightly raised in an almost priestlike gesture, Malcolm receives the approbation and attention of all his men, some on their knees, while above his head beams of light shine from the clouds as if heaven thereby showered its approval. He is bareheaded and walks down a flight of stairs to come closer to his subjects—seemingly a sign that he will be less dictatorial than his predecessor. Above Malcolm, however, the sky looms black, brown, and red, ominous colors, particularly because of their previous use. The illuminated text begins with witches' rising into a brown-black cloud as if evil now possesses even the skies—the same skies that finally beam red light on Malcolm. Throughout the book, Von translates Shakespeare's bloody imagery into an inundation of red. Page 31, in which Duncan's death is discovered, appears entirely in red, brown, and black. Page 45, in which Banquo dies, is bordered with dripping red as if blood flowed down along a camera lens—one of many devices that Von borrows from horror movies. Red is particularly associated with the villainous Lady Macbeth, who at first appears completely robed and cowled in scarlet cloth, the shade of her long, pointed nails, which maintain the same color until the hand-washing scene, where she merely imagines that they run with blood. Therefore, the black, brown, and red that beams down upon King Malcolm are disquieting. Directly following this picture, the final panel is even more ominous. In a brown fog, the three witches leer over Macbeth's grave, yet whether their glee comes simply from his downfall or from some more general triumph of evil is as unclear as the night in which they prowl.

Being a script, Shakespeare's *Macbeth* anticipates visual accompaniments, but on the Jacobean stage, not in a twentieth-century comic. The latter is as capable of foreshadowing the future as the former, but uses different conventions and assumptions about the universe. Thus, even where events in picture and text are the same (and they are not always that), the meaning of the occurrences foreshadowed may vary.

An example of polytemporal time, Samuel Taylor Coleridge's *Kubla Khan,* according to its author, occurred to him during a dream and reflects much of the confusion that one might associate with that state. In *The Road to Xanadu,* John Livingston Lowes has demonstrated that a hodgepodge of material from classical literature and various travel books coalesced in Coleridge's unconscious. For instance, "Alph, the sacred river," placed by Coleridge next to Kubla Khan's palace, not only did not flow there but was not called sacred in Coleridge's sources. The dreaming poet juxtaposed the supposed sanctity of the Nile in ancient Egypt with the Alpheus River of classical Greek myth and with Kubla Khan's thirteenth-century "pleasure dome" in Asia.[8] The poem slips from a consideration of the dome's construction to an uprush of the river at some contradictory time ("at once and ever / It flung up momently"). Then one reads of the timeless running of the river and of an undefined period when Kubla Khan heard "ancestral voices" (words from the past) prophesying future war. Finally, the unfinished poem switches to the present, immediately recalls a past vision of "A damsel with a dulcimer," and then predicts that if he could revive her song, he could rebuild Kubla's palace which would frighten "all who heard."

In *Poetry Comics,* Dave Morice, with his usual sense of humor, uses his pictures to turn "Kubla Khan" almost into a chronological story (pp. 71–78). Builders constructing something like Disneyland come upon a heart-shaped "romantic chasm" from which a woman crawls to meet a werewolf, "her demon lover." As they make love, the "earth in fast thick pants" emits "a mighty fountain," which knocks them into the river. At this point, Morice plays with chronology, suspending the thirteenth-century lover's story until the modern reader can solve a maze connecting them to the "lifeless ocean." Next Kubla Khan appears. Then Morice has the werewolf produce the previously mentioned woman, who solidifies from the smoke of his opium pipe (although Coleridge introduces a digression with new characters and little connection to what precedes). They end the travesty by escaping a mob and drinking "the milk of paradise" marked "paradise dairy." Although the pictures come somewhat closer to simple chronology than the poem, they form an additional counterpoint to Coleridge's polytemporal sequence. Because of the inherent difference between illuminations and texts, the graphics can only add to the complexity (even if, as here, they try to interpret the structure of the text in an almost chronological manner).

Numerous artists have made a living and sometimes even a reputation by adding pictures to classic texts. The artists need not be as idiosyncratic as Blake or as irreverent as Dave Morice to subvert the basic structures of the works. A text, even a polytemporal one, presents, one word at a time, a single line of print. With the introduction of speed reading, readers' eyes may now actually take a great many paths in perusing a page, but at least traditionally, one might assume that the author controls the readers' eyes, moving them down a row of letters in a predetermined order. With illuminated works, the eyes move between two different mediums (text and picture) seeing *almost* the same events repeated. The result is like hearing music in a canyon: the echoes never quite keep time to the conductor's beat. As Lessing and so many others have attested, pictures are primarily spatial. The reader/viewer thus alternates between patterns of time in language and frozen moments captured in the pictures. Before approaching the question of

Dave Morice, pictures for Samuel Taylor Coleridge's "Kubla Khan" from Poetry Comics: A Cartooniverse of Poems, *1982.* (Courtesy of Dave Morice, St. Louis.)

what kind of structure can reconcile time and apparent timelessness, we shall further examine the nature of imagery. Being seen at a glance, illuminations compellingly present seemingly eternal archetypal images, but such images also help to shape fantastic texts and form a common ground with myth, religion, and even cinematic fantasy.

6

Cinematic Magic: From Motion Picture to Comic-Book Adaptation

*T*HE FANTASTIC IN EVERY MEDIUM LARGELY CONSISTS OF IMAGES COMPARABLE to those that cinema buffs call "special effects"—strange, memorable, and self-contradictory. The light sabers in the *Star Wars* movies can well serve as a familiar example of these qualities. In a way that no laser beam could, these sabers vary in length. They consist only of energy, yet in the dueling scenes, when the swords touch, they seem solid as metal, thereby combining the science-fiction notion of a "force field" (energy rendered impenetrable) with the anomalousness of magic blades in the "sword and sorcery" genre. Since light sabers do not exist on earth, a special-effects department simulates them. They are among the key images of the movie and are associated with its other paradoxes, contributing to the mythical ambience. In Japanese legend, martial-arts experts possess such preternatural powers as the ability to predict their opponents' movements by sensing the enemies' *ki* (Chinese *Ch'i*), a universal energy in all phenomena, comparable to the Force in *Star Wars*. Even today, some older Japanese consult sword masters as fortune tellers.

Any society that could manufacture a light saber would certainly be technologically advanced enough for long-distance weapons (so the existence of light sabers also seems self-contradictory in terms of the evolution of weaponry). In *Star Wars,* the presence of the sabers is only plausible because of the existence of anachronistic martial artists (the Jedi Knights) willing to undergo excruciating training in order to win in fighting warriors with potentially superior long-range weapons. The characters include two opposing sword masters (Obi-wan Kenobi and Darth Vader), an apprentice (Luke Skywalker), and a scoffer (Han Solo) at first unconvinced about "Hokey religions and ancient weapons." Since extreme contrasts generally characterize fantasy, the Jedi Knights must fight something that is the opposite of their short-distance light saber—an ultimate long-distance weapon, the Death Star. The vast cost of this moon-sized assault vehicle implies an enormous organization to finance it, i.e., the Empire, while any group so evil that they are willing to use a planet-destroying machine ought to be resisted, ergo the Rebellion. The imagery of the *Star Wars* saga is a tightly interrelated structure, despite some inherent self-contradiction.

Although vast numbers of people enjoy these movies, science-fiction enthusiasts have often given them bad reviews for an obvious reason: they are based on such unexplained paradoxes as the light saber. For instance, in his science-fiction column in the July 1982 *Comics Journal,* Carter Scholz decries *Star Wars'* "retread nonsense." By this phrase, he names two of the characteristics of fantasy, its use of images that have a long history, and its being inherently self-contradictory, i.e., to a scientist, "nonsense." Scholz's mistake lies in letting a few science-fiction trappings lead him to conclude that *Star Wars* belongs to that genre in the first place. As has been mentioned, there is reason to hypothesize that "hard" science fiction and fantasy appeal to different personality types—the first to those wishing for consistent extrapolations from present knowledge about the external world, the second to those interested in psychological or religious mysteries. In *Star Wars,* not only is the light saber self-contradictory, but each of the following major appearances of it involves it with other old paradoxes:

Luke Skywalker acquires his father's saber. As with King Arthur's pulling the sword Excalibur from the stone, Siegfried's reforging his father's magic blade, etc., receiving the sword of one's father traditionally represents an abrupt entry into manhood and occasions the beginning of a mission. In a sense, the sword (with the responsibility it brings) takes over the youth. Similarly, one of Luke's later questions about the Force is whether it would control him. Obi-wan Kenobi replies in the affirmative but adds that a Jedi can also control the Force (a Jedi version of the Christian enigma of free will vs. predestination). In real life, fathers are generally both protectors and disciplinarians. Luke's father, Anakin Skywalker/Darth Vader, embodies this split in an exaggerated way. Indeed, there is even a hint of self-contradiction in Vader's appearance. Despite living in an age of medical miracles, Vader is so severely injured that he cannot live without a loudly wheezing respirator. Nonetheless, he is strong enough to lift a man's weight with one hand.

Obi-wan Kenobi protects Luke in the Mos Eisley cantina. Despite being dedicated to the cause of life, Kenobi kills. One of the chief functions of the scene is to show that the light saber does not disintegrate its victims but acts much like a real blade. This knowledge primes the audience so that they understand that when Kenobi later vanishes in the midst of Vader's saber thrust, the disappearance is mysterious, not a normal result of the searing light.

Luke practices swordplay on board the spaceship. After Kenobi instructs him, "Let go of your conscious self and act on instinct," Luke learns that he can "see" better without the use of his physical eyes and begins to have a kind of second sight that later guides his attack on the Death Star. Kenobi takes advantage of Luke's practice to continue explaining what various characters in the movie call the Jedi "religion"; thus saber and Force become more firmly connected in the audiences' minds. Swords have had a symbolic linkage to other religions, e.g., the association of cross-shaped swords with the crucifix by crusaders, or the phallic association of swords in some fertility cults. Appropriately, the blade of the light saber is pure energy like the Force itself.

Vader and Kenobi duel. Kenobi's body vanishes, yet his existence continues (a condition much precedented in myth).

Being itself partly inspired by the art of sci-fi and fantasy comics and pulps, *Star Wars* has appeared in a comic-book adaptation. Unfortunately, Roy Thomas's script and the art of Howard Chaykin and his assistants transform the Marvel Special Edition comic-book version into science fiction (for the alteration of even a few details can have considerable consequences). The graphics do virtually nothing to show the paradoxical nature of the saber, but the most significant change is coloring all its beams red. In the movie, Luke and Obi-wan have blades of bluish-white light suggestive of purity, while Darth Vader brandishes a blood-tinged one of reddish white. There is no obvious reason, of course, why the mechanical hilts of the sabers should make this color distinction. If, however, the beams are seen as symbols of the Force, then it is appropriate that the servant of the evil side has a saber with a different hue from that of the virtuous characters.

While this comic book shifts the story away from fantasy, the *Star Wars* movies employ devices comparable to the illumination/text discrepancy of fantasy books. For example, in these films, much of the humor derives from close-ups of C-3PO's immobile, metal face, while he expresses such sentiments as "Thank the Maker!" or "We seem to be made to suffer." He emotes with fear, confusion, and indecision, even once exclaiming, "My! My! I forgot"—scarcely what one expects from a thinking machine.[1] The comic book omits a large number of C-3PO's lines and frequently, instead of focusing on his face, shows the back of his head or includes his lines in word-balloons attached to no one, so that there is less apparent contradiction between the emotion expressed and the mechanical speaker. Nothing in the comic is funny. In the movie theater, the scene that usually draws the most laughs is when C-3PO and R2-D2 try to enter the Mos Eisley cantina. The camera pans a throng of varied creatures, strange almost beyond imagining, while the bartender yells at the robots, "We don't serve their kind here!" With its visual emphasis on his tolerance for so many nonhuman creatures and its verbal presentation of his prejudice toward another kind of creature (a robot), the scene's irony involves some picture/word disparity. The comic book omits it. Instead, Chaykin's considerable talents go to drawing space hardware and equally hard faces of people who often snarl, where the film actors look compassionate or amused.

The movie *The Empire Strikes Back,* the sequel to *Star Wars,* contains little humor or fantasy aside from the scenes with the muppet Yoda. As Andre Helfer observes in a July 1980 *Comic Times* review of the adaptation of that sequel, much of the comic is so close to the movie that it "seems almost traced" (p. 33).

Williamson's and Garzon's adaptation of *Return of the Jedi* is not particularly imaginative, but it is competent and colorful, particularly in the almost surrealistic backdrops of the final duel between Luke Skywalker and Darth Vader. It correctly incorporates the movie's sword imagery, such as the important scene where Vader tells his son, "You have constructed a saber to replace the one lost when we LAST met. Your skills are complete." This is the final evidence that the saber is more than a machine, for if it were simply like a gun, any of the mechanics on the rebel side could have produced it for Luke. If Luke has truly come into his power, he is right again to trust his instinct, which tells him that Vader is not totally corrupt. Unlike science fiction, where events are usually susceptible to reasoned, scientific investigation, the *Star Wars* saga, like most fantasy, provides a universe that can best be described through paradoxes and known through the unconscious, the part of Luke that Obi-wan and Yoda try most zealously to awake. When, in the movie *Star Wars,* Luke first begins to see without the use of his physical eyes, Obi-wan comments, "You've taken your first step into a larger world." All the comic-book adaptations of the *Star Wars* saga need to do more to suggest this "larger world." As the adaptation of the *Star Wars* saga demonstrates, the mere fact that a narrative appears in comic-book form does not mean that it is fantasy. Careful analysis is necessary in classification, requiring a thorough understanding of that genre.

Realistic movies are often made into novels, but virtually never into comic books (while fantasy films often become both). Turning a film into a book always necessitates changes, but *fantasy* movies are not so different from comic books as to require the significant alterations that the *Star Wars* saga has undergone. The crux of realistic plotting is that events flow into one another in a way that seems probable based on the audience's experiences from everyday life—an effect that movies can better capture than comics. In contrast, fantasy plotting depends on the close association of major images, with intervening, realistic detail largely excised. Comics can present such closely associated images. Thus they have potential for fantasy plotting comparable to that of the cinema. The *Star Wars* adaptations are comics that do not take enough advantage of this potential, so there is reason to examine a few that, whatever incidental changes they make, at least translate the films' fantasy into book form.

Consider, for example, *Conan, the Barbarian,* a movie based on Robert E. Howard's pulps of the 1930s. With subtle differences from the movie such as the merging of related incidents, the comic-book adaptation has generally more effective plotting. It begins with the pictured father's fashioning for his son the greatest sword that he has ever forged. Conan and his mother cower in the background, while the father, wreathed in smoky clouds in the foreground, resembles familiar pictures of smith gods such as Vulcan. In the next panel, the father holds up the blade, which seems to emit transcendent light, while he tells the boy, "Learn the riddle of steel and you won't need [the god] Crom! When the way of steel is yours, Conan, your sword will be your soul!" (p. 7). The scene reverberates with traditional associations: the inheritance of a magic weapon, the hero's receiving an enigma to solve, and the sword as the soul of the warrior (this last being one of many borrowings from Japanese samurai films).[2] Thus begins an elaborate saber motif, which creates a fantasy atmosphere and prepares the way for the many supernatural events, yet deliberately violates expectation. Instead of the weapon's being inherited, it is stolen by the warriors of the villain Thulsa Doom, who burns the entire village in search of steel. Like Conan's father, Doom also foolishly presumes that there is a riddle of steel. Seemingly set up to be the heart of the narrative, the sword that Conan was to inherit is never seen again in the comic. In the movie, however, it appears at the end, when Conan easily breaks it, takes it from the hand of a fallen enemy, uses it to kill Doom, then discards it, for it is no magic talisman, just broken steel.

Other sabers and the violence they bring pervade the narrative. As an adult, Conan becomes a gladiator sent by his master to the East to learn the secrets of swordsmanship. He heroically escapes (rather than merely being released as in the movie version) and finds a sword in a mysterious tomb. In a number of battles, he loses the weapon and much is made of his regaining it. When the hero disguises himself to infiltrate Doom's ranks, it is to a magician that Conan entrusts the blade. There is, nonetheless, nothing of sorcery about it. After discovering Conan's identity, Doom informs him that the mystique of steel is a fraud—not swords but the men who wield them are strong. Doom himself does not seem to fully grasp the implications of this insight, for instead of placing his lot with humanity, he breeds snakes, turns himself into a serpent on at least one occasion, and even feeds with human flesh a race of Neanderthal-like ape men (where the movie, less pointedly, has *human* cannibals). Despite its violence and sadism, *Conan, the Barbarian* (particularly the adaptation) offers a fantasy of *human* power raised beyond mortal limits.

In the world of Conan, the gods are indifferent or cruel. Swords are useful, but if overvalued, they bring the kind of madness that led Doom to massacre a whole village merely to steal them. As for the afterlife, the heroine Valeria returns from death and indicates that "e'en the gods could never sever" her from Conan. Similarly, in the rescue of the wounded Conan from death spirits, a magician who agreed to help flees from the apparitions, but Valeria's courage prevails. Despite the above-noted differences of method and interpretation, both versions of *Conan, the Barbarian* embody an ironic use of sword imagery that first seems magical until one learns that there is no effective power for good beyond the human will.

Like the film *Conan, the Barbarian*, the movie *Dragonslayer* also is among a number of popular films with a Marvel Comics adaptation. Both versions also are unified by an image of power—in this instance fire, associated with the pre-Christian age, its magic and ceremonies. At the beginning of the Marvel Comics version, the sorcerer Ulrich, staring into smoke and flame, sees a vision of a torchlight sacrifice of a virgin to a dragon. In this comic, his flaming magic appears real throughout, but in the movie he fakes sulfurous flames to impress the onlookers, although he does possess actual magical power. Quite the opposite holds for his apprentice, Galen. In one scene in the comic, he pleads to be sent to kill the dragon and tries to perform the old burning-bush miracle to prove his prowess. He imperiously cries in Latin, "Small bush burn! Thus I, Galen Bradwardyn, command you" (*Herbus minimus INCENDRE! Sic Impero Ego*, Galen Bradwardyn). The pictures reveal that nothing happens until Ulrich ignites the shrub. Throughout the comic, Galen's boasting runs in counterpoint to the visual exposure of his incompetence. When Marvel's Galen (incorrectly) believes that he has destroyed the dragon, he sets off a tiny fire ball to show that his power is greater than that of the Christians who try to take credit for the event. In the end, Ulrich, resurrected from the dead on a lake of burning water, must match his own power (glowing warmly within a magic amulet) against that of the dragon. When they both die in a blinding flash of flame, "half the powers of the universe vanish with [them]." Galen does not choose to join the Christians, who make dubious claim to the victory and hail the deceptive king as dragonslayer, while the latter ostentatiously plunges his sword into the already dead beast. In both versions of *Dragonslayer,* the use of fire for the magic of the last wizard and the breath of the last dragon has symbolic import, since the forces of good and evil are ultimately one. They cancel each other out, destroying an age of magic. Indeed, Ulrich speaks of himself and the dragon as "counterpart[s]" and "kindred spirits." Both the movie and the comic contain exciting moments of vivid parodoxical imagery (e.g., the wizard's resurrection from the lake of burning water and the subsequent explosion of both him and his counterpart, the dragon). These convey a different sense of time than everyday life—a period when "Time seems to have stopped" (no. 2, [p. 27]). The important concern for fantasists is to be assured that these meetings of time and eternity represent a hopeful vision. In the movie *Star Wars,* amid the flashing colored lights of hyperspace outside of the ordinary universe, Luke gains a perception beyond physical sight. The scene suggests that great powers are latent within human beings—an idea currently acceptable. In the adaptation of *Conan, the Barbarian,* "in [the] barest fraction of an instant," the deceased (yet magically alive) Valeria stops an enemy sword thrust, allowing Conan to recover his weapon. Her continuance beyond death implies the existence of eternal life (at least for those as willful as the heroine), another idea palatable to modern audiences. In contrast, in *Dragonslayer,* magic disappears from the world. To young audiences craving happy endings and the depiction of the supremacy of youth, this comic and movie only present tragedy and the incompetence of the youthful apprentice.

Another recent movie *Krull* offers fantasy that is actually repellent. Both *Dragonslayer* and *Krull* share fire as the symbol of magic, but employ it differently. After an insipid courtship scene, Princess Lyssa, as the bride at a wedding ceremony, takes fire from a basin of water. Flame contained in water is quite a traditional paradox, e.g., in ancient Meso-America, this combination symbolized the god Quetzalcoatl; in *Dragonslayer,* it constitutes the mythical underworld from which the dragon rises and Ulrich is reborn. What can be the justification in *Krull* where the princess is neither goddess nor sorceress? In the 1980s it is difficult to imagine, even in fantasy, that any writer would expect an adult audience, or even anyone out of nursery school, to believe that love between a prince and princess could kindle sorcerous flames. Nonetheless, the fire seems to flow from nothing more than their saccharine sentiments for one another. Before the hero, Prince Colwyn, can take the fire from Lyssa's bare hand, enemy warriors burn their way into the room and kidnap the princess. (Among various anomalies, the prince seems immune to fire some of the time, but at another time, a fire-producing ray burns him. The audience is never informed what distinguishes one occasion from another.) To save Lyssa, Colwyn first wades through molten lava; then he reaches bare armed to extract a weapon that looks much like the metal stars thrown so often in low-budget Kung Fu flicks. Strangely, Colwyn's new toy seems of little use, thus making his dramatic seizure of it seem almost extraneous to the main plot. The weapon is certainly not sufficient to kill the chief enemy. For that difficult task, the prince and princess must summon from their depths the fire of love. The creature perishes in the resulting conflagration. Both the movie *Krull* and the unfortunately faithful Marvel adaptation of it are riddled with inconsistencies, but much more than expensive computer animation (let alone mere inconsistencies *per se*) is required to constitute acceptable fantasy.

Fantastic images should be tightly associated and have an interesting religious or psychological import. According to the analytical psychologist Carl Gustav Jung, there are certain images that appear again and again throughout the world, as if they derived from basic patterns within the mind—patterns that he calls "archetypes [, which]. . . . are chiefly religious images" (p. 41). Not all swords, flames, etc., are archetypal; only when the artist or writer associates them with the paranormal do they deserve that epithet (and even then, the question of skill determines the value of the work). Because of the conjunction of archetypes with religion, the fantasist's task becomes an experiment in theology, building an alternative cosmos with its own religious structure. Furthermore, since fantasists draw on images from this world to create the new one, the difficult work is to reconcile the real and imaginary. Unless ordinary life and the seemingly paradoxical elements intersect convincingly, the result is not aesthetic. Before facing the problem of this intersection, the next two chapters will continue to examine these archetypal images themselves in terms of the Tarot cards, which Jung numbers among their many modern descendants.[3]

7

Legends of the Tarot

*I*N CHINA, THE GREATEST STOREHOUSE OF ARCHETYPAL IMAGERY IS THE *I Ching,* an obscure book employed primarily for fortunetelling. In Europe, the comparable work is the Tarot, a deck of playing cards used principally for divination. Jung has repeatedly explained that archetypes themselves are immersed in the depths of the unconscious and thus can be known only indirectly through the images they generate. Every fantasy contains some of these images, but shaped to fit a narrative context. In contrast, the Tarot cards (apart from the stories that interpreters read into them) consist of unconnected images, a good starting point for the examination of imagery. The Tarot is particularly relevant to illuminated fantasy, since each of the twenty-two Major Arcana or trumps (listed in chapter 8) has both a title and a symbolic picture, such as a falling Tower of Babel (generally signifying catastrophe) or the Sun (generally signifying success). As one might expect from the Tarot's aura of mystery, relationship between picture and label is problematic. Thumbing through Arthur Waite's version of the deck, for example, may leave one wondering why Death carries a rose on his banner, why the Sun shows a naked child on a horse, or why the Star depicts a naked woman pouring out vessels of water. Books exist explaining such details (not always consistently). Although one might presume that Waite's commentary must be definitive for his own deck, his work arises from an offshoot of an arcane society (The Golden Dawn), whose secrets he was sworn to keep. Consequently, the answers he published may not be the ones he privately taught. Furthermore, there exists the problem of whether his version accurately continues the tradition of older ones. In other words, the Tarot has an obscurity and ambiguity that makes it useful as a source of fantasy.

Like many other varieties of fantastic imagery, the Tarot has frequently encountered opposition from Christians. At least since 1423, when St. Bernardino of Siena announced them to be inventions of Satan, all cards have had an unsavory reputation, being termed "The Devil's books" as late as the nineteenth century in Scotland.[1] In the *Waste Land,* T. S. Eliot condemns the Tarot as a "wicked pack of cards," and this was even before his final conversion to Christianity.[2] The name "Devil's books" implies an inherent contrast to the Bible, God's book. According to Christian tradition, Holy Writ is sequentially arranged by revelation once for all time and has one true interpretation established by the Church. Since Tarot cards have any number of versions and possible arrangements, they can scarcely have any single orthodox meaning. Furthermore, Christianity has long complained that cards are an inducement to sloth, gambling, and fortunetelling. Some devotees even use them for non-Christian meditations. In *A Complete Guide to the Tarot,* the modern occultist Eden Gray promises: "Given an understanding of the inner meaning of the symbols, the cards yield, on the highest plane, mystic powers and esoteric wisdom."[3]

Sometime during the 1570s, a puritanical Englishman named John Northbrooke theorized that one of the devil's purposes in inventing cards was to lead the unwary into idolatry, for Northbrooke believed that cards originated as idols.[4] No one knows the Tarot's real origin, but legend attributes it to various pagan cults, several Christian heresies, and the migration of the Gypsies from Egypt (though the Gypsies probably were never there). Even in its history (or rather its lack of an authentic one), the Tarot is steeped in fantasy. At every level, it is a stimulus to the imagination.

Probably the Tarot is just a collection of stock images—large enough to seem fairly complete, small enough to be conveniently held in the hand. The number of cards varies from version to version, but the standard deck consists of twenty-two Major Arcana (the most obviously paradoxical cards) and fifty-six lesser Arcana. From this second group derive the fifty-two cards of the ordinary playing deck, which can be thought of as a truncated Tarot.

Even this ordinary playing deck has influenced literature, most famously Lewis Carroll's *Alice in Wonderland.* In the first sentence, Alice wonders, "what is the use of a book . . . without pictures or conversations" (Carroll, p. 5). Alice's observation marks one extreme of a continuum, the opposite end of which is pictures and conversations without a book, i.e., the talking playing cards. In her quest for amusement, events grow "Curiouser and curiouser!" (Carroll, p. 10). Finally, Alice encounters the three frightened gardeners, who are conversing playing cards. With his usual love of puns, Carroll assigns them the suit of spades, of which they represent the numbers two, five, and seven. These numerals may mark their fortune. The divinatory meanings of corresponding Tarot cards fit neatly: "Tension in relationships"; "Failure. . . . cowardliness"; "a plan that may fail" (Gray, pp. 109–14). Although Carroll had a passing interest in the occult, this correspondence may mean no more than that he conformed to a general tradition associating the image of spades with ill fortune or, of course, the correspondence may be coincidence. Where the gardeners hoped to allay the Queen of Heart's displeasure by painting the roses red, she ordered them beheaded. For the Tarot card corresponding to the Queen of Hearts, the negative meaning is "Someone who changes her mind constantly and is a prey to fantasies. Possibly, a vicious and depraved woman."[5] That is a fairly apt portrait of Carroll's Queen, though all he probably intends is to have her exemplify the worst aspect of the "heart" image—arbitrary, uncontrolled emotion. Alice, according to her sister, will mature, yet retain the opposite aspect, "the simple and loving heart of her childhood" (Carroll, p. 80).

For Victorians (including Carroll, despite his great love of childhood and the imagination), virtue must be of the head as well as the heart. Alice begins her dream desiring mere diversions, "pictures or conversations." In the concluding trial scene, she loudly advocates rationality, particularly when the Queen demands the sentence before the verdict. In a world of cards, arrangement naturally varies and is reshuffled. Alice, however, sees the Queen's behavior as "nonsense," rejects the royal cards she had previously longed to meet, and awakes. Only upon leaving her frightening, frustrating dream does it become "wonderful" to her (Carroll, p. 78). Her sister, however, manages to re-dream Alice's adventures while remaining partly awake and therefore in control. "So she sat on, with closed eyes, and half believed herself in Wonderland, though she knew she had but to open them again and all would change to dull reality" (Carroll, p. 80). This seems to be the ideal, neither atoss among the terrors of dreamland nor bored by "dull reality," but just musing about childhood on a summer afternoon.

As previously mentioned, Carroll's own drawings for Alice have a kind of primal power that captures the terrors of nightmare but Tenniel's render the calm that is the other side of Wonderland, the side that readers should experience—re-dreaming the events as did the older sister to whom they were told. Particularly in his treatment of the talking deck, Tenniel avoids realism, imitating instead the traditional stylization of royalty pictured on playing cards. Stylization is the customary way of representing psychic material. Stylization distinguishes itself from naturalistic portraiture through expressive distortions. Among the various ways that Tenniel stylizes his art is to give the playing-card people the proportions of children, regardless of

"Now for the evidence," said the King, "and then the sentence.

"No!" said the Queen, first the sentence, and then the evidence!"

"Nonsense!" cried Alice, so loudly that everybody jumped, the idea of having the sentence first!

"Hold your tongue!" said the Queen.

"I won't!" said Alice, "you're nothing but a pack of cards! Who cares for you?"

Lewis Carroll's own drawing from "Alice's Adventures under Ground." (Reprinted from The Complete Illustrated Works of Lewis Carroll, edited by Edward Guiliano, copyright © 1982, by Crown Publishers, Inc., by permission of the publisher.)

their age. Capable of accurate perspective, which he can use or ignore at will, Tenniel generally chooses a cartoonlike flatness. Without the distancing effect of perspective, a viewer might feel close to the picture, a child among children. Tenniel's stylization of the deck also inspires a sense of *déjà vu,* as the viewer beholds again card forms seen from infancy (a common experience), making them seem primordial images, exempt from the devastations of time. Whether or not Jung is right in contending that archetypes derive from the prehistory of mankind, he is correct that literature typically presents powerful images as being uncountably old or, at least, as dating from

Sir John Tenniel's picture from "Alice's Adventures in Wonderland." (Reprinted from The Complete Illustrated Works of Lewis Carroll, edited by Edward Guiliano, copyright © 1982, by Crown Publishers, Inc., by permission of the publisher.)

the childhood of an individual, if not the dawn of mankind.

A number of comics also draw on ordinary playing-card imagery, as with the villainous Royal Flush Gang, who have appeared more than once in DC Comics, or the heroic Jack of Hearts, who occasionally crops up in Marvel ones. For an example of comic-book treatment of these stylized images, consider the February, August, and September 1982 issues of *Master of Kung Fu*. The title pages of the first of these begins a complex series of interlinkings. The credits for the book and the main characters are both superimposed on playing cards. The name of the writer, Doug Moench, appears on the top of the arrangement surmounting a card king on whose figure is superimposed Shang-Chi, the major character. Both editors' names stand at the very bottom of two cards, each of a dark suit and bearing the face of a villain, perhaps evidence of the proverbial hostility between creative people and their supervisors. The villain Zaran, previously shown as Jack of Clubs (a warrior's card according to Lewis Carroll's symbolism), feels a need to "convince [himself] that he fits the perfect warrior stereotype that he has constructed for himself." Consequently, he throws a deck of cards into the air, attempting to pierce as many as possible before they all flutter to the ground, including the Queen of Spades associated with his mistress Fah lo Suee, who deserts him when she sees what he has done to her card. After six issues, card imagery resumes with the characters linked to the same cards. On the last page, a Joker appears, announcing the return of Shang-Chi's father, the insidious Dr. Fu Manchu, an unaging being who has lived for hundreds of years. To tempt his son into a trap, he sends him a pack of cards, the fronts of which peal off to reveal a jigsaw-puzzle picture of the young man's childhood home or, as Shang-Chi describes these cards in the next issue, a "mosaic [forming] the entire universe of my past." In a less skillfully made comic, associating characters with cards would be a redundancy, since most comic-book characters are already stereotypes. In *Master of Kung Fu,* however, the personalities seem like three-dimensional beings, forcing themselves into stereotyped hero or villain roles, sometimes against the grain. The cards represent the roles that fate compels them to act out. Fu Manchu, by the way, was originated by Sax Rohmer, a member along with Arthur Waite, W. B. Yeats, and other notables, of the Golden Dawn organization, which studied the occult lore of cards; thus there being ominous card imagery in these issues has a certain appropriateness.

The most famous novel of the Tarot is *The Greater Trumps* (i.e., the Major Arcana) by Charles Williams, another member of the Golden Dawn. According to Williams's fantasy, the Tarot exists in two forms, original cards from which all other versions have come, and seventy-eight matching golden images that move across a chessboard of their own volition or in magnetic rapport with the universe. Two wealthy families, the Coningsbys of Britain and the Lees of Gypsy descent, each possess half of the mystery. Since they are about to be joined through the marriage of Nancy Coningsby and Henry Lee, one might think that no obstacle hindered the union of both forms of the Tarot. Unfortunately, Lothair Coningsby, the head of one family, is loathe to part with his treasure, driving Henry Lee to a magical attempt on his future father-in-law's life by beating the air into a great storm with cards from the pack. Nancy interrupts him. The storm becomes seemingly uncontrollable, threatening to destroy the world. Ultimately, armed with spiritual insight fostered by her aunt Sybil, Nancy conquers the storm with laughter: "As if her laughter were a spiritual sword, the last great rush of spectral giants fell back from it" (p. 227). Williams does not explain this laughter beyond associating it with Christian joy and a divine power entering her from beyond the world. The only way to control the Tarot (as opposed to being controlled by the cards) is to match the mood of their sprightly free play or, as Williams terms it, their "dance." *The Greater Trumps* overflows with Christianity but not Christian orthodoxy. In the fashion of the Gnostic heresy, evil springs more from lack of esoteric knowledge than from corruption of the will. Indeed, as is common with fictions about cards, free will seems absent: "If you cry . . . [or] if you laugh, it's because some . . . step [in the dance] demands it, not because you will" (p. 107). At one extremely ecumenical point, Williams compares the cards to leaves from "the sacred bodhi-tree" of Buddhism, those of Yggdrasil, the world-tree of Scandinavian mythology, and of the "olives of Gethsemane" (p. 89). (It is left to conjecture whether Sybil, the saintly spokesperson of Christianity, ever went to church, and she explicitly rejects belief in the Devil.) From the Golden Dawn, Williams derives his interpretation of the Tarot card The Fool as a mystery associated with a transcendent Unmoved Mover, since The Fool is numbered zero in Waite's arrangement.[6] Although St. Paul advised each man to "become a fool, that he may be wise" (1 Cor. 3:18), Williams's linking God with The Fool sounds somewhat less orthodox, though it may merely mean that it is through the nonverbal side of the mind that worshipers contact Him, not an entirely heterodox notion.

Williams's idea of finding the original Tarot undistorted by subsequent corruptions perhaps inspired the similar aim in Piers Anthony's "quarter-million word novel of Tarot" *(God of Tarot, Vision of Tarot,* and *Faith of Tarot).* In this trilogy, the protagonist encounters living nightmares representing a hundred-card Tarot deck, allegedly a more complete set of archetypes than the usual seventy-eight card version. Similarly, in her multivolume *Chronicles of Tornor,* Elizabeth A. Lynn creates her own version, a feminist Tarot. Numerous artists have also reinvented the Tarot ranging from Koji Furuta's Zen-influenced "Ukiyoe Tarot" (available from U.S. Games Systems) to Salvador Dali's surrealistic "Universal Tarot," a collage of esoteric symbols and pictures from the history of art. Authors and artists seek archetypes but, significantly, they each come up with a strikingly different set of images.

Along with detailed new versions of the whole deck, there are also countless fictions employing some Tarot images. In his Amber series (*Nine Princes of Amber,* 1970, *The Guns of Avalon,* 1972, *Sign of the Unicorn,* 1975, *The Hand of Oberon,* 1976, and *The Courts of Chaos,* 1977), for example, the Hugo and Nebula Award-winning Roger Zelazny conceives of a few Tarot-like cards used for teleportation. In a Starmont Guide to that author, his close friend Carl B. Yoke notes that many characters and situations in the series are based on the Arcana of the Tarot, such as the amnesiac protagonist on the Fool, his royal father on the Emperor, and his red-haired enemy on the Devil. In *The Illustrated Zelazny* (1978), Gray Morrow provides "An Amber Tapestry," consisting of nineteen paintings shaped not like tapestries but cards. The first nine may be meant to represent the trumps mentioned in the series, but the remainder show scenes from the Amber fantasies, some paintings with several episodes impossibly compressed together or superimposed on one another.[7] In addition to books such as the above that have a relatively obvious connection to the Tarot, others make subtle use of it, e.g., John Fowles's *The Magus,* Samuel Delany's *Nova,* and Gustav Meyrink's *Der Golem.* One might easily devote a book-length study to them. Instead, this chapter will end by briefly delineating one avant-garde example.

The most difficult recent novel of the Tarot is Italo Calvino's *The Castle of Crossed Destinies* (*Il Castello dei destini incrociati,* 1969), which has quickly gained an international reputation. Fascinated by the interrelationship of images and interpreting language, he makes his text a speculation into the meaning of a series of Tarot cards, pictured in the margin of his book. The first section of the volume concerns wanderers rendered mute by experience in a dark forest (life). Having "faced so many trials, encounters, apparitions, duels, that [he] could no longer order [his] actions or [his] thoughts," the narrator, along with the other guests of a mysterious castle, seems to have been temporarily deprived of verbal ability but, presumably, he later regains that power, using it to tell what he experienced during his aphasia.[8] While mute, the wayfarers choose Tarot cards that resemble their bodies, using the deck to tell their tales wordlessly. The story is the result of Calvino's odd method of composition for, as he reveals, he first laid out the cards at "random" (if laying out cards is ever truly at random) and then constructed narratives suggested by the imagery (p. 126). As Calvino explains in a note to the Italian (though not the English) edition, Paolo Fabbri's paper on cartomancy (delivered at a 1968 international symposium on the structure of the narrative) inspired Calvino's using the Tarot for story telling. The structuralist understanding of language as an arrangement of images and other elements underlies Calvino's work. If a small number of components constitutes all narrative, then these must recur again and again; and all humanity, to the extent that each person is part of his own story, his own life, must be the double of some fictional character. Calvino, though, subtly undercuts this contention by using very different Tarot decks as illuminations. He further undermines it by showing the wide variety of interpretations possible for the identical cards. In the same set of Tarot, Faust and Parsifal (sinner and saint) each sees his own life, yet arrives at opposite conjectures:

> "The world does not exist," Faust concludes . . . "there is [only] . . . a finite number of elements whose combinations are multiplied. . . ."
>
> Whereas this would be the (still temporary) conclusion of Parsifal: "The kernal of the world is empty . . . around absence is constructed what exists, at the bottom of the Grail is the Tao," and he points to the empty rectangle surrounded by the tarots (p. 97).

The word *Tao* refers to an unexplainable reality, the Way of the Universe as intuited, not reasoned. In Chinese metaphysics (from whence Calvino derives the term *Tao*), "empty" often means that everything is void of separate existence because all is so interrelated. Not merely the cards but their relationship to one another and to the very spaces that separate them make up a single pattern. Not realizing this, Faust sees only the individual cards, while Parsifal recognizes that since the meaning of the parts blends together, there is a total world, one so complex that it cannot be comprehended short of eternity. This is why the conclusion is "still temporary." In structuralist terminology, the word "absence" in the above quotation designates the almost infinite possibilities excluded each time a choice is made. In the story of "The Waverer" told by one of the castle's guests, Calvino plays with this idea. A young man, desiring everything, cannot choose between two women, two roads, two fountains. Thus he deprives his double who was to have had the other woman, other road, other fountain. Structuralists associate absence with the unconscious, which includes the sum of memories absent from consciousness. There the double seems a personification of the unconscious. In "The Tale of Astolpho on the Moon," earth and moon are complements, the latter containing all the possibilities not explored on the former. Thus, totality of life involves both presence (what one has actually had) and absence (what one has not had but merely dreams about), i.e., both reality and fantasy. Calvino describes the balance of nature being broken, the repressed or suppressed excluded too long, women revolting against men, the wild against the city, the sea against the land, until order shatters, and in the reshuffling, all is undone. Not to make the mistake of suppressing anything, he does not wish to exclude from his work what might be contained in its double—the other book that might have been written if he had made different choices. Consequently, he tempts his readers to make their own interpretations of the pictures of cards in the margin, since the narrator is untrustworthy. Not only are the narrator's readings often far-fetched, but he lacks knowledge of the traditional meaning of the Tarot, as when he reads the Eight of Cups as meaning a wedding. Actually it signifies "disappointment in love" or "decline of interest."[9] Ironically, the wedding described by the narrator appears to bring such disillusionment. In the midst of it, the groom jilts the bride to run after a naked boy, who turns out to be his son (pp. 10–12). The narrator's mistakes render the relationship of picture and text problematic. The open endedness of the book also derives from its three-part structure: the first, a castle resembling an inn with mute story-tellers' employing a Renaissance Tarot deck embellished with deities; the second, an inn resembling a castle with another silent group (some of them virtual doubles of the first) using cheap, eighteenth-century Tarot cards; and the third, Calvino's indefinite plan for an unwritten section left to the readers' imagination—a motel with another group of mute story narrators employing scraps of comics for cards. Calvino, who had previously written *Cosmicomics* (1965), recognizes the presence of archetypes in comics.

His suggestion is intriguing, partly because some comic books are even inspired by the Tarot, e.g., the June, July, and August 1982 issues of *Justice League of America,* when the title team fights magically vivified Tarot cards. More significant for the study of imagery are the great number of comic books that, without alluding to the Tarot, nonetheless share stock images with it. Back in the 1930s, with her *Archetypal Patterns in Poetry,* Maud Bodkin began an era of the study of archetypal imagery in serious literature. Comic books, though, are only beginning to receive academic attention. Thus there is still some novelty in showing that yet another subgenre of fantasy abounds with paradoxical, inherently religious imagery (the subject of the next chapter).

8

Archetypal Arcana: A Catalogue of Imagery

COMIC-BOOK CHARACTERS TYPICALLY HAVE UNUSUAL COGNOMENS—E.G., Batman, Lightning Lad, Abomination—and these names have a not-always predictable impact on the way they are drawn. What makes their epithets so evocative is partly ambiguity. Until one sees them, one does not know if Batman is part bat, if Lightning Lad is pure energy, if Abomination is physically abominable, and so forth. The other evocative quality of these names is their suggestion of some paradoxical, archetypal image, e.g., a being who is part man, part animal; a being who is part child, part Lightning God; a being who personifies abomination itself.

For a catalogue of common archetypal images, one may well examine the Major Tarot Arcana. Naturally, the Tarot does not devote an entire card to each of the possibly infinite number of images in existence, and even when the Tarot includes archetypal images, they are not always among the Major Arcana. Sword motifs, for example, are more thoroughly treated in the lesser Arcana suit of swords (comparable to spades in more familiar playing cards). The Minor Arcana, though, generally lack written labels on the cards, usually have far less elaborate pictures than the Major Arcana, and have been less influential on art and literature. Even Major and Minor Arcana together do not contain all images. For the purposes of the present study, the Major Arcana suggest a sufficient number of widespread patterns.

*The twenty-two Major Arcana of the Swiss Marseille Tarot
cards.* (Reproduced by courtesy of the Trustees of the
British Museum, London, and the Robert Harding Picture Library Ltd., London, as agent for the Rainbird
Publishing Group's photographic archive, London.)

Arcanum O: The Fool (Le Fol)

The Tarot Fool (symbolic of the primary stage of spiritual development) is
usually shown as a young man accompanied by a playful or threatening dog
or other animal, his link to the nonreasoning level of life. Some versions

show him holding a mirror, an invitation to the quest for self-knowledge. The occultist Richard Cavendish exemplifies the Arcanum with Parsifal.[1] This figure is "the chief of fools," according to Patrick Mason's *Parsifal* (1977)—a variety of beautifully produced comic book called a graphic novel to distinguish it from less expensive, pulp publications. *Parsifal*'s artist, P. Craig Russell, discloses in an October 1982 *Epic* interview that his art has been influenced by Symbolist paintings (which here probably inspire the etherealized portrayal of the Fool), Buddhist mudras (from which he clearly derives the magic hand positions), and Theosophical pictures of the human aura (which apparently serve as sources for the coloring of mysterious light). In contrast to Russell's eclecticism (typical of fantastic illuminations), Mason, at the beginning of his comic, informs the reader that he intends to make his story of the Fool consistently Christian.[2] Almost inevitably, he does not quite achieve this purpose. According to Jessie Weston's classic study *From Ritual to Romance,* the grail legend (including the story of Parsifal) and the suits of the Tarot both derive from ancient rites that initiated innocents into sexual mysteries.[3] In Mason's work, Parsifal drifts as in a dream, deprived of memory or understanding. He cannot redeem Amfortas, chief Knight of the Holy Grail, until the evil woman Kundry ends Parsifal's innocence with a kiss. Making sexual awakening a stage in the Fool's spiritual growth evokes fertility cults rather than Bible school; but then, as archetypal figure, the Fool is too paradoxical and multi-faceted to fit neatly into any dogma. In *Parsifal,* the (unintentional) contradictions suggest this unavoidable multiplicity.

The only Major Arcanum to survive in the ordinary playing deck, the Fool therein bears the title "Joker," which is also the name of a famous comic-book villain. That "grim jester, arch-criminal, master fiend" (*Batman,* December/January 1941–42) leaves a Joker card at his crimes and has a laughing hyena as a pet (perhaps a carry-over from The Fool's dog). Similar villains abound, among them the Riddler, the Prankster, and Mr. Mxyzplk, a joking "imp" from another dimension. Some of the younger, more playful superheroes are also trickster figures, the most famous of them that master of the wisecrack, Spiderman. Despite his name, he is a fairly ordinary-looking grad student except for his red and blue costume. Coincidentally, Anansi, a trickster-god popular in Africa, is also a spider-man. African slaves brought stories of his mischief to America, where they mixed their own tales with those of the rabbit-trickster-god common among Indians of the Southeast; thus was born Br'er Rabbit, hero of books, animated cartoons, and comics. In the Southwest, the comparable deity was a coyote, father of the Indian people and cunning thief of fire. He inspired Steve Englehart's series of graphic novels entitled *Coyote* about an eighteen-year-old called "Sly" Santangelo (i.e., mischievous holy angel) who becomes not a coyote, as his name implies, but a shadowy creature usually pictured as flying. In the premiere issue (April 1983), the youth's mobster enemies try to track him down by drugging and interrogating local anthropologists. To the gangsters' frustrations, instead of giving them information that would lead to discovery of his whereabouts, their scholarly informants spend much time reciting tales of his namesake, the Indian trickster-god, and making the usual academic comparisons of the latter to such other trickster divinities as Hermes and Loki.

The most popular comic-strip manifestation of the trickster archetype is the perfect Fool's dog, Snoopy—a character who has turned "Peanuts" into a multi-million-dollar industry. Able to walk on two legs, pull money out of his fur as if he had pockets, fly by rotating his ears, and type parodies of novels with his paws, Snoopy is not an average canine. As the Easter Beagle, he appears as a kind of spring demi-god, an incarnation of youthful folly and sprightliness. While the bodily members of the chaotic Amerindian trickster-spirit occasionaly war one against another,[4] Snoopy often argues with his stomach and talks to his limbs when they take on a will of their own (e.g., "Peanuts," 17 May 1982). In his deeply theological *Gospel According to Peanuts* (pp. 86–101), *The Parables of Peanuts* (passim), and a series of slide lectures delivered nationwide, Robert Short identified Snoopy as "a little Christ," what each Christian should be. Seen from a less profound perspective, Snoopy seems usually to be one of the most selfish and mischievous characters in the strip. Concerning the theology of trickster figures, however, Carl Gustav Jung observes:

> If we consider . . . the daemonic features exhibited by Yahweh in the Old Testament, we shall find in them not a few reminders of the unpredictable behavior of the trickster, of his pointless orgies of destruction, and his self-appointed sufferings, together with the same gradual development into a savior and his simultaneous humanization.[5]

The paradoxes of the Trickster/Fool underlie all the other major Arcana, for Tarot tradition considers them stages that he undergoes in his movement from infantile insouciant jests and dreamy innocence to full humanity.[6] Only then will he truly deserve the oxymoronic title "Wise Fool."

Arcanum 1: The Juggler or Magician (Le Bateleur)

The Juggler or Magician is the Fool's first new role, where he acquires power. The magician has been so important a type in comics that one critical compendium entitled *The Comic-Book Book* dedicates a chapter to the magicians of the 1930s and 1940s when at least thirty of them mingled sleight of hand and miracles, e.g., Phantom Magician, allegedly the first of them, and Mandrake, the best known.[7]

Students of the Tarot commonly associate the Magician with the ego. While prayer beseeches the supernatural, magic egotistically attempts to command it. The Magician, however, is not a rational ego like his modernist incarnation, the scientist. Rather, the former juggles both sides of the mind in eternal peril of losing sanity and soul. In comics, magicians' trafficking with dark powers seems demonic, but ambiguously so, for a good number of them are heroes; and even the villainous ones seldom are literal Fausts awaiting a Christian hell.

Dr. Strange, the most popular magician at present, learned altruism as well as occultism in Tibet. Despite his heralded reform, he virtually always appears arrogant, commanding spirits and mere mortals. He is like an ego forcing itself into the unconscious, where control is resented and resisted. This condition is often quite distinctively presented as in the premiere issue of *Doctor Strange: Special Edition,* where the protagonist plunges into the hostile world of "unreality" attuned to his "unconscious." He fights death sent by a former Roman Catholic Cardinal turned wizard-killer. When Doctor Strange proclaims, "I must ONCE AGAIN confront DEATH," he believes the threat is external (p. 39). In contrast, the illumination depicts the left side of his face as a skull for, as he eventually learns, his fear of dying is the real peril, opening him to death from within. Once he conquers that fear, he is immortal.

Arcanum 2: The Priestess, Popess, or Goddess Juno (Junon)

The fool next encounters the magician's feminine counterpart, the desirable enchantress, termed by Jungians the *anima* (Latin for soul), an image of a man's unconscious as a seductive woman who may, nonetheless, terrify a man who fears his own less masculine side. Tarotists name her the Priestess or Popess, the latter in memory of legendary Pope Joan, who allegedly gained the papacy before the Romans, in horror, discovered that she was a woman.[8] A quick survey of the paperback racks may show the anima in a hundred guises, her nubile breasts bulging through gold-filigree armor or a torn space suit while some male creature molests her with green-scaled tentacles. She may be a mermaid singing by an alien sea, a winged Valkyrie flying above battle spears, a virgin stroking a unicorn, or a naked sacrificial maiden awaiting the plunging knife. She sells fantasy—indeed, *is* fantasy. Any similarity between her and a real woman is probably coincidental.

Too often being merely the hero's girl friend, feminine figures usually do not rise above a stereotype, although they are sometimes given a slightly larger part as in *Isis* magazine. On the cover of the November 1977 issue of that comic book, the title character cowers in chains while a giant serpent prepares to assault her (another example of the picture/text discrepancy motif, since the story presents the incident differently). The comic-book episode begins when Isis's boyfriend, Rick Mason, suspects that Andrea and Isis are the same character. This upsets him; he is sure there must be something sinister in his girl friend's becoming a powerful goddess devoted to helping the needy. Already afflicted by his masculine pride, Rick is ripe for possession by the sorcerer Serpentotep (the male ego personified), who is pictured with a large gold cobra rearing virilely from the bottom of his wide belt.

Comic-book males often show hatred of anima figures. In the August 1982 issue of *Kazar,* for example, the title character, high on psychedelic mushrooms, spends the episode trying to shoot his girl friend Shanna because he thinks he is a Chicago detective stalking an evil seductress. Hallucinations follow a quarrel with Shanna in which he resents her emasculating attempt to take his gun away from him and also her words about "the phallic symbolism of the pistol and its role [with regard] to [the] insecure male psyche" (p. [8]). Comparably, in the November 1980 issue of *Wolverine,* the title character first dreams of a former woman friend's piercing him with an arrow, plunging him "into the abyss" (p. [11]). Then he seeks to murder his treacherous present love. He pauses before finishing the execution, gangsters eliminate her instead, and he suddenly feels a fresh serenity, a renewed sense of being, a consciousness that he is not a beast (which he physically resembles) but "a Man!" (p. [15]).

One of the most obvious personifications of the anima in comics is Dr. Strange's disciple Clea, pictured with coiffeur rising in unexplained horns, a counterpart to the hornlike streaks in Strange's hair. Not even allegedly an earthwoman, she comes from a dark, chaotic, magical dimension, i.e., the unconscious. Usually reduced to fixing snacks for her master or staying at home meekly wondering if she deserves so great a friend as Dr. Strange, she occasionally receives more opportunity for adventure, as in the April 1981 issue when she becomes a priestess warding off an invasion from another dimension. In the epilogue, Clea plays in the sea, voluptuously enticing him to join her, while he stands back, summoning a great storm so that she will cease her seductive gestures and be "the disciple again" (p. 30). Considering her love unworthy of Strange, Clea leaves him and in his sorrow he feels as if "his soul had died" (*Doctor Strange,* October 1982, p. 2).

Arcanum 3: The Empress or Great Mother (L[']Emperatrice)

If the Magician and Priestess mate, they become Emperor and Empress, adult man and woman. As the previous section suggests, comic books generally prevent their heroes from reaching this stage, which places them above the comprehension or sympathy of their youngest readers—one rea-

Mike Vosburg and Frank Chiarmonte, picture from Isis, *October/November 1977.* (ISIS is a trademark of DC Comics Inc., New York, and is used with permission. Copyright © 1977 DC Comics Inc.)

son why these figures appear less frequently than the previous ones. They do occur, though, e.g., the "Mother of Memory" in *ElfQuest;* Azar, matriarch of Azarath in *Teen Titans;* and Hippolyte, ruler of Paradise Island in *Wonder Woman.* There are also a few Terrible Mothers (the other side of the Arcanum) such as Granny Goodness, who runs a concentration camp for children in Jack Kirby's now defunct *New Gods* series. Even more psychologically suggestive, the title character of *Arion, Lord of Atlantis,* has a mother of pure energy who wishes to possess him, even if she must destroy his physical body and imprison his spirit within herself. Sadly, the depiction of maternal figures (and women characters in general) seldom evidences much sophistication. Although the writer Christopher Claremont has sometimes been praised because his heroines are less objectionable than the average, his partner, the artist John Byrne, accurately criticizes Claremont, for the latter's stupid mother characters whose only important role seems to be giving birth—"when they've dropped the kid . . . [t]heir intelligence comes out with [it]" (*The Comics Journal,* Summer 1980, p. 68). In many comic strips such as "Momma," mothers and mothers-in-law are meddling, ignorant, and quarrelsome. They resemble much less the Empress than the Fool. Comic books in all their irreverence well suit their chief readers, adolescents, in their rebellion against parental authority.

Arcanum 4: The Emperor or Great Father (L[']Empereur)

George Lucas, author of the *Star Wars* saga, has revealed that he "wanted a name that suggested dark Father and arrived at the blend Darth Vader"[9] (ambiguous sounds that also suggest death and invader). When, in the movie *The Empire Strikes Back,* Vader reveals Luke Skywalker to be his son, comic-book readers should not have been very surprised. That does not mean that previous issues of *Stars Wars* comics (inspired by the movie of that name) contained specific preparation for the disclosure. There was no necessity for that. The father as villain is a comics' cliché (and Lucas has kept every comic book he ever bought, though he also drew on world mythology[10] and other sources). Among those comic-book heroes compensating for paternal malevolence are Shang-Chi, son of Fu Manchu; Wolverine, son of the villain Sabretooth (though not in the first story that tells the origin of the character); Raven, daughter of Trigon (the Devil of another dimension); Orion, son of Darkseid (evil personified); and Daimon Hellstrom, son of Satan himself. With contradictory evidence, Satan also claims paternity for Hellcat, a particular embarrassment to her since she loves Daimon Hellstrom (*Defenders,* Sept. 1982) and eventually marries him (*Marvel Universe,* March 1984). In the premiere issue of what the Marvel Company hoped to make a series, the new male character Star Lord finds that a white-bearded "Master of the Sun," who bestows powers upon him, is his father, though once a villainous member of an alien race. The father assumes human form "to accomplish good works by sending his son in his place" (*Marvel Spotlight,* May 1980, p. 30). The episode ends with Star Lord's paraphrasing the Christian Lord's Prayer in his decision to do the will of his God/Devil father.

In their series "The Alchemist Supreme," Godard and Ribera depict an extremely lecherous, fat old man, who claims to be God (*Heavy Metal,* July 1980, p. 56). Apparently this image is what is desired by some readers, among them David Stallman who actually praises the series' theology in his review article entitled, "God Isn't Dead! He's Just Blitzed Three Sheets to the Wind!" (*The Comics Journal,* October 1980, pp. 46–47). Dave Sim's and Fabio Gasbarri's 1977 story "I'm God" also shows an impotent Deity, self-exiled on a distant planet because the Creation expended most of his energy.[11] Although one might trace blasphemies against the gods at least as far back as ancient Greek comedy, these comics' most obvious predecessor is Blake's character Nobodaddy, a god of materialism and, as his name implies, no one's spiritual father (Damon, p. 301).

Paradoxically, youths may also have a strong need for parental figures. For years the psychological researcher Lloyd Silverman conducted still-controversial tests using a flickering picture "of a man and woman merged at the shoulders" to instill the message "Mommy and I are one" in male subjects and "Daddy and I are one" in females. This subliminal image allegedly helped bring college undergraduates sufficient peace of mind so that they performed more effectively on final examinations than a control group.[12] Comparably, in the October 1977 issue of *Mister Miracle,* written by Steve Englehart, the title character takes into his own body the power of the magical "mother box." This connects him to the "Source" and fills him with the knowledge necessary to use his own abilities (pp. 4–5). In the dialogue, motherhood is ironically reduced to a "box." The pictures, though, show a shadowy woman's face next to a bearded man unmentioned in the text—a paternal archetype mysteriously added to the maternal one in the text. More dramatic (and perhaps even stranger), in the final issue of *Iceman,* the title character's girl friend, Mirage, chooses to re-enter the body of her divine father, Oblivion. Absorbing her, he cries ecstatically, "Now come, my daughter . . . my sister . . . my mate" (p. [26]). She has scarcely an alternative, for Oblivion argues persuasively that all is void. With more self-doubts than usual, Iceman returns home and tries to improve his relations with his own parents, but he now fears that life is a mere dream and that only the archetypal father Oblivion exists.

Arcanum 5: The Hierophant, Pope, or God Jupiter (Jypiter)

While the Emperor represents the father per se, the Hierophant presents a slightly different image, that of the person who has accepted paternal values, shaping his or her conscience or superego. Less a free agent than the Emperor, the Pope stands for the Church and its orthodoxy. Since orthodoxy is not particularly popular in comics, the Hierophant fares little, if at all, better than the Emperor. Children's comics, though, tend to avoid religious controversy by sparing the Catholic hierarchy, as in one episode of *Arak* that contrasts a benevolent but weak real Pope with a dynamically evil "Black Pope," who rules a literally subterranean church underneath the city of Rome. Adult comics are somewhat more direct, as in Enki Bilal's "The Immortals' Fete," where a neo-Pope of the future Church fakes miracles and cooperates with the fascist government (*Heavy Metal,* November 1981, p. 28). More psychologically interesting, in "The Further Adventures of John DiFool," Alexander Jodorowsky and Moebius show DiFool's escaping the savage minions of the despicable "Techno-Pope" by destroying his temple with a magical object called the Black Incal. As the Techno-Pope tries to murder DiFool, a beautiful semi-nude maiden named Animah arrives from the depths of the earth to save DiFool by killing the Pope. Recognizing her as the woman of his dreams, DiFool gives her his most precious possession, the Black Incal. Despite this loss, DiFool will eventually have to combat the ruler, an imperial hermaphrodite (Emperor and Empress combined). Such blatant use of all of the aforementioned archetypes suggests that Jodorowsky and Moebius had in mind something very like the Tarot Fool's journey (*Heavy Metal* 5 (March 1982): 18).

Instead of Popes, per se, comic books and strips more often show cult leaders and evangelists with their individual religions or heresies. In Charles Schulz's "Peanuts" strip, Linus is an amusing parody of the type, because of his frequent Biblical quotations, evangelical faith in the Great Pumpkin, and, of course, Snoopy's choice of him to act as minister at the dog's wedding. Faced with the somewhat premature fear of not getting into a desirable college and with a mother who packs guilt-producing, lengthy notes with his lunch, Linus staggers to school even when sick, and apparently turns for consolation to religion and his blanket (sometimes called a "spiritual tourniquet").[13] Like most cartoonists, Schulz, the creator of "Peanuts," does not glorify any authoritarian, priestly figure. Of his own religious position, Schulz remarks, "I now shy away from anyone who claims to possess all of the truth" (*Peanuts Jubilee,* p. 100).

Arcanum 6: The Lovers (L[']Amoureux)

This card signifies that learning affection through human love may serve as preparation for deepened spirituality—in Medieval Christian terms learning to love God by first loving a fellow mortal, or in Taoist yoga the heightened spiritual energy achieved through special sexual practices (see the discussion of the *Hsi-yu-chi* in chapter 10). Comic-book erotica are still very popular in Europe and, during the 1950s, melodramatic romance comics dominated the American market until television and film sensuality made them obsolete. Nevertheless, these narratives of literal love do not usually represent the spiritual aspect of the Tarot card: psychological growth through affection. Many superheroes, however, have at the beginning of their careers the death of someone (parent, sibling, fiancé or fiancée) in whose memory they dedicate themselves to a life of self-sacrifice. Thereafter, they periodically lose loves, charging the heroes with almost uncontrollable energy and resolve. In between these maudlin scenes, the life style of most of the heroes is single. Admittedly, Spiderman finally tired of one-night stands and married in 1987. Reed Richards, head of the Fantastic Four, married long ago, and has even begotten a child, but love only becomes the focus of the comic when his family is threatened, spurring him to greater heroism. The less popular characters Aquaman and Mera wed but spend much time apart. Heroic figures are most often bachelors, spinsters, widowers, widows, divorcés, and divorcées.

Arcanum 7: The Chariot (Le Chariot)

Having (at least temporarily) acquired an intimate friend in the last Arcanum, the Fool now gains the *sine qua non* of such a relationship: "wheels," e.g., a chariot. A considerable number of heroes treasure vehicles that are extensions of their personalities. Dazzler, a relatively modest heroine, contents herself with wheels in their simplest form—roller skates—but young women do not need mega-horsepower vehicles to prove virility. Almost equally unostentatious, Wonder Woman flies an invisible plane. Gadget-mad Batman, however, has land, sea, and air transportation so well-equipped with special devices that they make James Bond's seem like stripped-down models. The mechanic/race-car driver/stunt motorcyclist Ghost Rider can project a cycle of hellfire from his demon soul. Comics approve extensions of personal freedom ranging from the hot rod to the intergalactic cruiser. Artists seem fascinated with the look of vehicles, sometimes lavishing hours to make their creations far more elaborate and detailed than is required by text or plot. The Chariot signifies the triumph of man over matter or, in a paradoxical way, the union of man and matter.

Arcanum 8: Strength (La Force)

In this Arcanum the Fool learns that power requires no such external trappings as the Chariot but flows into his own body from the energy of the universe. Some of the older Tarot decks associate the symbol with Hercules, a muscle-bound idiot who adventures his way into godhood, a prototype of lumbering superheroes. A particularly juvenile line of comics, *Charlton Classics,* presents a bowdlerized version of Hercules' Greek myths in which he seems no more dull witted than the other characters, all of whom sound as if they have been lobotomized by a jackhammer. The Marvel comics group has issued a more promising Hercules mini-series beginning with *Hercules, Prince of Power,* September 1982. In an interview in *Comics Scene* (May 1982), the series creator, Bob Layton, describes the god's character as a "budhead" who "starts out being vacuous and shallow, and . . . ends up being vacuous and shallow, but realizing it." This description capsulizes the Marvel approach to characterization. If a hero remains static, he is uninteresting; if he matures to another stage of psychic growth, he no longer embodies the type that his readers anticipate; thus he must progress, but only within his type. At most, Hercules can recognize himself to be mindless strength. Such a realization is really necessary for him to fulfill the archetype or he will be merely a Fool with a diploma from Charles Atlas. Some versions of this Arcanum depict a young girl taming a lion to show the conquest of the brute part of the mind by its seemingly weaker, higher nature, while Hercules represents strength paradoxically derived from a weak intellect, which does not interfere with the power of nature flowing through his body.

Arcanum 9: The Hermit (L[']Ermite)

Certain affinities tie together the Hermit and superhero. Both reputedly have miraculous powers, which they can use to help others, though hermits specialize in healings and heroes in monster battling. Hermits, rather, tend to tame dangerous creatures, as with St. Jerome and the lion—a link to the lion-taming symbol sometimes used for the previous Arcanum.

Consulting the wise man on the mountain is a cartoon cliché, where he occasionally appears with an anachronistic book or computer by his side to link him with more prosaic sources of knowledge than silent contemplation. Some superheroes make retreats from society, notably Superman at his "Fortress of Solitude," its name borrowed from the arctic hermitage of Doc Savage, another star of the adventure pulps. Superheroes, however, can spend little time away from close involvement with the outside world, though their retreats equip them with greater self-knowledge for such encounters. Dedicated recluses are only interesting for the brief periods when visited by would-be disciples who, of course, are turned away, or the hermits would cease to be hermits.

Arcanum 10: Fortune (La Roux de Fortune)

The superhero Dr. Fate has an abode that might befit the Hermit, a tower without windows and doors on top of a high hill, but instead of trying to investigate his own mind, he sees "prophecies" and "destinies" inside a crystal ball. "He is possessed" by fortune personified (*Flash,* February 1982, p. [24]). When Dr. Fate was a child, a god of order killed his father accidentally (if any act of a god of destiny can be accidental) and took on that role himself, first declaring the boy to be his predestined servant; then he hypnotized the lad to follow orders. Similarly, in the aforementioned story of the Justice League vs. the Tarot, there is an ultimate merger of dream and reality, for life becomes art; the villain Amos Fortune, who animates the cards, at last finds himself absorbed into one of them—the Tower, symbolic of the overthrow of pride. With a cry "like a MAN who'd LOST HIS SOUL!" Amos Fortune (now a stylized image) is shown perpetually falling from the pictured edifice to suffer "for all ETERNITY!" (*Justice League of America,* September 1981, p. 26). In his book *The Archetypes and the Collective Unconscious,* Jung writes, "The unconscious no sooner touches us than we *are* it."[14] In the Arcanum of Fortune, the Fool begins by looking into the unconscious to predict the outside world and may finally be unable to distinguish himself (and external reality) from its strange, ominous patterns.

Arcanum 11: Justice (Ivstice)

Comic books love the word "justice" as in the "Justice League of America" and its predecessor the "Justice Society of America," but what does their "Justice" actually mean? Trial by combat! In comic books, human relations must appear visually. However clever a writer is in rendering the nuances of a relationship, the villain is not vanquished until the final punch, the girl not won until the final embrace. Therefore, in order that superheroes can have a visual relationship with one another, they occasionally even fight their friends. Thus, after years of cabin-fever-close friendship with Batman, who in early episodes sleeps next to him in a twin bed, Robin, in a trance, tries to punch his former guardian and vents long pent-up resentment with the ambiguous words: "NOBODY uses me any more—including YOU!" (*New Teen Titans,* February 1981, p. 16).

For an exemplary compendium of the treatment of law and morality in *humorous* comic books, one may turn to a series of volumes collected from the pages of *Mad* magazine, one of the most notable of which is entitled *The Mad Morality or The Ten Commandments Revisited.*[15] In the lower corner of the cover, standing on a soap box, Alfred E. Newman, imitating Moses, prepares to smash the Tablets of the Law. A crowd drawn with the magazine's

THE MAD
MORALITY
OR
THE
TEN COMMANDMENTS
REVISITED
Vernard Eller

Picture for the front cover of The Mad Morality or the Ten
Commandments Revisited *by Vernard Eller.* (Copyright
© 1970 by Abingdon Press, Nashville, the publisher;
Alfred E. Newman © 1986 by E. C. Publications, Inc.
New York. Reprinted by permission of both publish-
ers.)

usual lack of subordination of detail to overall design mills about, one man holding a little golden calf, which is not worshiped but generally ignored by the rest. Individuality runs joyously rampant, to Newman's moronic approval. This accords with the "disclaimer" of *Mad*'s publisher and editor printed in the front of the volume to reassure the magazine's usual patrons that nothing "we print is moral, theological, nutritious or good." Nonetheless, the author of the book is Vernard Eller, B.A., B.D., M.A., Th.D., Professor of Religion. His unenviable task is to make something edifying out of *Mad*. Thus begins a war between his words and the pictures. Even before he began the effort of selecting tractable material from *Mad,* the features embodied a comic relationship between text and illumination. For example, the *Mad* writer Max Brandel took U.P.I. photos and affixed a commandment to each of them (pp. 9–14). To a snapshot of groupies on their knees before the Beatles, he adds, "Thou shalt have no other Gods before me." Since most of the features are drawings rather than snapshots, word and picture have a more complex relationship. At one point, a man appears with a beard made of text, which describes him as a clod masquerading as "masculine and distinguished" (p. 41). Another cartoon, this one seemingly carved from stone, purports to be Abel's Mother's Day card to Eve. The words praise her, though with reservations about the way she is "raising Cain." The picture, however, shows his presenting an apple to her—obviously an allusion to the Fall. His gift's recalling the cause of all human suffering subverts his gesture of respect, giving it a vaguely sinister undertone, while her kneeling in front of him suggests a childish fantasy of dominance over a parent. Abel's card decorates Eller's little sermon on the theme, "Honor your father and your mother." Abel, however, is neither clearly honoring nor dishonoring his parents. Far from satirizing disobedient children, it draws its humor from Bible parody, for its young readers presumably enjoy seeing the scriptural foundation of ethics being undercut. According to Eller, the man with a beard made of words illustrates the commandment, "You shall not make for yourself a graven image," which Eller redefines to mean that you shall not "treat something [such as a beard] as more valuable and important than it actually is" (p. 50). Looking at the cartoon, instead of thinking of God or Biblical morality, the reader probably just laughs at an authority figure, a typical target of *Mad*. Eller ignores the subtler nuances of his visual material, forcing them into categories they almost but not quite fit. He mentions in his own "Disclaimer" (p. 71), but generally ignores thereafter, that his theological position may differ from the message (or as he phrases it "garbage") that *Mad* wishes to convey.

According to another of the *Mad* religion books, Dave Berg's *Roger Kaputnik and God, Mad*'s publisher, William Gaines, is an atheist. What is Berg's attitude toward God? On the cover, the monumental hand of God descends from the upper-right corner to dispense the Ten Commandments to a bandaged Kaputnik. God advises, "Take these two tablets and call me in the morning." The words imply that the deity is like an indifferent doctor who prescribes aspirin instead of ministering to a seriously injured patient; so the religious aspirin, the tablets of morality, are virtually all we know of the Divine. The few cartoons depicting God show no more than the Divine hands. The moralistic text defines God as "Mitzvah," explained as people secretly helping one another (p. 141). The pictures, though, show Him as a Force beyond man, creating the world (p. 11) and secretly supporting the spacecraft of astronauts who foolishly presume that technology alone preserves them (p. 154). Berg's choosing to show only the Divine hands may also be significant. Indeed, in his previous book of *Mad* theology, *My Friend God,* Berg, in a parody of Michelangelo's *Creation of Adam,* startlingly omits all of God's Body except one hand. This pious reluctance to portray Deity apparently evidences a reverence for the supernatural, but the text of *Roger Kaputnik and God* overflows with reason and morality while avoiding discussion of the supernatural. His book appears to evidence that even the same author may be of two different minds about authority and divine law when he writes text and when he draws cartoons.

Arcanum 12: The Hanged Man (Le Pendu)

According to the symbolism of this card, the hero hangs on the cosmic tree, sacrificing himself for the world. In the October 1980 issue of *Thor,* Odin crucifies himself on the tree Yggdrasil to achieve "atonement" (p. [14]) with "the elder gods who spawned him" (p. [10]). Mother Nature convinces him that such an unnatural, despairing act would only betray the earth that he tries to save. Most crucified heroes of comic books do not imagine that their suffering is redemptive. They arrive at the predicament only because of a temporary loss in battle, as in the aforementioned story, where the Royal Flush gang bound each Justice League member on a giant playing card. Conan the Barbarian occasionally finds himself in one form of crucifixion or another, such as hanging nailed to the "tree of Woe" in the Marvel adaptation of his 1982 movie. In the October 1977 issue of *Mister Miracle,* the deity Scott Free, son of the divine ruler of New Genesis, is tied to two rockets. Granny goodness jeers:

> It is a form of CRUCIFIXION!
> Is that not what HAPPENS to Gods
> who dwell on PLANET EARTH? (p. 10)

A professional escape artist, Free releases himself before blast-off. Then he decides to become a messiah somewhat like Christ, except that he does not wish to aid the "forces of RELIGION" but those of "FREEDOM" (p. 17). Similarly, the cover of the October 1983 issue of *E-Man* shows the heroic title character crucified at the back of a stage, at the front of which a television evangelist screams, "Face the righteous WRATH OF GANTRY BABBITT!" This scene never precisely takes place in the story, but the minister does confine E-Man on a cross for later torture. A being from outer space who feeds on fear causes the evangelist to frighten his viewers with right-wing paranoia, but E-Man escapes from crucifixion in time to expose the fraud. As Donald Palumbo has demonstrated in his article "Adam Warlock: Marvel Comics' Cosmic Christ figure," Warlock's life closely follows that of Jesus, including trial, crucifixion, and resurrection.[16] His death, however, is not seen as an atonement.

Despite the rejection of redemptive sacrifice in the comics, it manifests itself in many ancient religions. In his article, "The Psychology of Transference" (*Complete Works,* vol. 16, par. 470), Jung explains:

> Nobody who finds himself on the road to wholeness can escape that characteristic suspension which is the meaning of crucifixion. For he will [be thwarted by] . . . the thing he has no wish to be (the shadow) . . . the thing he is not (the "other" . . .) and . . . his psychic non-ego (the collective unconscious).

Blake, however, speaks for the modern sensibility in his repeated denunciation of sacrifice. Similarly, comics generally repudiate the idea of a Just God's imposing crucifixion, an act to be attributed to enemies (perhaps personifications of Jung's "shadow," "other," and "collective unconscious").

Arcanum 13: Death (La Mort)

Following Durer, the Tarot of Waite shows Death as an armored knight. In the complex mythology of Marvel comics, which contains many death gods, the skeleton figure is usually female, the third phase of the goddess who appears as Priestess and Empress in the Tarot. As any number of figures from Diana, patroness of childbirth, to fairy godmother, the goddess welcomes infants into the world; as princess or priestess, she is the cherished female; and, as the many-named crone Death, she takes humanity back into the darkness. The mythology of Marvel comics calls her beloved "Thanos," who plans to destroy the entire solar system as a sacrifice to his love. (Freud argued that mankind has a death-wish, which modern Freudians call "Thanatos," a Greek term he used in conversation, but not in his writings.)[17] Although most comics' protagonists survive magazine issue after issue, some do not, e.g., twenty-one from the Marvel universe alone, according to an obituary page near the end of *Contest of Champions* (August 1982, p. [26]). One recent major superhero to expire was Captain Marvel. Since 1967, when he ceased being a villain, he fought crime off and on until years of weak sales brought his demise (allegedly from cancer) in the 1981 graphic novel *The Death of Captain Marvel*. Ironically, it sold very well, leading the list of trade paperbacks for the first part of the year. At the story's end, Marvel kisses the female, skull-faced Death and follows her away. A problem that the comic book does not explore is that Captain Marvel lost his soul in *Marvel Spotlight* (January 1980). Thereafter, he has the soul of the character Primus—a repellently bizarre idea if "soul" means here what it does in Christianity. However, drawing on primitive religion, Marvel comics distinguish between souls and selves. Deprived of a soul, characters sometimes only go mad, the fate that threatened Captain Marvel if he returned to earth without one, while for Christianity, separation of soul from body is death. For Marvel comics, the soul appears to be an energizing link with the unconscious, though this has not been made explicit. After death, the destination of a comic-book character's soul often seems to have less to do with the morality of his life than with the mythological figure who claims him—a primitive concept indeed. Souls captured by the character Vonndha go to his Master Erlik, Yellow God of Death (*Conan, the Barbarian,* March 1981, p. 3), those slain by John Daltry to Thog, the Nether Spawn, and those touched by a once human with the unangelic name of "Kowalski" to his unspecified patron. Back in the Golden Age of comic books when there was generally presumed to be only one God running the universe, He commissioned the deceased Jim Corrigan (a.k.a. the Spectre) to return to earth, fight crime, and send souls to perdition. Even this was a revision of the old notion that the Church held the keys to heaven and hell and was God's sole agent on earth. Modern comic books expand the *Spectre's* paradigm to a swarm of death gods competing for souls as a variety of religions do for the living.

Arcanum 14: Temperance (Tenperance [sic])

Having undergone Death (a temporary loss of separate selfhood before rebirth), the Fool is ready to learn moderation of individual desires and cooperation with others—the lesson of this Arcanum. In identifying with them, he faces the paradox that many separate beings can, in a sense, unite (see chapter 9). Throughout the history of comic books, teams both of heroes and villains have become ever more common, partly because of the variety they present but also because they resemble that basic human association, the family—an institution whose decline in reality has made it all the more attractive in fantasy. The ultimate of such coordination is the character

Collective Man, the Tao-Yu identical quintuplets, who through meditation can fuse their atoms into one body possessing the total of their strength and intelligence. By even more intense concentration, Collective Man can draw on the power and skill of China's billion inhabitants (*The Official Handbook of the Marvel Universe,* Feb. 1983, p. 30).

Arcanum 15: The Devil (Le Diable)

In the September 1982 issue of *Defenders,* Satan explains a significant part of the mythology of Marvel comics. Mephisto, Thog, Asmodeus, Satanish, and Satan are all "physical projections of mankind's collective unconscious" (p. 15). Claiming no knowledge of the Biblical Lucifer, Satan remarks that he himself serves "man's GOOD" by strengthening him through trial, though Satan must also continue to corrupt mankind so that there will be evil to project a devil. As the term "collective unconscious" suggests, the writer, J. M. DeMatteis, has psychology in mind. In fact, Devil and God representation in the comics coincides fairly well with psychological theory. Drawing on H. Golding's study "Themes of the Phallic Stage" and on Freud's equation of both God and Devil with the father, Ana-Maria Rizzuto, in *The Birth of the Living God: A Psychoanalytic Study,* argues that all children go through a series of stages in which their fantasy is dominated first by monsters, then by a devil, then a hero, and finally a superhero. The figures grow progressively more positive as the child gains greater mastery of his environment and thus sees himself less estranged from it. Since the child's sense of self arises partly through identification and interaction with parents, their demanding attitudes and the sense of shame that they instill in the child significantly affect formation of a devil concept and of a related God concept. The latter also involves such diverse sources as personal psychic experience, the superhero, and ideas taken from organized religions.[18] The evidence of comic books supports the complexity of the God concept, both in the variety with which He is represented and in the reluctance of writers to present Him in one unambiguous way or another. Rizzuto's idea of stages of development helps to give one of the reasons for children's accepting as credible that superheroes usually win: heroes evolve from a time in children's progress when they are older and stronger. (Naturally, the convention of happy endings in children's literature also contributes to the heroes' notable run of victories.) Rizzuto wonders why the Devil always derives from the father, since demanding mothers could equally well contribute to the image; yet she has never heard of female devils (p. 197). There are, though, devil-like death figures in literature: for instance, in *Thor* comics, Hel, a malevolent Norse goddess of the underworld. Nonetheless, since male writers have long dominated literature in general and comic books in particular, the fearful father figure predominates.

Arcanum 16: The Tower (La Maison Dieu)

At the close of a good number of James Bond movies and the comics made from them (e.g., in *Live and Let Die,* when Bond escapes with Solitaire, the beautiful priestess of the Tarot), the villain's stronghold explodes, bringing the destruction of his insidious schemes. Similarly, in Tarot imagery, the falling tower of Babel, toppled by a lightning bolt of the Lord, symbolizes the collapse of ambitious human efforts. A common paradox in religion is that human effort is insufficient for spiritual progress. In Buddhism, desire for nirvana (desirelessness) prevents attaining it, yet one cannot gain it without seeking it. One can merely meditate until Enlightenment comes as if by itself. Christians are encouraged to pursue a religious life, yet they cannot achieve salvation without God's grace. Thinking that one has accomplished some great achievement brings pride and destruction. At least as often as superheroes savage a villain's citadel, their own is totaled so that they can be shown standing in the rubble, learning humility and loss.

Arcanum 17: The Star (Le Toille)

As in the titles of *Star Reach* comics, *Star Trek* comics, Jim Starlin's *Dreadstar,* and Alfred Bester's now partly illustrated science fantasy, *The Stars My Destination,* stellar imagery implies a distant region, perhaps "long, long ago" as in *Star Wars,* but more often far in the future when man may inhabit other galaxies. Tarotists generally associate this Arcanum with hope and high aspirations. Idiosyncratically, Blake makes the stars represent one of the four faculties: "Sun (imagination), Moon (love), Stars (reason), and Earth (the senses)" (Damon, p. 386). These bodies (which, by the way corrrespond to four of the five final major Arcana) were more mysterious in Blake's time than in ours: even in his period, the Newtonian beginnings of astrophysics had so reduced the heavens to clockwork that Blake associates them with his least favorite category, reason. Since then, technological progress has inspired science-fiction writers to fantasize this faculty's being carried to its highest (though not always its most humane) potential by dwellers among the stars. So many habitable worlds may exist among the nebulae that the interstellar spaces promise anything imaginable; thus, in a sense, they have become a screen on which all the workings of the imagination are projected. At one time, constellations were literally presumed to be the bodies of deities. In comic books, they are inhabited by numerous monsters and heroes, but astronomy has virtually killed the idea of literally seeing God seated among a stellar choir of angels. Thus, in the premiere issue of *Epic,* the Silver Surfer, having crossed the cosmos without discovering "The Answer," returns to "the most remote asteroid in all the universe," still ignorant. His companion Galactis informs him that he could better have found in legend, literature, or within himself the solution that "Time and space are one . . . and God is all" (p. 17).

Arcanum 18: The Moon (La Lune)

Aside from a few exceptions such as the Moon Valley in the "Dick Tracy" comic strip, the basic assumption of modern fantasy is that lunar inhabitants must come from earth. Occasionally, as in *Paradox* (*Marvel Preview,* Winter 1980), these earth people genetically engineer themselves for survival until they look as strange as aliens; even so, the moon could just as well be any barren, airless planet. The Tarot associates luna with the subconscious (Gray, p. 54), while the comic books most often link it with an event when the subconscious dominates reason, i.e., lunacy. Typical of this, the woman friend of the hero Moon Knight complains that he's "schizo" because of the multiple identities and personalities he adopts in his crime fighting (*Moon Knight,* January 1981, p. 14). At the close of that episode, he mentions his liking the villain for being "refreshingly psychotic" (p. 27). The latter wears a costume that is almost a black double of Moon Knight's own silver one, rendering them Doppelgänger. A June 1985 episode reveals that Moon Knight's mental problems derive partly from his being "the living embodiment of an ancient Egyptian [lunar] deity" (p. [6]). Long associated with the dream world of the imagination, the moon represents the nocturnal realm through which the Fool passes into the dawn.

Arcanum 19: The Sun (Le Soleil)

In the Waite Tarot, this card shows a child with a banner in his left hand to signify that the Fool's level of mastery over himself has now become second nature and can be resigned to the left side considered by Gray to be that of the subconscious (p. 56). The card represents heightened control of energy streaming from the unconscious. Perhaps comparable, in the September 1981 issue of *New Teen Titans,* Hyperion, a puissant deity of the sun, leaves the underworld of Tartarus and attempts to introduce a golden age. Elsewhere in comic books, solar light frequently figures as a source of energy. In the latest version of Superman's powers, they derive largely from solar light. Because of its vital connotations, the word "Sun" (or the equivalent) also appears in the name of some characters, e.g., Sun Boy of the *Legion of Superheroes;* David Oliphant's *Solarman;*[19] or the Japanese hero Rising Sun (*Super Friends,* June 1981). According to one book on therapeutic imagery, "Visualizing [the sun] helps a person to return to ordinary consciousness refreshed."[20]

Arcanum 20: Judgment (Le Iugement)

This card evokes the apocalyptic end of the world, a common image in comics. On the cover of the ninth *Thor Annual,* for instance, Odin, the "All Father," looms majestically in the upper right-hand corner. In the lower left sits "Dormammu Lord of the Dark Dimension." Extending a hell-fire red glove, the latter reaches for Thor, who stands diminished in size, a pawn on a cosmic chessboard. Aside from the spatial arrangement (good, upper right— evil, lower left), all of the figures contrast with Christian convention. Odin, a *horned* god, but also a god of order, confronts a lord of darkness; however, instead of cowering in torment, Dormammu flames forth, threatening Odin himself. In the comic book itself, emerging from the sea's depths, Dormammu's dragons injure Thor. Suffering from a concussion, Thor, through his "fevered imagination," learns the existence of the game, a reality closed to those around him. Roused from a boat-shaped sickbed, as if sleep itself were a voyage—a journey into the unconscious—he plunges into Dormammu's dimension of the dead. After perilous adventures, Thor learns that by attempting to aid Odin he has almost jeopardized the game. If he had succeeded, Odin's side would have been disqualified for Thor's unauthorized actions and Armageddon would have destroyed the world. The aim of Odin's side (Order) is anti-apocalyptic—balance, not victory. Thus, the comic book's cover masks an irony: Thor appears to be defending Odin, but Dormammu's reaching for him as for his own chessman truly suggests that Thor is already (unwittingly) a pawn on the side of darkness.

Much science fiction and fantasy is apocalyptic—Deathstars incinerating planets, rebels and imperial storm troopers locked in Armageddon, interstellar powers descending to judge the world and destroy it if it proves wanting—so there is virtually no limit to comic books that deal with the End. Two series, however, are particularly notable for their extensive treatment of this theme: *Forever People* and *Metamorphosis Odyssey.* The former, a series of DC comics begun by Jack Kirby, employed the Eden and Armageddon motifs as cosmic opposites. Appearing in the magazines *Forever People, New Gods, Mister Miracle,* and *Jimmy Olsen,* the Forever People inhabit paradisiacal New Genesis under the leadership of Isaya, the All Father. Deities themselves, they serve the Source, a mysterious "wall of glowing ENERGY" from whence they have come (*Forever People,* February 1978, p. 3). Their enemy Darkseid rules another planet, constantly at war with them.

Jim Starlin's *Metamorphosis Odyssey,* an even more grandiose Armageddon, starts with twenty-four chapters serialized in the first nine issues of *Epic* magazine, then continues with the graphic novels *The Price* and *Dreadstar,* followed by a series of comic books. In order to save the universe from The evil Zygoteans, Aknaton, the last survivor of a race destroyed by those savage imperialists, begins *Metamorphosis Odyssey* by laboring to annihilate the entire Milky Way Galaxy. Cosmic euthanasia! As Starlin contends in an interview accompanying the last installment, Aknaton's mentality resembles that prevalent during the Vietnam War, when the American military personnel expressed such sentiments as "In order to save the village we had to destroy it" (*Epic,* December 1981, p. 28). Starlin believes that his fantasy treatment captures the Vietnam War's essence better than more direct portrayals such as the movie *Apocalypse Now.* With the free scope of fantasy, he focuses on what he considers the root of Vietnam—fanaticism causing mass annihilation. The name of his character Aknaton derives from the differently spelled Pharoah Akhnaton (fourteenth century B.C.), who lost his empire through devotion to one God. In the interview, Starlin mentions that his works frequently attack organized religion because he reacts against the dogmatism as well as racial and political prejudices that he feels the nuns in parochial school tried to instill in him (p. 28). The evil that Zygoteans do is "blessed by the holy offices of the CHURCH" (*Epic,* August 1981, p. 46) and Aknaton also seems to be on a crusade. In a moment of doubt, though, he tries to summon the God Ra to aid him in his moral choice. The being who appears (perhaps only in his imagination) remarks that the gods have nothing to do with ethics (*Epic,* June 1981, p. 64). Compelled to seek the answer within himself, Aknaton predictably decides to continue what he has already planned, a galactic holocaust. At the heart of the destruction, three of Aknaton's companions become gods, and a fourth named "Vanth" kills Aknaton, precisely what Aknaton wanted, his martyr complex fulfilled. Dying, he urges Vanth to continue fighting to help the inhabitants of a distant galaxy transform "their worlds into scientific GARDENS of PARADISE" (*Epic,* December 1981, p. 22). Behind Aknaton's willingness to wreak vast destruction lies an obsessive desire for purity and perfection—a dangerous manic symptom. In a photograph accompanying the interview, Starlin (who left the American military after his disillusionment with the war) stands dressed as his character Vanth, the warrior dragged along by Aknaton's madness (p. 28). In the sequel, *The Price,* Lord High Bishop Syzygy Darklock turns against the evil Church and acquires great occult power. In the next book, *Dreadstar,* he joins forces with Vanth in trying to overthrow the Church (called the Instrumentality) and its opponent, the equally evil Monarchy, each a superpower spanning a league of planets. Vanth, however, suspects Darklock of plotting widescale carnage, as did Aknaton. Having learned his lesson that Armageddon does not lead to New Jerusalem but merely to more Armageddons, Vanth insists on proceeding in a slow, noncataclysmic manner. In comic books, even when apocalypses occur, they do not really tend to lead to a universal end. After all, sequels are too profitable.

Arcanum 21: The World (Le Monde)

After the judgment, a revived Eden appears. The theme of Eden is one of the easiest to find (or read into) literature. In a provocative article entitled "The Politics of Comics," Arthur Berger applies the same approach to his subject that Richard W. Lewis gave to nineteenth-century literature in the *American Adam*.[21] The basic idea of both is that Americans, severed from the old world, are like orphans or like Adam and Eve without human parents or heritage, inventing civilization from day to day. According to Berger, *Little Orphan Annie* has an underlying political theme: "Into the natural paradise of America the serpent of European ideas [i.e., socialism] has glided, and when this snake is destroyed [as Daddy Warbucks repeatedly attempts to do], we can return to the 'good old days' " (p. 18). Similarly, orphaned from Krypton, Superman grows weak in the presence of pieces of his home planet like "Puritans [who] feared . . . that exposure to old-world practices and ideas was morally corrupting and destructive" (p. 19). Berger's analogies sound more inventive than convincing, yet he approaches an important topic: what (if any) attitudes toward Eden do actually exist in comics?

In action comic books, time is typically cyclical. Destruction often precedes pseudo-Eden, which then falls, leading to a new apocalypse and new corrupt genesis . . . for as long as sales continue. In recent Marvel magazines (as in myth), characters move from one story to another, linking plots, tending to preclude narratives with absolutely clear beginnings and endings. This confused, mythic time is as close as fantasy can come to timelessness. The Christian conception of temporality is more linear, flowing from Creation to Judgment, each moment being ordered by providential plan.

Jack Katz's *First Kingdom* indicates by its very title a comparison with the Biblical first kingdom, Eden. This comic book's premiere issue prophesies a nuclear holocaust because "a brainwashed society is desensitized away from feeling and nature by its artificial rules, from its religious laws to its deodorants." Katz's narrative focuses on the time after the apocalypse and the problem of restoring order, with one leader after another failing. A whole pantheon of gods interferes with the nude and semi-nude humans. Unlike most writers of comic books, Katz intends to stop *First Kingdom* after twenty-four issues (like the similar number of sections in Homer's epics). True to the cyclic tendency of comic books, the two concluding words of Katz's series will be "the beginning." In a two-part interview in *Comics Scene,* where he reveals this intended ending, Katz describes his work as "a story of Man after the Fall" (May 1982, p. 53). The imagery of the work derives partly from vivid dreams that Katz had as a child. His verbal abilities developed slowly, since he couldn't talk until he "was almost five" (*Comics*

Scene, July 1982, p. 38). Katz assigns considerable importance to his early dreams, speculating that they may be recollections of previous incarnations or racial memories. They sound like comic books, even though he had not yet read any. Thus, according to him, they tie the imagery of comic books, particularly his own graphic novel, to earlier experiences of the human race.

Myths and fairy tales generally take place in an indefinite once-upon-a-time, long ago.[22] The vagueness suggests not a real period but a mental condition—the blurred, impressionistic vividness of images first emerging from the timeless mists of the unconscious. Whether in dream, myth, or artistic fantasy, consciousness shapes a narrative around them, but not a realistic one with consistent historical location. Skillful fashioners of word and picture may give them an illusion of historicity—a characteristic of the best recent fantasy that combines the attractions of novel and fairy tale—but the images still hark back to a supernatural epoch when gods walked with men. The interviewer, Howard Zimmerman, sees the many, often-contradictory flashbacks in *First Kingdom* as being "perhaps in search of the original state of grace" (May 1982, p. 53), but seeking is not necessarily finding either in Katz's work or in other graphic fictions. Zimmerman's comment could be generalized to apply to most adventure comic books, but with the understanding that glimpses of an "original state" are few and far between, particularly in recent comic books.

To see the reason for this, consider a comic book from the early days. The clinical psychologist William Moulton Marston began writing *Wonder Woman* comic books to combat the patriarchal tendencies of the Judeo-Christian tradition. He writes of an original paradise made, not by God, but by Aphrodite, who preserves it under the antarctic ice, for the earth has fallen beneath the sway of Mars (here an evil god of machismo). To save the world, she sends Wonder Woman, miraculously conceived without divine or human father. Another of Aphrodite's Edens is Wonder Woman's home, Paradise Island, which will remain perfect only so long as no man sets foot on it. Having a clear-cut myth of origin gives the early *Wonder Woman* comic books a doctrinaire sense of direction. If people were made for a known reason, revealed by a god or goddess (such as the promulgation of femininity), then ethical implications and limitations follow immediately. Everything becomes too clear-cut. To avoid restrictions, comic books frequently redo their origin stories (e.g., *Wonder Woman,* February 1987) so that the powers and backgrounds of the heroes can be brought up-to-date and opened to new possibilities. This is particularly evident with Superman, who was first shown as an adult in the 1930s. Now, in *Superboy* magazine, he is depicted as having been a child in the 1960s. Indeed, a January 1983 issue of *Legion of Super-Heroes* reveals that the original sin was seeking to know the origin of the universe. Krona, a member of an immortal race, builds a device by which he glimpses "the BEGINNING" (imaged as a blue hand holding the stars). At that moment, he is "STRUCK DOWN—by a bolt of force from the cosmos itself" and "EVIL [is] unleashed in the universe" (pp. 14–15). Whether evil or not, an interest in origins is widespread. In fact, the appeal of archetypes themselves comes partly from their seeming to be basic patterns from the most distant past.

III

Mysteries of Identity

9

Narcissus and the Theory of the Double

A NUMBER OF RECENT BOOKS, INCLUDING M. C. NELSON, ED., *THE NAR-cissistic Condition: A Fact of Our Lives and Times* (1977) and Christopher Lasch, *The Culture of Narcissism* (1979), argue that narcissism is widespread in modern America and underlies such phenomena as the increase in "psycho-religious cults" during the 1970s.[1] The 1970s and 1980s have also been marked by the proliferation of literary and cinematic fantasy. In her pre-viously mentioned *Fantasy: The Literature of Subversion*, Rosemary Jackson demonstrates the close relationship of literary fantasy and narcissism.[2] Clinical observation of this condition since the time of Freud consistently notes the subjects' mental flux and fragmentation as if they had regressed to a period in childhood before the formation of the ego and before the mastery of any language (since most languages provide a convenient word meaning "I" to use in thinking about the self). Before the acquisition of language (at least according to the psychologist Jacques Lacan), a child's sense of self may derive significantly from visual sources: single or multiple mirrors and distorted reflections in metal or water.[3] For most people, verbal and visual conceptions of self are eventually reconciled but, for extreme narcissists, the various fragments of self present a problem of unity as challenging as the contradictions and discrepancies of illuminated fantasy. Jackson notes that literary fantasy frequently involves imagery of instability and fragmentation of the mind, as in a character's seeing his double (Doppelgänger), or undergoing transformation into a new personality, or splitting in two, or suffering metamorphosis into a completely different being. Since she draws her psychology almost exclusively from Freudian sources, which fairly consistently consider adult narcissism to be pathological, she makes it sound pejorative. In contrast, the Jungian analyst Murray Stein writes:

> Narcissus gazing in the pool becomes an image for imaginative activity. . . . To reach imagination . . . requires the functioning of Narcissus in the psyche; the psyche moves toward imagination and the imaginal realm through the functioning of narcissism.[4]

Creative work, with all its cultural and scientific fruits, arises from a *healthy* narcissism involving withdrawal from everyday life into the world of thought.

Narcissism apparently takes a number of forms, of which two are particularly relevant to illuminated fantasy. In her article "The Dual Orientation of Narcissism," the psychological pioneer Andreas-Salomé calls the first of these "identification with the totality" (a feeling of oneness with the whole universe, a sense of psychic unity).[5] Descriptions of this state abound in Romantic poetry, other mystical literature, and clinical studies of narcissists who, following an acute depression, sometimes find within themselves an exhilarating sense of energy and wholeness. In talking about the results of such depression, the Reverend Allen Whitman in *Fairy Tales and the Kingdom of God* remarks, "It is as though at that moment you are opened to a power greater than yourself and unconsciously something occurs—God and you are united."[6] Whitman, drawing on Jungian analytic psychology, recommends fantasy as a spiritual discipline. In writing of this condition, Jung himself, however, worried about those patients who took this sense of power too literally and started calling themselves gods after identifying with archetypes, most of which represent some form or manifestation of the Divine.[7]

Andreas-Salomé calls the opposite kind of narcissism "self love" and illustrates it with one of her childhood experiences: she felt alienated upon looking into a mirror, because she saw how separate her image was from the rest of the world. Loss of "identification with the totality" was for her very painful (Andreas-Salomé, p. 7). Her account partly anticipates Jacques Lacan's famous treatment of a child's recognizing itself in a mirror as a significant stage in the maturation of its identity—a stage marked by acute alienation.[8] In their article "The Mathematician as a Healthy Narcissist," Reuben and Benjamin Fine present a character type who has a tendency toward the following psychological problem: "abstraction deteriorates into isolation and withdrawal, aggression becomes constant quarreling."[9] Here there is no sense of oneness with the universe but the alienation of "self-love." Charles Dodgson (Lewis Carroll), who was both an amateur poet and a professional mathematician, appears to have incorporated both kinds of narcissism in *Through the Looking-Glass*.

On the one hand, he depicts alienating "self-love." A step beyond the mythical Narcissus, who drowned upon trying to enter the world of his own reflection, Alice survives. She revels in the thought that the looking-glass, through which she has walked, now protects her so that people "can't get at [her]!"[10] At first, she is so cut off from her surroundings that the creatures of the mirror world cannot see or hear her. Even when she is able to make contact with them, misunderstandings often occur. The characters' physical conditions also sometimes impede their interactions: the talking flowers are rooted and thus relatively immobile; Tweedledum, Tweedledee, and Humpty Dumpty are all approximately egg-shaped, too fat for much motion; the sleeping Red King is, of course, as isolated from the world as a fetus; and the White Knight and "four thousand two hundred and seven" soldiers are all protected from their environment by stiff armor.

On the other hand, Carroll expresses a potential for "identification with the totality." In the "Nameless Wood," Alice befriends a fawn, but only as long as they are both partially deprived of language by the magic forest. The moment they can name each other, the animal flees. This is not a unique incident but part of a general motif—the repeated association of names with name-calling, scolding, and aggression. When, however, language is non-referential, it can be more pleasant. Upon first encountering the nonsense poem "Jabberwocky," Alice says: "It seems very pretty. . . . Somehow it seems to fill my head with ideas—only I don't exactly know what they are!" (p. 97). In addition to arrogant scolding, the narcissistic characters she meets also use virtually nonreferential talk, usually in the form of absurd puns or nonsense poems. Alice sometimes finds both kinds of language threatening, but in different ways. She shies from the verbal aggressions of the self-infatuated characters, but the nonsense only bothers her because she keeps trying to make sense out of it, as with Alice's meeting with Tweedledum and Tweedledee. She is able to dance around with them while music replaces talk. The twin brothers give one another an "affectionate hug" upon preparing to recite the longest poem they know, for a long poem means a long period without quarreling (p. 115). To Alice, however, the prospect of having to listen to more nonsense makes her want to escape. When the poem concludes, she tries to discriminate which of the characters in the verse was most admirable—i.e., the one with whom she should identify. She cannot identify with the totality for, as Carroll sadly tells the reader at a number of points, Alice has already grown a bit too old.

In real life, when his child-friends reached adolescence, Lewis Carroll (or

should one say Charles Dodgson) generally broke off contact with them—
the kind of breach he anticipates in his prefatory poem to *Through the
Looking-Glass*, where he writes: "No thought of me shall find a place / In thy
young life's hereafter."[11] The following lines from the concluding poem
show that Alice no longer seems very real to him (if she ever did):

> Long has paled that sunny sky:
> Echoes fade and memories die:
> Autumn frosts have slain July.
>
> Still she haunts me, phantomwise,
> Alice moving under skies
> Never seen by waking eyes (p. 176).

The character Alice has matured from seven to seven and a half between
her *Adventures in Wonderland* and the sequel. Humpty Dumpty laments that
she had not stopped her life at seven, and the flowers describe her as faded.
Actually, Dodgson first told the earliest version of the *Wonderland* saga to the
ten-year-old Alice Liddell. One wonders why he even bothered conversing
with someone so aged. In the prefatory poem to *Alice-in-Wonderland,* he
contrasts the "dream-child . . . [who is] / In friendly chat with bird or beast"
with the real children of his audience, who nag and interrupt him. Even a
quick perusal of that book makes obvious that the "dream-child" is actually
not in Edenic communion with animals but is caught in a series of distinctly
unfriendly and bewildering verbal confrontations (though many of Tenniel's
pictures come close to this Edenic calm). In looking-glass land, Alice, who
escapes there to be on her own, finds the characters even more absurdly
demanding than mundane adults. In particular, she falls prey to the tyranny
of the queens. These, however, themselves suffer a number of embarrass-
ments. Proud Humpty Dumpty insults Alice, only to fall himself to destruction. An alleged self-depiction of Dodgson, the White Knight, absorbed in
his own impractical schemes, spends much of his time being tossed from his
horse. Dodgson laughs at disturbed complacency, even that of his persona,
Carroll, who is nagged and interrupted by the children he is trying to amuse.
Andreas-Salomé theorizes that in dreams (and in the "healthy, intact narcissism" of the creative artist) there is "identification with the totality . . .
transcending the personal wishes of the dreamer and making him come off
second best in respect to others" (Andreas-Salomé, p. 28).

The two principal aspects of *Through the Looking-Glass* are its caricature of
self-love and its creation of a total world where no character can entirely have
its own way. In more normal fiction there are also non-narcissistic attach-
ments; people come to conventional understandings of one another and

develop strong relationships of liking or hatred. In contrast, Carroll goes little beyond the two kinds of narcissism, yet so skillful is he that their combination is complex and elusive.

In addition to disruptions within the text, there are also disruptions of the text by the pictures, which in some instances form an impressive counterpoint to Carroll's words. Andreas-Salomé furnishes a case history that suggests some of the psychological implications of the picture/text relationship applicable to *Through the Looking-Glass*. Although her example sounds quite trivial and ordinary, her clinical experience causes her to recognize that it exemplifies a general characteristic of psychological fantasy. A small boy sees the picture in a children's book of "a merry youth leaping forth from a band of children crowned with flowers, with the caption, 'May has come.'" That "merry youth . . . exist[s for him] from then on as [his] double, with fate supplementary to [his] own" (Andreas-Salomé, p. 6). Whenever the boy is happy, the "youth" is sad and vice versa. Andreas-Salomé suggests that the real boy transforms the pictured one into his complement, so that the two together constitute a totality, with both good and evil, sorrow and joy, each experience and its opposite. Andreas-Salomé sees the boy's childish fantasy as an instance of the more widespread human desire to encompass the totality of experience.

If one credits her theory, it may help to explain some of the strange anomalies in *Through the Looking-Glass*. For example, Tenniel's drawing of the Jabberwock stands as complement to the text in a number of ways. The poem concerns a boy who ignores his father's cautions, kills a monster, and then earns paternal congratulations. The drawing shows a feminized figure with long hair and dresslike tunic battling a monster wearing a vest, who resembles an old man, as if the child were battling a figure of adult authority. Because Tenniel has turned the face of the pictured hero/heroine from the audience, he renders the Jabberwock-slayer's gender and identity ambiguous, being either Alice or the boy from the medieval past. Thus, the drawing strangely links the two opposite characters together, acting as a mediation between them and enhancing the psychological unity of the total book. In fantasy, one of the characteristics of "identification with the totality" is that the structure of a work often incorporates contrasting pairs (e.g., illumination/text, or split personality).

From the very first chapter of the first Alice book, Carroll has made division into contrasting aspects an important part of the characterization of his main character. He recounts:

> She generally gave herself very good advice (though she very seldom followed it), and sometimes she scolded herself so severely as to bring tears into her eyes; and once she remembered trying to box her own

Sir John Tenniel, picture from Through the Looking-
Glass. (Reprinted from *The Complete Illustrated Works of
Lewis Carroll,* edited by Edward Guiliano. Copyright ©
1982, Crown Publishers, Inc., by permission of the
publisher.)

ears for having cheated herself in a game of croquet she was playing
against herself, for this curious child was very fond of pretending to be
two people. (p. 9)

The book itself has two sides, a dreamy, passive one, and an aggressive,
active one. Carroll's prefatory and concluding poems, as well as Tenniel's
drawings, generally constitute the former, the body of the text the latter.
According to Carroll's text, once Alice is through the looking-glass, she
"jump[s] lightly down" and contemplates committing acts forbidden on the
other side of the mirror. Tenniel, though, shows her pausing, virtually
expressionless, to look at "the face of a little old man" on the clock, while in
the description she only observes the timepiece after she leaps down and

excitedly looks about. Here Carroll's Alice is actively curious, Tenniel's a more wary, passive observer. Tenniel adds a protective bell jar to both the clock and vase (also personified). Thus, their isolation under glass mimics that of Alice behind the glass wall through which people "can't get at [her]." Carroll originally intended to call the book *Behind the Looking-Glass,* but at Dr. H. P. Liddon's suggestion, he changed the word "Behind" to "Through,"[12] more in keeping with the text's general emphasis on action and movement, such as in the many scenes of running. Tenniel, however, often takes advantage of the natural motionlessness of drawing to stress moments of stillness and introversion. The next picture, for example, is very far from a predictable illustration of Carroll's sentence, "The chessmen were walking about, two and two!" (p. 93). Only four of the sixteen chess pieces are clearly "walking about, two and two," both pairs of them in the background.

There are a few pictures of rapid movement, such as Alice's running with the Red Queen (p. 104). In general, though, the art shows little action, even when the text is more dynamic. Carroll writes of Alice's walking with a fawn, which then wildly shakes itself loose from her grasp and bolts away. Tenniel, however, depicts the deer with one hoof timidly raised in hope of progressing along the trail, but Alice firmly holds him, the position of her feet showing her as being unlikely to move at all. Similarly, Tenniel portrays relatively little movement among the "toves" who, according to the accompanying poem, habitually "go round and round like a gyroscope" (Carroll, pp. 96–97). With a very few exceptions, chiefly the violent "Jabberwocky" engraving, which demonstrates that Tenniel could be dynamic if he wished, Victorian calm characterizes the pictures, suggesting a bemused withdrawal from the real world. Carroll's prose, however, emphasizes the energy of beings pursuing their own selfish paths, most of them free from the inhibiting effect of social ties.

The majority of Tenniel's drawings prepare the reader for Carroll's dreamy final poem where the selfishness of the individual characters fades into the background and the author identifies with the whole. The two kinds of narcissism in the book reflect its two governing metaphors: life as a chess game and life as a dream. Chess is egoistic combat played according to logical rules. Far less orderly in arrangement, dreams are solipsistic—a total world arising from a single individual's imagination. In the final poem, Carroll states his preference for life as a timeless dream of childhood, where one may linger in the undifferentiated "golden gleam," untroubled by the passing of time. Rather than expressing a desire to return from his own imagination to the real world, Carroll casts doubt on the existence of reality in the very last line of the book where he asks: "Life, what is it but a dream?" (p. 176).

According to the most famous recent investigator of narcissism, the psychoanalyst Heinz Kohut, narcissistic adults may feel as if their lives were empty or not completely real. Instead of maturely admiring others' accomplishments and trying to emulate them, narcissists often succumb to "disjointed mystical religious feelings" and psychological fragmentation. Kohut theorizes that small children all have a grandiose image of themselves, but if external circumstances (particularly parents) fail to reinforce a sense of self-esteem and self-assurance, the children begin to repress the grandiose image into the unconscious. Thereafter, they find the internal world more interesting than the external one. [13]

In Jungian psychology, introspection is an even more positive quality than it is for Kohut because it is necessary for individuation, a mental journey through the unconscious during which a person encounters archetypal fantasies before uniting the conscious and unconscious into a coherent self. Putting aside the question of the accuracy of Jungian analysis for all literary fantasies, it is at least relevant to works by writers whom Jung influenced. One of the most famous of these is the Nobel Prize–winning author Hermann Hesse; English translations of his novels have played a role in the growing popularity of fantasy in Britain and America. In addition to reading Jung's works, Hesse underwent analysis under one of Jung's pupils as well as meeting and corresponding with Jung himself. The total extent of Jung's influence on Hesse's novels is still controversial but the two writers certainly share much common imagery as, for example, in the latter's illuminated fairy tale *Pictor's Metamorphoses* ("Pictors Verwandlungen," 1922). Many of Jung's patients painted elaborate symbolic art usually involving geometric designs. So similar are the styles of these paintings that one might talk of a Jungian school of art—a school to which Hesse appears to belong, first because of the similarity of styles. Second, his passion for painting began in the summer of 1916 directly after his brief psychoanalysis in April and May. [14] "Pictor's Metamorphoses" is admittedly the work where his writing and painting are most integrally related. Concerning that narrative, the scholar Theodore Ziolkowski somewhat exaggeratedly remarks:

> Here the text is so closely tied to the watercolor illustrations—indeed, the text emerges from them, as Hesse wrote to Romain Rolland when he sent a presentation copy—that the full meaning is apparent only when word and image are taken together. [15]

This seems to suggest the existence of a definitive relationship between the two, but Hesse continued re-drawing holographs for about thirty years, though in 1954, when he published a facsimile edition, he chose an early version to be reproduced (Ziolkowsky, p. xx). The following comments pertain to the version given to Hesse's second wife, Ruth Hesse, née Wenger, who inspired the work.

The first full-page watercolor represents a garden called "Paradise," where a serpent coils around a tree. Unlike the tree in the Biblical Eden, though, this tree has two human heads in separate clusters of foliage: one masculine, one feminine. In the story, the protagonist named "Pictor" (i.e., "painter" in Latin) questions the personified tree and numerous flowers (also with faces). In the *aquarelle,* however, he stares ahead of him, ignoring the fauna (all of which, aside from the one tree, are faceless). Furthermore, the tree's two depicted faces disregard each other. Thus, the personal interactions described contrast with the isolation pictured. This contrast establishes the central theme: involvement vs. narcissistic withdrawal. In the narrative, Pictor finds a magic "stone" (probably an image inspired by the alchemical philosopher's "stone" of which Jung wrote so much). With the aid of this enchanted object, Pictor transforms himself into a tree, thereafter growing old and lonely (an allegory of Hesse's own long retreat at Montagnola before he married his second wife).[16] Finally, a young girl (i.e., Ruth Wenger, twenty years Hesse's junior) adds her soul to Pictor's, becoming his *epipsychidion*—a very Jungian version of the double where the two selves are of different sex. The story ends with Pictor's becoming "[f]ulfilled, complete . . . a double star in the firmament" (*Pictor's Metamorphoses,* p. 120), for, in Jungian terms, he has united with his anima and completed the process of transformation. The final picture, however, shows the stars not touching; indeed, part of one lies beyond the horizon of the sphere they occupy. (Actually, Hermann and Ruth Hesse parted after only eleven weeks of marriage.)

"Pictor's Metamorphoses" is an example of the German *Kunstmärchen* (artistic fairy tales), a genre characterized by an attempt to turn juvenile material to higher aesthetic purpose. Today, their closest counterpart is the more sophisticated variety of comic book recently emerging. While earlier comics used doubling, mistaken identity, transformation, etc., primarily as superficial plot devices, the new breed explores psychological implication of the motif.

These newer comic books conform to a general tendency diagnosed by Robert Rogers in his study, *The Double in Literature,* "doubling in literature usually symbolizes a dysfunctional attempt to cope with mental conflict."[17] Marvel comics have led the way in the portrayal of agonized heroes who come close to schizophrenia. What makes comic-book treatment of the double unusual is its attempted reconciliation of two contrasting notions: multiple personalities as psychic dysfunction or as potential for heroic action. To combine pulp adventure and novelistic psychologizing, comic books draw on yet another tradition—the double in the folk tale and the Romantic tradition. German folk stories and legends call the external soul or double *fylgja* and identify it with such disparate phenomena as guardian angels, dream selves, and werewolves.[18] Romanticism refashioned the folk double motif in terms of a new religious aesthetics influencing a host of Doppelgänger narratives that descend from one of the earliest Romantic fairy stories, a tale as strange as any comic book, Wackenroder's "Wonderful Oriental Fairy Tale of a Naked Saint" in *Outpourings of the Heart of an Art-Loving Monastic.* Its protagonist mundanely "lives with the people who pass in the caravans, experiencing with them fear, hope, danger."[19] His naked-ness, celibacy, and horror of time leave him acutely sensitive and vulnerable, aware of his inability to do or create anything. But he also has a latent second personality, that of an artistic "Genius," able to overcome time and ascend into the eternal heavens. Even in the so-called "Golden Age" of comics (late 1930s to early 1950s), the double personality was at least implicit, as in Clark Kent/Superman dualism, in which the former identity is confined to daily life; the latter is a conqueror of temporal limitations. Superman can travel through time or move with blurring speed, sometimes represented by multi-ple images of himself on the page. With a few exceptions, Golden Age superheroes sublimated everyday desire for sexual reproduction (self-du-plication) so that they could be totally dedicated to their roles, much as early Romantics often advocated such renunciation for the sake of art (e.g., in E. T. A. Hoffmann's "The Doubles").[20]

Since the Golden Age, particularly in the last few years, superheroes seem more human and psychologically complex, while their relationship to their creators becomes more explicit. Indeed, in the July 1981 issue of *Man-Thing,* its actual writer, Chris Claremont, appears as one of the characters. Thrust into the fantastic world that he has so long envisioned, he is at first inept, a pathetic form huddled over a drink; but near the end of the book, a demon transforms him into the monstrous Man-Thing (a comic-book character he invented). As this green hulking swamp beast, he overcomes the villain, saves the universe, and returns to his human form to write about the adventure (although he also turns in his resignation to Marvel comics). Similarly, in the June 1982 issue of *New Teen Titans,* both its writer, Marv Wolfman, and artist, George Perez, serve as characters who rescue the Teen Titans from a mad scientist. Another narrative in the same issue shows the character Wally West/Kid Flash drawing his own story. In the January 1984 issue of *Peter Parker, the Spectacular Spiderman,* two principal artists of the magazine (Al Milgrom and Fred Hembeck) appear fighting over the appro-priate style for it. Consequently, the art shifts from the former's realistic manner to the latter's comic illumination. There is even a final page that is done in neither style. It shows a host of tiny Doppelgänger of Spiderman and his secret identity, Peter Parker, arguing with one another over whether

Spiderman should sleep with his superpowered girl friend at the cost of revealing his secret identity to her.

The gradual disappearance of the line between creator and creation, reality and fantasy, belongs to a growing tendency. Frequently, the illustrators and writers of comic books refer to themselves or one another as heroes, even to the point of describing comics' innovator Stan Lee as one of the "real all-fathers," ascribing to him a title of his superhero god Odin.[21] Fans lionize comic books' creators at conventions as if the writers and artists were the heroes that they invent. At first, young readers who take comic books too literally may send away for the muscle-building kits, karate correspondence courses, and books of magic words advertised therein; but eventually readers are likely to realize that the only way they can instantly become their ideal selves is through their imaginations as consumers or creators of fantasy. The NBC program "Drawing Power" preached this to small children. Jules Feiffer shows in the introduction to his compendium *The Great Comic Book Heroes* that his fascination with superbeings led him to a cartooning career, where he eventually used satire as a weapon against the degeneracy of the real world.[22]

Because of the Comics Code Authority (which censures children's comics), many superheroes have corresponded rather closely to what Rogers calls "superego" doubles.[23] Typical of these (with a few exceptions such as when Superman and Clark Kent split apart in the movie *Superman III*), the DC character Superman forces his unobtrusive personality, Kent, to live a humdrum life, sacrificing his time to the compulsive altruism of his other role. Although not the first to do so, Marvel comics organization has pioneered in personifying the id as a superhero. The Man-Thing, for example, is a mass of muscle and emotions, void "of intellect [and] of the very capacity of conscious thought."[24] Also recognizable as an id figure is the Hulk, a huge, green embodiment of pain and rage, who in recent comic books emerges when his brilliant scientist self undergoes stress, as if he suffers from periodic madness. In a 1972 *Journal of Youth and Adolescence* article, Lawrence Kayton argues that in schizophrenia a "regressed portion of the ego" (analogous to a monster in its infantile emotionality) splits from the rest.[25] Numerous Marvel heroes are from time to time in fear of losing their sanity or are beyond fearing like the Man-Thing.

Many of the superheroes, most obviously the Hulk, directly or indirectly come from one of the most popular prose works of the Romantic Movement, Mary Shelley's *Frankenstein*.[26] Victor Frankenstein, the monster's creator, is described as leading "a double existence: he may suffer misery, and be overwhelmed by disappointments; yet when he has retired into himself, he will be like a celestial spirit, that has a halo around him, within whose circle no grief or folly ventures."[27] His monster, a creation of his imagination (his "celestial spirit") represents in extreme form another common Romantic motif, the difficulty of transferring a dream self into the real world. There the great power and oddity of the unconscious estrange its manifestation from an overly conventional society. Similarly, Superman's imperfect double Bizarro terrifies those he rescues and, like Frankenstein, Superman unsuccessfully strives to destroy this hideous duplicate.[28] When either Frankenstein's creation or the Thing (a slightly more intelligent Marvel character than the Man-Thing) appears, mobs may attack before the creature has a chance to prove his benevolence.

Another common id image in comics is the werewolf, e.g., Werewolf by Night, the Beast, Timberwolf Boy, and Wolverine. Although the Germanic word *fylgja* could mean either a benevolent being (a guardian of individual, family, or nation) or a werewolf, it does not mean both simultaneously. The id superhero, however, to protect the innocent, draws power from his monstrous self.

Comic books teach that a despised quality, an evil characteristic, an unconscious drive, or a seeming handicap may serve the forces of virtue. With sharpened senses because of his blindness, Matt Murdock, dressed as a horned red imp, undertakes daring deeds under the name "Daredevil" (or "Devil," for short). Johnny Blaze, the Ghost Rider, is often possessed by the demon Zarathos, who dwells in his unconscious. Blaze, though, manages to force the demon to serve justice. Similarly, Dr. Strange "uses his Satanic powers on the side of good," performing such feats as sending forth his soul double while his body remains in trance.[29] Such a small difference separates villains and heroes that they occasionally switch from one to the other as drastically as did Jekyll and Hyde in Stevenson's classic. An example of this ambivalence, Jessica Drew (alias Ariadne Hyde), able to change to Spider-Woman (also called "the Dark Angel"), no longer belongs to the malevolent organization Hydra, but is now a superhero in her own magazine.[30]

In their early years, comic books were Manichean, glorifying a struggle between good and evil. Heroes took sadistic delight in murdering their foes. Nowadays (partly because of the Comics Code Authority), if a hero kills his enemy in self-defense, he may renounce his career, as with Star Boy. Even for justifiable homicide, he is expelled from the Legion of Superheroes.[31] Similarly, Flash is brought to trial when he kills the villain "Reverse Flash," his complementary opposite. The one-eyed god Odin tells the once human, blind god Korgon:

> [W]ithout such [villains] as Wiglif and Loki, the balance is meaningless. Thou needest thy followers, Korgon, all of them, and they need thee. Shorn of his followers, a god ceases to exist . . . and too, thy followers have no reason to exist without their god.[32]

This new emphasis on balance between ideal and actual, god and devotee, superhero and mundane alter ego pervades recent comic books.

Even counterpart universes must maintain balance. In *DC Comics Presents,* "Mallo, keeper of the COSMIC BALANCE," notes:

> Two parallel worlds which you know as EARTH-ONE and EARTH-TWO, are the homes of numerous super-heroes . . . with similarly powered counterparts on each world: The sole exception is the pair of ATOMS . . . and it is this lack of parallelism in their powers which is upsetting the COSMIC BALANCE![33]

To prevent universal destruction, Mallo preternaturally exchanges the powers of the character named Atom on Earth-One with those of his double on Earth-Two. According to this theory, a countless number of other parallel universes exists, each with a double of all familiar superheroes. These universes contain all the choices not made, the alternatives not taken, the unrealized potential, what the structuralists call "absence" and identify with the unconscious. Thus, the comic book entitled "What if Dr. Strange Had Been a Disciple of Dormammu" shows a double of Dr. Strange choosing evil, when the original Dr. Strange chooses good.[34] In "What if . . . Spiderman's Clone Had Survived?" Spiderman and his double first fight, then decide to live together sharing dates, adventures, and schoolwork, while in another universe the clone dies after the fight.[35]

The setting of each adventure comic is a time when the balance is broken (corresponding to a stage of psychic disharmony) and then restored, a scenario of regaining sanity after psychic conflict. Along the way, the labyrinthine mysteries of identity and of the unconscious arise in all their seeming irrationality. The lame physician Dr. Donald Blake merges with his other self (the immortal god Thor) despite their strikingly different speech pattern, powers, and parents. Rob Reed becomes simultaneously both Castor and Pollux, twin gods; Ronnie Raymond and Professor Martin Stein combine to form the single superhero "Firestorm." The villain Kamo Tharnn contains within his body thousands of people, some of whom take over his mind from time to time. And these identities appear in a context of doubling, with characters meeting clones, robot doubles, or former incarnations of themselves, or even other stages of their lives (through time-travel) until the normal boundaries between self and other, time and eternity, conscious and unconscious lose all solidity. As A. E. Crawley reasons in his pioneer article on the double: "It is natural that when once the notion of 'spiritual' duplication has been formed, it may be applied to anything that strikes the fancy."[36] The superhero's reconciliation of his multiple personalities is at most temporary, a lull before the next adventure. Yet it is sufficient to bring empathetic readers a feeling of union with their ideal selves, as powerful as the imagination and as profound as the depths of the unconscious.

Elaborate doubling increases the complexity of the text; thus, doubling necessarily affects the relationship of words and pictures as may be seen by a brief analysis of the premiere issue of *Cloak and Dagger* (a comic approved for children but slightly above average in sophistication). It commences with a quotation from Psalms 129:12–14: "The darkness and light are both alike. . . . / I am fearfully and wonderfully made." In the original psalm, the speaker (traditionally considered to be King David) praises God for his ability to preserve his people even during darkness. The comic book's truncated version is more obscure. In the context of the magazine, the first line seems to apply to the title superheroes: Cloak, a young black man in an indigo robe, possessed of the powers of darkness, and Dagger, a young white woman capable of projecting blades of light. In the first picture, they patrol a rooftop, while below them walk a black pimp and a white prostitute. The four together suggest extreme diversity. Here darkness and light do not look the same.

On the next page appears the text, "Me, too! Save me!" The picture shows the speaker to be a taunting, scantily clad woman, seductively fingering the priest's clerical shirt, so her intention is the opposite of her words. In torment, the priest returns to his church, where he prays, "Bring your light into my . . . darkness?!" (p. 3). At the last word (which occupies a different panel from the beginning of the sentence), the drawing depicts Cloak and Dagger suddenly materialized. The former looks demonic in his enormous black cape. The latter resembles a seductress in her skin-tight body stocking as she sits demurely on the holy altar. Are they the answer to his prayer or a manifestation of darkness? The comic book gives no clear answer. They are vigilantes on "a mission of vengeance." Those whom they kill, however, are criminals, but so, according to the police, are Cloak and Dagger.

Doubling in comic books is bizarre, but no more so than in more reputable literature. A number of Romantics, including Nerval and Hoffmann, sought a resolution of a mental disease called "autoscopy" (seeing their Doppelgänger walking near them).[37] Blake's great illuminated poem *Milton* contains a complex, interlapping series of doubles: the characters Milton and his "sixfold emanation" (his three wives and three daughters) appear to be *epipsychidion,* as are William Blake himself and his wife as depicted in the poem, while William and his dead brother, Robert, are treated as Doppelgänger. In illuminated fantasies that are this complex, unity often derives from the identification of opposites (e.g., antithetical doubles, discrepant pictures and texts, etc.). It resolves what Rogers calls "mental conflict," leads toward the Jungian unity of the "Self," or satisfies Andreas-Salomé's desire for "totality" (depending on which psychological terminology one may prefer).

Despite considerable insights, depth psychologies have long had difficulty establishing scientific credentials, their technical terms (e.g., Oedipus complex, narcissism) sounding more like the metaphors and allusions of poetry than the precise abstractions of mathematics. According to the critic T. E. Apter, not only suspect figurative language in psychoanalysis but also its indeterminacy and fascination with the bizarre demonstrate its kinship with Romanticism. This affinity, however, has not prevented psychoanalysis, particularly the Freudian variety, from generally reflecting a notion common in our culture—that fantasizing is an immaturity or infirmity.[38] Need thus exists to investigate further approaches to the fantastic such as the Oriental ones surveyed in the next two chapters. (Indeed, Jung, the major psychologist most tolerant of fantasmagoria, also studied Asian religions, particularly in his last years.)

10

The Yin and Yang of Taoism

U NLIKE WESTERN CULTURE WITH ITS FREQUENT SCORN OF FANTASY, TAOISM, a Chinese philosophy, has been relatively sympathetic to the imagination, considering dreams and waking consciousness interrelated, indeed, entangled. The great Taoist sage of the fourth century B.C., Chuang Chou (usually called Chuang-Tzu), reminisces:

> I, Chuang Chou once dreamed that I was a butterfly. . . . I did whatever I wished! I knew nothing about any Chuang Chou. Then I suddenly awakened. . . . Now I don't know whether Chuang Chou dreamed he was a butterfly, or a butterfly is dreaming that he is Chuang Chou.[1]

Modern fantasy often plays with similar themes, such as Kaze Shinobu's graphic story "Heart and Steel" (*Epic,* 1 [Feb. 1982]: 92–97), which ends, "I no longer know whether I am a robot, who wishes to become human . . . or a woman who is dreaming she is a robot." In "Let Fancy Roam," the first section of Chuang Chou's writings, he suggests that people should allow their minds to soar above the narrow views of the materialistic, even if an imaginative and intuitive life earns charges of selfishness and uselessness.[2] To explain this position, he narrates one of the "tall tales" of Chinese legend about a monstrous winged creature called the *p'eng* (or, as Kuang-Ming Wu translates it, "Big Bird").[3] It flies at an altitude of ninety-thousand miles and raises tornadoes by the beating of its wings. Ironically, two talking birds

172

(themselves small but fantastic beings) express their disbelief in the *p'eng.* Chuang Chou summarizes: "Petty knowledge [such as that of the small birds] is not comparable to knowledge on the large scale [i.e., that of the sages]" (p. 2). He uses fanciful examples because, as Taoists have always emphasized, the Tao, the Way of the whole universe, is not literally expressible.

One reason for turning to China to study illuminated fantasy is that great artists, who are *both* writers and painters, are more common in that country than in the Occident, e.g., Wang Wei, Su Tung-p'o, Shen Chou, Wen Cheng-ming, and T'ang Yin, to name but a few of the better known. Admittedly, before about the ninth century, Confucians, the defenders of reason, propriety, and morality, were reluctant to consider painting a scholarly activity, but the visual arts encountered less resistance in China than in the West, and by the eleventh century A.D., the Chinese alliance between writing and painting was firm and fruitful. In his essay, "Some Relationships between Poetry and Painting in China," a professor of comparative literature, Jonathan Chaves, notes: "in Blake, as in Chinese art, the relationship between text and picture was often complex, each offering a counterpoint to the other."[4] Again he speaks of text and picture as "complementary elements" (p. 90). Taoist thought often examines complementary relationships because of its emphasis on the dichotomy *yin* (dark, passive, cold, etc.) and *yang* (light, active, warm, etc.). In *The Tao of Painting,* Kai Wang remarks:

> The *Tao* is manifested through the primary elements or forces, the *Yin* and the *Yang,* and in painting the *Tao* is expressed through understanding and transmitting by every means possible this balance and fusion of the *Yin* and *Yang,* and so achieving harmony and coherence among the ideas expressed as well as in the elements of the painting itself.[5]

Because of the nature of the Chinese language, writing is not as inherently different from painting as in English. Each Chinese word is an ideogram, originally derived from a stylized picture, seldom with any portrayal of time. Chinese verbs lack tenses, time being conveyed (if at all) by separate words. Furthermore, as François Cheng explains in *Chinese Poetic Writing:*

> Often, in an effort to create an ambiguous state, where present and past may mix, or dream become confused with reality, the poet may break the linear logic of a line either by omitting elements that indicate time, or by the juxtaposition of different times.[6]

Chinese aesthetics does not stress a crude contrast between *yin* and *yang,* but seeks "balance and fusion." The very symbol for *yin* and *yang* is a circle with an S-shaped curve separating the dark side (*yin*) and light side (*yang*). The curve shows that the one bends into the other. Furthermore, a spot of white appears in the black section, a spot of black in the white, forming a dark fish with a light eye and a light fish with a dark one.

Some Western fantasists owe particular debts to Taoism and thus are especially appropriate for Taoist analysis. For instance, Ursula Le Guin (winner of the Gandolf, Hugo, Nebula, and National Book Awards) achieves a subtle blending of masculine and feminine, reality and dream, action and introspection related to her childhood readings of Taoist texts. She has explained this on a number of occasions and even employs her own translation of parts of the *Tao Te Ching* (*The Way and Its Power,* the first great Taoist work) throughout her novel *The City of Illusion.*[7] In her essay "Is Gender Necessary?" she writes, "Our curse is alienation, the separation of yang from yin."[8] In her most famous book, *The Left Hand of Darkness,* the title derives from a scene where the narrator draws a symbol of *yin* and *yang,* identifies it as such, and then adds, "Light is the left hand of darkness."[9] Light and darkness are as integrally related as if they formed one body.

As Barbara Bucknall remarks in her book-length study of Le Guin, "The Earthsea trilogy is the work in which [she] has expressed her Taoism most artistically."[10] It is also unusual among her works because, in addition to very striking covers, it has maps and a woodcut-like picture at the head of each chapter. Publishers have a way of changing a book's cover from time to time, almost as if they hoped that fans would become confused and buy a book twice; and there is no reason for presuming Taoist influence on the illumination of Le Guin's work, yet because of the Taoist affinities of the text, there is reason for wondering if the pictures appropriately conform to a Taoist aesthetics or conflict with it. Pauline Ellison's cover of the current (twelfth) printing of *A Wizard of Earthsea* shows a confrontation with a dragon.[11] The scene comes from the fifth chapter, except that the picture makes the monster about twice as large as the text does. Furthermore, the cover depicts the hero with a distinctly feminine hairdo, an androgynous face, and dresslike robe, perhaps to make him seem all the more vulnerable to the dragon. In a way, the figure on the cover is the opposite of Le Guin's masculine hero, Ged. The latter grew up in a war-filled, male-dominated world, where such chauvinistic expressions as "Weak as woman's magic" or "Wicked as woman's magic" had become proverbial. The subject of the trilogy, though, is the coming peace and Ged's growing appreciation of his *yin* side. Throughout much of the first book, he runs from a dark, amorphous or polymorphous being, an embodiment of this *yin* side, which he accidentally summoned while trying to show off his (imperfect) magical skills. (The image of trying to escape a shadow also occurs in *The Sayings of Chuang Tzu,* chapter 31, p. 400.) Ged finally takes the shadow into himself, recognizing it to be part of his own nature. His acceptance of his other side comes when he has learned to be less boastful and self-assertive. Further-more, only at the end of the book does he have close contact with a young woman, Yarrow (named for the sticks used in Chinese divination). Pre-viously he had devoted himself exclusively to what on Earthsea is a man's world—power and adventure. Although the movement toward the *yin* side of life progresses further in subsequent volumes, he perhaps achieves enough in the first one to justify his feminized portrait on the cover of that volume. In the text, however, Ged grows more androgynous within, while his body becomes "lank," "harsh," and "scarred"—an appearance admired by a "com-ely" boy, who sees it as an embodiment of virile adventure (p. 162). Pauline Ellison's manner of feminizing the hero naturally differs significantly from Le Guin's, because visual art can only present psychological insights through external details. Comparably, Taoists shift viewpoints and manners of ex-pression, from picture to text or even within the text. As the Sinologist A. C. Graham remarks, Chuang Chou lets "conflicting meanings explode against each other in apparent contradiction."[12]

Ellison's cover of the next volume of Earthsea trilogy, *The Tombs of Atuan,* has only one clear figure, not Ged the hero of the series, but a young woman, probably the character Tenar, as she is the main female figure in the book. Again, Ellison exaggerates a tendency also evident in the text. Admittedly, Tenar does have a major role in the book, the opposite of Ged's in the previous one: while Ged learns to be less assertive and to accept the shadow side of life, Tenar, a priestess of the sacred blackness of the tombs, learns to be more assertive and to accept the light side of existence. This lesson, though, requires Ged's help. Bearing magic light, Ged breaks into the tombs so that he can find the other half of a magic talisman that should be made whole. When he encounters Tenar, she does not even have a name of her own but is merely called Arha (the eaten one) to signify that she no longer has a separate will to assert but must devote her life to the interminable, tedious rituals of the Dark Powers. Ged frees her and does not even bind her to himself—the closest the trilogy comes to anything even resembling con-ventional feminism; but the structure of the series has far less to do with feminism than with the Taoist balance of *yin* and *yang,* a dichotomy most evident in the third volume, *The Farthest Shore.*

Ellison's cover for it shows no clear characters, just two blurred figures on the back of a dragon. Once more this exaggerates a tendency in the text, a surrender of individuality and entry into the blurring darkness of death. Taoists believe that people have two souls, one of them *yang* that may become part of the Tao, and the other *yin* that continues as a kind of ghost.[13] Similarly, Ged explains that part of the dead remain in the world, becoming "the earth and sunlight, the leaves of trees, the eagle's flight" (p. 180). The other part continues as a phantom in a shadowy kingdom of death.

Throughout all the books, the wizards of Earthsea emphasize the importance of "the Equilibrium" or "balance" of contrary forces. (The appearance of these terms in other recent illuminated fantasy, particularly comic books, may derive from Le Guin, so that a Taoist approach to it becomes more-and-more appropriate.) Because of the precariousness of this balance, Le Guin's wizards repeatedly advocate restraint and inaction (the Taoist concept of *wu wei*, not doing). In *The Farthest Shore* the balance is particularly between life and death. A sorcerer who lacks true wisdom ignorantly attains immortality, thereby destroying the balance and threatening the whole world. Here Le Guin's story reflects the history of Taoism. The great Taoist sages Lao-tze and Chuang Chou accept death as part of the natural order, but later Taoism was preoccupied with a search for immortality, which, ironically, shortened the lives of its adherents because they began experimenting with poisonous elixirs. To heal the world, Ged must exhaust his magic and thereafter accept an inactive life (like that of the Taoist sages). At the end, far from being an assertive individual reveling in fame, Ged cannot even be found by those who seek him (a common theme in Chinese legends as with the sage Han-shan, who reportedly hid in a hole, then pulled the hole in after him).[14]

When Le Guin began the Earthsea trilogy, one of her first acts was to draw a map.[15] Ruth Robbins's professionally re-drawn version of it appears at the beginning of *A Wizard of Earthsea*, complete with scenes from each of the chapters, as if the whole book's timespan were simultaneously present in the map. From one point of view, the action (or at least its symbolical frame-work) is inherent in the map. Ged, for example, was born on the north-ernmost point of a cold northern island inhabited by a dark-skinned race—north, cold, and dark all being *yin* characteristics. In Taoist literature, the Tao is most frequently described in terms of *yin* qualities, particularly water,[16] the most conspicuous feature on the Earthsea map. Not surprisingly, the people of Ged's northern island are the greatest wizards, since (in the trilogy) magic seems largely a kinship with the natural order, a oneness with the Tao. The story begins with Ged's island being raided by a "savage people [without magic], white-skinned, yellow-haired, liking the sight of blood and the smell of burning towns." These people from the Far East form a threat in the first two books, while by the third book, one of them has even become a great and good wizard. In Le Guin's subtle contrasts and blendings between *yin* and *yang*, she sets up stereotypes merely to break them down. The threat in the third book comes from the Far West, a land associated with fairy tales (p. 190) and with death—a proper setting for her parable of the sorcerer's unwise search for immortality. Thus, as is often the case in epic fantasy, the map is to some extent a diagram of psychological states as well as of places. Virtually no fantasist, certainly not Le Guin, makes every scrap of territory in an imagined world psychologically significant. Therefore, the relationship of map and text is problematic in that one cannot be absolutely certain how much symbolism is implied.

As to the internal illuminations, each one has its own mystery. For instance, in *The Tombs of Atuan,* when Ged creates the illusion that Tenar is wearing royal robes, Gail Garraty's picture adds five angelic beings and structures the whole like a stained-glass image of the Madonna. This exaggerates Tenar's glorification, but why there should be such an exaggeration is not clear. The chapter is called "The Great Treasure," so the artist perhaps uses religious imagery to suggest that Tenar is such a treasure herself— possibly also implied in the text. Nonetheless, in her well-known dislike for Christianity, Le Guin certainly does not rely on angelic iconography to show Tenar's glorification. The text is secular, urging Tenar to renounce her role of priestess. The drawing seems religious, except that the angels are ugly and the Madonna untraditional, as if Garraty were also rejecting religion— specifically the Christian religion. Relationship between picture and text arouses more questions than it settles. Certainly one can imagine pictures that more perfectly embody the Taoist side of the work and yet at least these illuminations have some of the requisite tastefulness and subtlety.

After the publication of *A Wizard of Earthsea,* some critics remarked the similarity of Le Guin's concept of the shadow with that of Jung's, who saw it as a collection of all the character traits that a person represses. Never having read Jung, she immediately turned to his writings and eventually composed an essay, "The Child and the Shadow" (1975), in which she registers her general agreement with his psychology, particularly his almost Taoist insistence on uniting conscious and shadowy sides of the mind.[17] Some of Jung's followers (such as the Jungian analyst Jean Shinoda Bolen in *The Tao of Psychology*) have continued his interest in the East, but his own fascination with the idea of the Tao appears (among other places) in his forward to a German translation of the *I Ching* (Book of Changes).[18] This book is a Chinese classic used in Taoist fortunetelling, though the work predates Taoism and may even be the source from which Taoism derived the terms *yin* and *yang* (the first recorded use of which occurs in a fourth-century B.C. commentary on that classic). The *I Ching* consists of sixty-four sections, each representing what Jung considered an archetypal image (e.g., heaven). These images are in the form of Chinese characters, i.e., ideograms (stylized depictions of some object or event). In a manner that may seem arbitrary to the Westerner, these images stand for sixty-four patterns of lines, each pattern consisting of six lines, each line either broken (*yin*) or whole (*yang*). Thus, the *I Ching* is a fantastic compendium of images based on the complementary opposites, *yin* and *yang,* a systemization of the metaphysics that shapes Taoist fantasy. Indicative of the degree to which the *I Ching* once pervaded Chinese culture, one Chinese artist during the fifth century A.D.

wrote: "Painting should correspond with the *I Ching,*" delving into the interrelationships of spirit and nature, as does that classic.[19] For fortunetelling, each of the hexagrams (sets of six lines) offers a slightly different prediction such as the hexagram "Shang," which stands for advancement. The *I Ching* is beginning to find its way into Western illuminated fantasy. In 1973, the comic-book writer Steve Englehart chose the hexagram "Shang," coupled it with "ch'i," spirit (or in his simplified orthography, chi), and used these two as the name of the protagonist of *Master of Kung Fu* comics. This character (who wears a *yin-yang* symbol on the back of his costume) devotes himself so exclusively to the advancement of his spirit that his current love, Leiko Wu, often ends up sleeping with virtually everyone else. (Committed to balance, the *I Ching* counsels against such blind devotion to advancement.) Finally, to preserve the cosmic balance that his actions have unsettled, Shang Chi retires to obscurity in the village of "Yang Yin," China.

There is some advantage in looking at one of his adventures before this retirement to see how its treatment of *yin* and *yang* as a structural principle compares with Le Guin's. Howard Zimmerman, editor-in-chief of *Comics Scene,* has called issue no. 118, November 1982 (written by Doug Moench) "what may be one of the 10 best comics published since the end of the Golden Age."[20] The comic begins with Shang Chi and friends parachuting past monumental religious sculptures from Asian antiquity. All the time that his parachute is falling and subsequently during one fight scene after another, his thoughts run on in an improbable, philosophical commentary. He thinks that his unconscious craving for either death or psychological rebirth has forced him to abandon Taoist inaction for violence. He considers this "a paradox—only by DEFYING the ways of the Tao can I again face the true path with new eyes" (p. [2]). Despite these musings, a close-up of his face shows his features transfixed in that expression of mindless fury that Kung Fu actors use in place of acting. An even more obvious disparity of word and pictures appears near the center of the comic in one of its most violent moments. Shang Chi sees his reflection in a mirror; then a human being almost identical to him crashes through it and attacks him. He throws his double down the stairs, dives after him, engages in a mêlée; yet through most of this, he is reportedly devoting his mind to the production of an elaborate sustained metaphor, likening his agony in combat to that of a scholar entering a burned library. His meditative thoughts contrast with his pictured concentration on violence, even though the skilled artist Gene Day does as much as he can to make some connection between the two. The figure of the Buddha, for example, may remind the viewer that Chinese martial artists have traditionally honed their concentration through Buddhist meditation, thus uniting dispassion with violent action. Far above Shang Chi appears a stone relief of a phoenix to symbolize that out of mental con-

Gene Day, illustration from Kung Fu, *November 1982.*
(Copyright © 1982 by Marvel Comics Group. Reprinted by permission.)

flagration the protagonist will be reborn. On the left of the phoenix are carved a "k," a *yin-yang* symbol, and a playing-card king of spades—all symbols of Shang Chi. On the right of the phoenix these images appear again but reversed as in a mirror and with scars on the king—symbolic of Shang Chi's imperfect double. A common theme in *Master of Kung Fu* comics is that rebirth comes through battle with oneself, and issue no. 181 is certainly built around that idea. In his childhood home, he fights a clone, a being grown from his own flesh and trained by his old teacher. Shang Chi describes his clone as "yin to my yang." They are indeed opposites—too opposite. The double is incredibly unquestioning and obedient, ready without the slightest hesitation to give his blood to Shang Chi's father, Dr. Fu Manchu, who drinks it as part of his magic Taoist elixir of life. Shang Chi, however, questions everything and dedicates his life to killing his villainous father. *Master of Kung Fu* is subtler than the most juvenile comic books but far less so than *A Wizard of Earthsea*. There Ged's shadow is not in any simple way his opposite. At first, it is a formless monster and in the end his Doppelgänger. As R. L. Wing explains in *The Illustrated I Ching, yin* and *yang* "are not considered opposites at all, but interdependent polarities that bring all of existence into being" (p. 14). In the Earthsea trilogy, pictures and texts achieve such subtle interrelationship; in *Master of Kung Fu* no. 181, the structural contrasts show some sophistication but not enough to be even remotely close to the *yin* and *yang* of so many great Chinese illuminations that convey a sense of tranquillity, even in the flying of dragons or the epiphany of gods.

Another kind of juvenile Occidental literature, the variety of fantasy that most children's librarians are now happy to stock, does tend to be fairly peaceful and thus, with the growing vogue of Oriental thought, one may be temped to reinterpret such Western classics of illuminated fantasy from a Taoist perspective. In A. A. Milne's books about Winnie-the-Pooh, there are many bucolic scenes such as one where E. H. Shepard's picture shows young Christopher Robin and his stuffed bear Pooh romping through the fields, while in Milne's text the boy says that they are going "nowhere" and doing "nothing." Confused by this seeming discrepancy between word and deed, Pooh asks for clarification. Christopher Robin then defines doing "nothing" as "just going along listening to all the things you can't hear, and not bothering."[21] In the context of the Pooh books, this is merely one more idyll before Christopher Robin must abandon his toys and go off to boarding school. Benjamin Hoff, however, in *The Tao of Pooh*, sees Christopher Robin's "just going along" as the central Taoist principle of life, the *wei wu wei*, doing by not doing, according to which all that needs to be accomplished will unfold if one simply permits the Tao to continue its own path without human interference. Whatever relevance *The Tao of Pooh* may have

THE TAO OF
POOH

Benjamin Hoff

Nancy Etheredge, jacket picture for The Tao of Pooh *by Benjamin Hoff.* (Reproduced by permission of E. P. Dutton, New York, a division of New American Library, and Methuen Children's Books, London.)

to Milne's books, it is itself a fantasy complete with philosophical dialogues between Hoff and the stuffed bear. Nancy Etheredge's cover for *The Tao of Pooh* depicts Winnie-the-Pooh dressed in a Chinese jacket and flying a kite with a *yin-yang* symbol on it. Pictures within the volume, though, have been extracted from Milne's Pooh books and replanted within the context of Hoff's imaginary dialogues. Ernest Shepard's drawing of a group of trees (the "hundred-acre wood" of Milne's books) appears next to Hoff's "Backword" [*sic*], where he and Pooh sum up Taoist philosophy, including the doctrine of the "Uncarved Block" (*P'u*). Taoists believe that people should remain childlike, undistorted like a block that has not yet been carved. The pictured trees are, in a sense, uncarved blocks, though Hoff and Pooh aren't precisely talking about trees. The tranquillity of the picture, however, evokes that natural state that Hoff and Pooh are noisily trying to define, so illumination and text are subtle complements in the best Taoist tradition.

Hoff's transforming Pooh into *P'u* obviously exaggerates the affinity between Eastern and Western fantasy, but there is a growing number of actual Chinese fantasies being imported to the Occident, including the *Hsi-yu chi* (*The Journey to the West*), a sixteenth-century narrative about the travels of Hsüan-tsang from China to India in search of Buddhist scriptures. From this bare sketch of its plot, one might think it to be totally Buddhist but, as its translator Anthony Yu has demonstrated, "the themes and rhetoric of Taoism appear in every part of the work."[22] Taoism is most obvious in the long prefatory section treating the acquisition of magic powers by a talking monkey (later Hsüang-tsang's disciple but at first interested only in the acquisition of Taoist immortality). The Italian writer Silverio Pisu and artist Milo Manara have collaborated in a very free adaptation of this prefatory section, which appears translated with the title "The Ape" as a serial in *Heavy Metal* from August 1982 to April 1983.

As Yu states in his Introduction to the *Hsi-yu-chi,* "Unlike any typical Western work of prose fiction written since the Renaissance, *The Journey to the West* is made up of prose heavily interlaced with verse of many varieties and lengths" (p. 21). Although such an extreme mixture of styles is not common in modern Occidental work, the genre that comes closest to it in the West is fantasy. A number of epic fantasies, e.g., Tolkien's *Lord of the Rings,* actually contain inset poems (though not to the extent of the *Hsi-yu-chi*), but the most widespread alternation in style in Western fantasy epics is from fast-paced narration to dreamy descriptions often resembling Romantic poetry. Yu partly agrees with another scholar Jaroslav Prusek, who considers poetry and prose in Chinese stories to be "two levels of representing reality," but Yu adds that both poems and prose are "integral parts" of the *Hsi-yu-chi.*[23] Thus, Yu seems to see the work's connection of prose and poetry more or less in terms of the *yin-yang* aesthetic that stresses the integral relationship of contrasting parts. The *Heavy Metal* adaptation is a kind of abridgment deriving from Arthur Waley's incomplete translation, and is less complete than his, except that it adds something new: pictures. To what extent do illuminations serve the same function as the omitted poetry? The answer requires investigating the poetry of the original. Yu categorizes the verses of the *Hsi-yu-chi* into three kinds: dialogues, descriptions, and commentaries (p. 24). Poetic form such as verse distinguishes dialogues from everyday conversation, constantly reminding the readers that they are not perusing real speech but a fiction. Similarly, the sight of word balloons coming from a talking monkey and other more preposterous characters constantly reminds the viewer of the fantasy of the adaptation. Even more obviously, drawing takes the place of lyric description, showing the waterfalls and crags, the celestial palaces and magical caverns. Finally, pictures serve as a commentary. In the text the ruler of heaven orders the arrest of the monkey, *Heavy Metal* 6 (February 1983), 28. So that the reader/viewer does not miss the point that members of the ruling class are not always benevolent, the picture provides a visual commentary. It shows a twentieth-century factory streaming clouds of smoke that form a kind of political cartoon. In it, grotesque images of a pope, a fascist general, and a plutocrat gloat as a prostrate worker is devoured by a batlike demon. Modern Chinese communist commentaries also tend to interpret the *Hsi-yu-chi* anachronistically, as if it were an allegory of the alliance of religion, finance, and politics in a capitalist society. The pictures abound with nudity and graphic sex, virtually absent from the characters' words. Here, though, there is a complication, for a basic theme in the prefatory section is the monkey's acquiring magical power through Taoist sexual yoga, in which "the sexual force is aroused, conducted through pathways in the body (balancing the polarities of *yin* and *yang*) and transmuted [into spiritual energy]."[24] The text of the adaptation devotes half a page to listing the cryptic terminology of this process, *Heavy Metal* 6 (September 1982), 32. Erotic pictures abounding throughout "The Ape," however, seem to have little or nothing to do with spirituality, Taoist or otherwise. As with *Master of Kung Fu,* the various contrasts in the work, including the difference between illumination and text, are too extreme to meet any aesthetic standard requiring the subtle integration of complementary parts.

The gradual rapprochement of East and West may lead to the rise of an increasingly Taoist spirit in fantasy and this would present a real alternative to Occidental paradigms. Unity in each Western fantasy lies in its representing the dreamscape of its author's mind. Fantasies often purport to represent the totality of existence, but Western tradition tends to discount such claims. In Taoism, however, a fantasy (illuminated or otherwise) may be viewed as reflecting the unifying Tao of the cosmos rather than the mere fancies of a solipsistic author. Taoism, furthermore, is not the only Oriental approach to fantasy available. The following (and final) chapter explores a second, alternative perspective—one where all illuminated fantasy, tasteful or garish, serene or violent, may be seen as possessing some real value.

11

Zen and the Ultimate Illumination

IN DOUGLAS HOFSTADTER'S PULITZER PRIZE-WINNING BOOK, *GÖDEL, ESCHER, Bach,* which he described as "a metaphorical fugue on minds and machines in the spirit of Lewis Carroll," the character Achilles tells a talking tortoise:

> I have always had a yen for the yin and yang, you know—the whole Oriental mysticism trip, with the *I Ching,* gurus, and whatnot. So one day I'm thinking to myself, "Why not Zen too?"[1]

Of the many methods that Zenists utilize to try to go beyond preconceptions to an ultimate view of reality, Hofstadter focuses on one, using *koans,* which he calls, "absurd answerless questions" (p. 255). In actual Chinese practice, Taoism and Zen are often intertwined, the Japanese using the word *doshaku* to refer to their combination, though *koan ga* (koan pictures) are a subvariety of *doshaku* stressing Zen elements. Hofstadter's focus on koans as "triggers" to jar people out of logic coincides with Zen *koan-ga,* which are done in a startling, cartoonlike style contrasting with other *doshaku* pictures "of a more . . . popular nature."[2] Although Hofstadter ignores many aspects of Zen (since he only treats it in passing), his approach to it is adequate as a starting point for an examination of shocking illuminations in Western works that are somewhat analagous to that Eastern philosophy. Hofstadter himself likens "Zen" to the lithographs of the Dutch artist M. C. Escher (1902–1972), whose works are notable for optical illusion and visual paradox. In a 1956

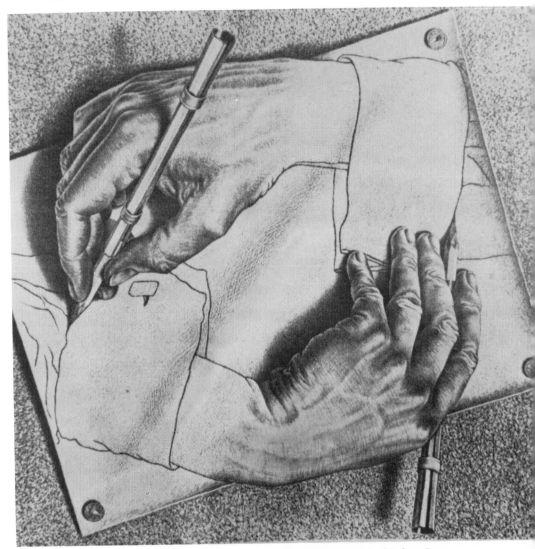

M. C. Escher, lithograph of "Drawing Hands" from Bruno Ernst, The Magic Mirror of M. C. Escher, *1967. (Reprinted by permission of © M. C. Escher Heirs c/o Gordon Art–Baarn–Holland.)*

letter to the art critic Bruno Ernst concerning one of these, Escher admits his desire to "shock" the public.[3] Typical of his works is one showing a hand sketching another hand, which is drawing the first one. The boundary between creator and created, real and imaginary, seems to break down. Escher once said that he felt "controlled by the creatures" he invented.[4] Escher's lithographs, however, are less jarring than much illuminated fantasy, the latter combining the former's visual tricks with vivid, even crude images. For instance, in the last episode of his occult Western serial, "Tex Arcana," *Heavy Metal* 6 (November 1982), the writer/artist John Findley portrays himself being dragged by one of his own grisly creations to a drawing board. Beside it, a bookshelf conspicuously contains Hofstadter's *Gödel, Escher, Bach*. A later panel shows Findley's hand drawing the disgusting creatures, who coerce him to create them. His wife, pictured next to him in the studio, also appears in the sketch. There she is "The Mysterious Woman in White," who in previous episodes has talked on and on in untranslated tenth-century A.D. Anglo-Saxon.

In addition to Escher, Hofstadter also cites, as being Zenlike, the visual paradoxes of the surrealist René Magritte. One of Magritte's paintings is strangely titled "The Air and the Song" (p.494). It depicts a pipe accompanied by the words, "*Ceci n'est pas une pipe*" (This is not a pipe)—a striking example of problematic picture/text relationship. In his book *Les mots et les images,* Magritte explains, "No object is so inextricably linked to its name that one could not give it another name that would suit it better."[5] In 1940 he declaimed:

> The titles of the paintings were chosen so that they would provoke in the observer an appropriate mistrust toward that unthinking tendency to indulge in easily attained self-satisfaction. [The astonishing juxtapositions of hardly related paintings and titles suggest] extraordinary events that are still by no means subject to reason.[6]

Surrealism shares with Zen both the notion that reality transcends logic and an emphasis on spontaneity and shock.

At present, one of the best surrealist illuminators of popular fiction is Philippe Druillet, who resembles Magritte in his usually puzzling picture/text relationships. In the recent work "Yragael," with pictures by Druillet and words by Demuth, even the text contains Zenlike paradoxes, e.g., "I never deceive with my appearance. To fool you I disguised myself," *Heavy Metal* 6 (November 1982), 30. Each of Druillet's pictures possesses some elements derived from the text and others purely from his imagination. Typically, at the beginning of the fourth episode Demuth mentions "mad priests" while Druillet presents figures with feminine hands and bizarre hieratic costumes including masks. (Obscuring the features is a common surrealist device to make characters seem mysterious.) The part of the picture that is purely Druillet is the macabre frame surrounding the words. It seems to be part of the picture, since the ornamentation is too elaborate for a mere word-balloon. How, though, can this floating frame fit into the rest of the scene? On the page opposite this picture, there is nothing but a rococo scarab with a galaxy at its heart. It has no obvious connection to any text. Certainly the extreme isolation of picture from word supports rumors of disagreements between the collaborators but the alien quality, so brilliantly achieved throughout Druillet's works, always makes his art illumination.

The psychological richness of fantasy, however, does not require extraterrestrial scenes. In the book *Zen Art for Meditation,* the Buddhists Stewart Holmes and Chimyo Horioka explain that one of the insights often embodied in Zen art is that "The realities of life are most truly seen in everyday things and actions."[7] One of the recent illuminators who best combines the commonplace and fantastic is Paul Kirchner. On rare occasions, he evokes a traditional Zen setting as in "Mirror of Dreams," *Heavy Metal* 5 (December 1981): 43–55. It begins with a medieval Japanese Buddhist priest who lives a normal life, even though he possesses a mirror that reflects the mind (a stock image in Zen literature). A thief purloins the mirror, then tries to use it as a magic device to grant wishes. Instead, all it gives him is the hell of his chaotic mind. More typical of Kirchner is the modern setting of "My Room," *Epic* (Fall 1980): 82–84. A suited man sits upright in the midst of very ordinary surroundings. He says that he has made the room a "reflection" of his mind. (Zen has as one of its predecessors the Buddhist *Yogacara* school, which affirms the doctrine "mind only": the whole world arises from thought.)[8] When the man drops a teacup and swears in anger, a monster slithers upward from the puddle of spilled liquid. With great concentration, beads of sweat flooding from his brow, the man restores order. His situation is reminiscent of a famous Zen legend where an advanced but not yet Enlightened monk composed the following poem:

> The body is the Bodhi tree [the place
>   where the Buddha attained Enlightenment].
> The mind is like a clear mirror.
> At all times we must strive to polish it,
> And must not let the dust collect.[9]

(Kirchner's unenlightened man is like this monk, always struggling for control.) In the Zen legend, an Enlightened monk corrected the poem to read:

> Bodhi [Enlightenment] originally has no tree,
> The mirror also has no stand.
> Buddha nature is always clean and pure;
> Where is there room for dust?[10]

Kirchner's Buddhist priest seems more like this monk, secure in his attainment.

For several years, Kirchner has graced virtually every issue of *Heavy Metal* with at least one episode of "The Bus." Prosaically set in a modern city, the feature is a series of fantasies honed to haiku-like brevity. Each begins in everday reality and then shifts into the impossible with a kind of visual metaphor. In an average episode, a bald-headed man enters a bus and walks toward the rear. From one panel to another, the bus fades away, its long seat slowly transformed into a bench in a park, yet all is drawn with realistic care (August 1981, p. 96). In another strip (March 1982, p. 96), the man exits a bus marked "All the Way" to find himself on a stage. He re-boards only to discover that the bus has become a cardboard prop. Fantasy and reality intermingle. In a third episode, a youth calmly lounges against a lamppost while a policeman walks nervously about, apparently fearing mischief. Nonetheless, as a clean bus passes the boy (who does not seem to move at all), it is seen to be completely covered with graffiti. One of the bus's signs, eventually obscured by scribbling, displays an ad for "Occam's Razor Hair-styling." This alludes to Occam's Razor (the fourteenth-century scholastic doctrine that a hypothesis should be as simple as possible, a doctrine that has become a basic tenet of science). No simple, scientific explanation, however, can show how the bus is changed. In a letter to *Heavy Metal* (September 1980, p. 96), Timothy Cummins, one of the readers, writes about Kirchner, "He's seen it!" by which Cummins seems to imply that Kirchner has attained great spiritual insight.

The major surrealists also often make use of everyday imagery, e.g., Max Ernst's *La femme 100 têtes,* which extracts images mostly from ordinary life but juxtaposes them in bizarre ways and furnishes them with mysterious labels. On an etching of prosaic industrial construction, for instance, Ernst superimposes a sumo wrestler and two naked women, positioned as if they were flying. It is titled, "And Loplop, Bird Superior, has transformed himself into flesh without flesh and will dwell among us" (*Et Loplops, le superieur des oiseaux, s'est fait chair sans chair et habitera parmi nous*).[11] Surrealist illuminations are amusing as an antidote to convention, but they tend to stay largely on the plane of dream and nightmare, while Zen expects the Enlightened to cope with external existence as well as the depths of the mind.

Much more obviously connected to Zen than surrealism is Ioanna Salajan's *Zen Comics.* In 1971, after five years of meditating in Holland, she began the series in an Amsterdam magazine entitled *Cosmic Papers.*[12] Her style derives from that of the *sumi-e* (paintings in black watercolor) of Japanese *koan-ga* and from the *i-p'in* (untrammeled style) of Chinese Ch'an (Zen) *p'o mo* (spilled ink).[13]

Before treating her adaptations of this style, a few words about traditional Zen art may be useful. The pioneer interpreter of Zen to Westerners, Daisetz Teitaro Suzuki, writes that the unconscious spontaneity "of which the Zen master makes so much . . . is also eminently the spirit of the Sumiye artist."[14] Japanese Zen artists catch the wonder of everyday reality as in a simple sketch by Sengai Gibon (1750–1837) of a frog about to eat a snail. The problematic caption reads, "The Buddhas of the Three Worlds [past, present, future] / Gobbled up in one mouthful."[15] On a superficial level, this means that the meditator who can sit with the concentration of a frog waiting for food will attain the ultimate realization, but the true meaning of the picture is the wordless intuition that it evokes in the receptive. Comparably a picture of Bodhidharma (the founder of Zen) by Takuju (1760–1833) contains the caption, "The voice of the spring in the middle of the night; and the mountain scenery at sunset."[16] The words specify two proverbial scenes of placid beauty ironically juxtaposed to the fierce beauty of meditation.

Salajan adapts Zen styles into comicstrip form. This joining of East and West is an odd amalgam. In comicstrips, the young usually best the old but, true to her sources, Salajan has the "Old Monk" (Zen master) almost always outwit the young ones. This happens, however, because the Old Monk is more childlike than the youths. The latter take themselves very seriously. Some of them try to exhibit the perfect meditational posture to impress him. Instead of encouraging them, he tells them that he needs no more "stone Buddhas" (p. 5) and that meditating to gain Enlightenment is as pointless as polishing a floor board to make a mirror (p. 43). Designed for the already converted, *Zen Comics* neglects to explain what the readers of *Cosmic Papers* already knew—that Zen *does* advocate meditation. (The word "meditation," by the way, is used in this chapter as a translation of *zazen,* alert sitting, without thought). The point of the Old Monk's disparagement of meditation is to set up a double bind: unless one meditates, one will probably not gain Enlightenment; nonetheless, in and of itself, meditation does not guarantee Enlightenment. Every part of *Zen Comics* is challenging, including the picture/text relationship. In one cartoon, the Old Monk stands next to a corralled goat and exclaims: "Whenever I see horns behind a fence, I know there's an ox!" In another strip, the young disciple's word-balloon (filled with a mixture of words, pictures, and indeciferable scribbles) crowds out the figures. Neither picture nor text is sufficiently clear for one to be sure that they either agree or disagree. In a third cartoon, the Old Monk appears walking into a room where he seems to be already seated in meditation. The caption consists of the first two lines of an aphorism by Yün-men (ca. 862–949), "When walking just walk[.] When sitting just sit[.]"[17] The next panel shows Old Monk's delivering Yün-men's punch line: "Above all[,] don't wobble[!]" The play here is with the comic-book convention that the same person's appearance more than once in the same panel tends to signify speed. The monk's stroll, however, is leisurely and his seated position seems the antithesis of haste. One might assume that the monk's third sentence imme-

Ioanna Salajan, pictures from Zen Comics (Copyright by the publisher, Charles E. Tuttle Co., Inc., Tokyo, 1974. Reprinted by permission.)

(21)

when sitting
just sit

when walking just walk

Above all
don't wobble

Ioanna Salajan, pictures from Zen Comics. (Copyright by
the publisher, Charles E. Tuttle Co., Inc., Tokyo, 1974.
Reprinted by permission.)

diately follows on the other three, yet he is standing in a new locale.

The essence of Zen art is to present everyday reality in such a way that it seems fantastic and impossible. As the great Chinese lay Zenist P'ang proclaimed:

> How wondrously supernatural,
> And how miraculous, this!
> I draw water, and I carry fuel![18]

This sense of life as extraordinary is, of course, not confined to Zen. The modern Roman Catholic monastic Thomas Merton considered "the experiences of the Old Testament prophets . . . [to be] as factual . . . and as disconcerting as any fact of Zen."[19] There is beginning to arise an ecumenical body of Zenlike fantasy such as the illuminated play *EveryOne* (1978) by Frederick Franck, author of *The Zen of Seeing* (1973) and *Zen and Zen Classics* (1977). *EveryOne* is a modern adaptation of the fifteenth-century drama *Everyman,* itself a version of a story in *Barlaam and Josaphat,* a collection of Buddhist tales in Christianized form. With their Buddhist origins forgotten, these narratives enjoyed a great vogue in Europe at the end of the Middle Ages. The earliest extant version of the story of *Everyman* is the Buddhist parable, "The Man and his Four Wives" (*Miscellaneous Agamas,* no. 101).[20] A man about to die finds that he will lose the company of three wives, symbolizing respectively his body, riches, and companions, but his fourth wife, his "True Nature," will not desert him. In the fifteenth-century Christian *Everyman,* the title character, summoned by God, dies, leaving everything but his Good Deeds behind. Franck's version has Insight (man's "True Self") as the final companion, a return to the Buddhist interpretation, though *EveryOne* also includes God as a character like the Christian version. Franck reports that "Christians saw it as a Christian play. Buddhists called it a Buddhist play in disguise. Jews declared it to be essentially Jewish" (p. 144). To accompany the text, Franck drew a number of pictures which, as he explains, "are not 'illustrations'" but relate to the words in less clear-cut ways. When, for instance, God summons EveryOne to death and rebirth, Franck appends the sketch of a scarecrow, a corpselike form. What, precisely, Franck means by such juxtapositions is "to be visualized by the inner eye, to be listened to by the inner ear, to be experienced in the heart." All the drawings are of everyday life, common people, ordinary scenery, and European architecture. In *The Zen of Seeing,* the very similar sketches have as their stated purpose to lead artist and viewer to a sense of oneness with all creation. To this effect, he cites verses by the modern Zen Master Sokei-an, "I saw people coming towards me / But all were the same man, / All were

Frederick Franck, picture from EveryOne, The Timeless
Myth of "Everyman" Reborn. (© 1978 by Frederick
Franck. By permission of Joan Daves, New York, the
agent for Frederick Franck.)

myself." On the same page, Franck then quotes words of St. Nicholas of
Cusa, "In all faces is shown the Face of Faces, veiled and as if in a riddle."[21]
Franck's afterword to his play contains a comparable vision of oneness, this
time in the words of William Blake, "As in your bosom you bear your
Heaven and Earth and all you behold, tho it appears without, it is within."
To evoke a sense of closeness to the reader, Franck hand printed the play's
text "as if [he] were some medieval monk." The book has its roots in the
illuminations of the Middle Ages, the realistic drawings of Franck's Dutch
forebears, and the *koan-ga* of Zen.

turtle
explaining
don't act
but act

Another fairly successful ecumenical illuminator is the American Paul Reps, best known for his *Zen Telegrams* (1959). It consists of seventy-nine "picture poems" originally displayed in one-man shows in Japan, then collected into a volume.[22] In words reminiscent of Franck's, the book's jacket announces that it "aims at the inner ear, the inner eye, the inner self." His turtle-picture has as its text, "turtle explaining don't act but act." How the turtle explains this paradox is left to the intuition of the reader/viewer.

Paul Siudzinski, picture from Japanese Brush Painting Techniques (© 1978 by Paul Siudzinski). Reprinted by...

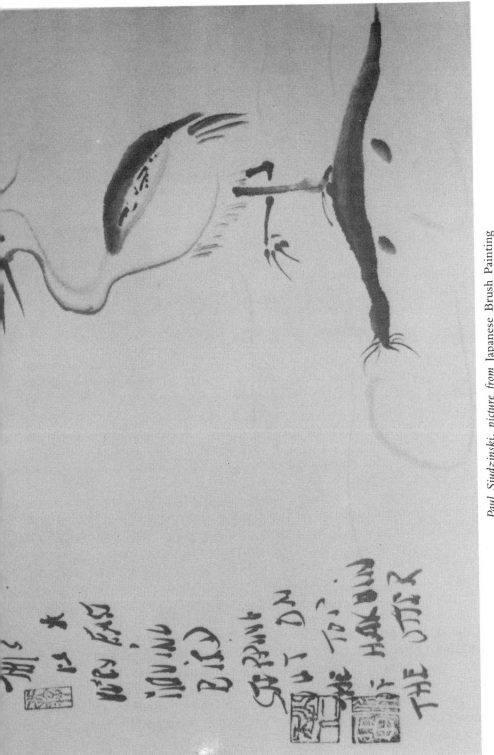

Paul Siudzinski, picture from Japanese Brush Painting Techniques. (© 1978 by Paul Siudzinski. Reprinted by permission of Sterling Publishing Co., Inc.)

Another drawing picturing a hand compares the fingers' touch to the compassion of Buddha and love of Jesus (p. 96).

Paul Siudzinski's *Sumi-e: A Meditation in Ink* also follows *koan-ga* tradition, sometimes mixing it with other sources as in his painting of an intoxicated Japanese. Siudzinski mentions that it was inspired by the American expression, "I have to get a hair of the dog that bit me," yet he titles the section "The Tail of the Tiger" (after an "Eastern myth") and draws neither a dog nor a tiger but a horse. His *sumi-e* sketch "Hakuin the Otter" is a parody of a well-known drawing by the eighteenth-century Zen master Hakuin, who was himself parodying an earlier Zen tradition about Bodhidharma. Nonetheless, Siudzinski stated in his preface that although his book "is intended to produce paintings that communicate directly the spontaneous, intuitive perception of the inner eye . . . it is not Zen meditation."[23]

Ecumenical works, such as Franck's, Reps's, and Siudzinski's, evidence that Zenlike art is not necessarily limited to that faith. For the precise nature of Zen illumination, however, one may best turn to a work totally within that tradition, such as the Ox-herding (also called the Cow-herding) pictures.

In Sung Dynasty China (A.D. 960–1279), the Zen Master Seikyo painted six allegorical sketches, using as imagery the herding of an ox or cow (the Chinese character means either one). His series (no longer extant) was elaborated to ten stages by the monk Kakuan. From this latter, present editions reputedly descend, although, as with the Tarot, there are many versions. The Reverend Seisetsu Seki, Abbot of Tenryuji, Kyoto, painted a modern set for Suzuki's *Essays in Zen Buddhism* (1st ser.), 1927. These pictures begin with a young man alone in the wilds, reminiscent of the Fool of the Tarot. According to the Chinese verses, he is "lost in the jungle" (*po ts'ao,* literally, spreading grasses), but the picture lacks the cluttered vegetation that one might expect.[24] Rather, there is much empty space, a common part of Far Eastern art, where areas of blank paper may suggest *sunyata* (emptiness, signifying the Buddhist rejection of all categories).

The second scene reveals that the youth has found traces of the ox (his true nature). All Zen drawings and calligraphy are called *bokuseki* (traces of the inspiration or Enlightenment of previous masters). The fantastic Chinese verses state that the ox's "nose reaches the heavens and none can conceal it," yet the sketch shows only its hoofprints (Suzuki, facing p. 358). The beast that cannot be concealed is as invisible to the viewer as to the youth.

The third poem asks rhetorically: "The splendid head decorated with stately horns, what painter can reproduce her?" (Suzuki, facing p. 359). With typical Zen humor, the picture shows not the animal's head but its buttocks. Seisetsu Seki's version leaves these white, while, inexplicably, the creature is always thereafter black.

Seisetsu Seki (Abbot of Tenryuji, Kyoto, Japan), Cow-herding (Ox-herding) picture I in Daisetz Teitaro Suzuki's Essays in Zen Buddhism (1st ser.), 1927. (Reprinted by courtesy of Mr. J. B. Knight of Luzac and Company Limited, London, the publisher.)

The fourth poem describes the ox as being "lost in a misty unpenetrable [*sic*] mountain pass" but the picture shows the youth still holding its rope (Suzuki, facing p. 360).

Despite the title of the sequence, the fifth scene is the only one depicting the youth's herding the ox (Suzuki, facing p. 361).

Seisetsu Seki (Abbot of Tenryuji, Kyoto, Japan), Cow-herd-ing (Ox-herding) picture VI in Daisetz Teitaro Suzuki's Essays in Zen Buddhism *(1st ser.), 1927.* (Reprinted by courtesy of Mr. J. B. Knight of Luzac and Company Limited, London, the publisher.)

In the sixth poem, the youth rides the ox home, playing a flute that disappears in the mist. The painting shows no such disappearance. Indeed, a fifteenth-century version by Shu Sun is even less misty. Zen terms the ecstasy of spiritual freedom gained through meditation *yuge-zammai,* which may seem dreamy and erratic to the laity, but is a condition of absolute clarity to those experiencing it.

Seisetsu Seki (Abbot of Tenryuji, Kyoto, Japan), Cow-herding (Ox-herding) picture VII in Daisetz Teitaro Suzuki's Essays in Zen Buddhism *(1st ser.), 1927. (Courtesy of Mr. J. B. Knight of Luzac & Company Limited, London, the publisher.)*

The seventh poem describes the youth as indoors at home; the painting shows him sleeping outdoors next to his house. From this point on, the ox never appears again, because the youth has realized his identity with it. Whether he is indoors or outdoors is unimportant, since all is one.

The eighth scene may seem the strangest to Occidental eyes, since all it contains is blank paper within a circle. The poem reads, "All is empty, the whip, the rope, the man, and the cow" (Suzuki, facing p. 364). This sentence calls the objects to mind, yet explains that they are only apparently separate, for emptiness (*sunyata*) does not signify vacuum but is a technical term meaning that the ultimate nature of the world cannot be divided into categories. The words (resorting to imagery) cannot adequately convey the emptiness of the world nor can the blankness of the picture evidence that all the objects in some sense remain. Illumination and text are here profoundly interdependent. According to the Zen Patriarch Seng-ts'an, "The circle is like the Great Emptiness, / Nothing lacking, nothing too much."[25]

The ninth painting presents flowers, branches, and leaves. The poem is even more puzzling than its predecessors:

> To return to the Origin, to be back at the Source—
> already a false step this!
> Far better it is to stay home, blind and deaf,
> straightway and without much ado,
> Sitting within the hut he takes no cognisance
> of things outside,
> Behold the water flowing on—whither nobody knows;
> and those flowers red and fresh—
> For whom are they? (Suzuki, p. 365 1st ser.)

The first two lines warn against presuming that one has accomplished anything when the Enlightened are simply in the natural condition that they should never have abandoned. The last two lines deny that the youth "takes . . . cognisance" of the outdoors. Then why does the painting show scenery? According to Zen, observer and observed are one. The flowers and the youth are interdependent whether he "takes . . . cognisance" of the fact or not.

The last picture shows the one-time youth grown fat and old. According to the verse, he is "Daubed with mud and ashes" and in the "market-place," while the painting shows him immaculate and in a rural setting (Suzuki, facing p. 366). The words make him sound like the most abject of beggars, but the *sumi-e* depicts his basket and enormous sack of possessions. In the fantasy of the verse, "he touches, and lo! the dead trees come into full bloom" (Suzuki, p. 366). In the painting, though, he stands away from the tree and talks to a youth much like his earlier self. Like the Major Arcana of the Tarot, the series ends with renewal, though of varying kinds. The discrepancies and mysteries in the Ox-herding pictures ranging from the trivial to the more meaningful remind one that Zen considers the world paradoxical. What to Zen constitutes reality is to logic mere fantasy and vice versa.

In his *Zen and Japanese Art,* Toshimitsu Hasumi paraphrases the Ox-herding series, then asserts: "All Japanese arts must mount unswervingly by these steps."[26] As Hasumi suggests, since the series represents stages of Zen consciousness, it also describes levels of paradoxical aesthetic awareness; and as such, it is relevant to an important problem: whether anything as self-contradictory as illuminated fantasy can be classified. Consider, for example, Todorov's famous attempt to separate works into the three classifications, "fantastic," "marvelous," and "uncanny." As Han-liang Chang has demonstrated, the categories at least occasionally blur into one another.[27] Categories only make sense if they are mutually exclusive, but nothing is mutually exclusive in the paradoxical world of fantasy. To analyze phenomena one must divide them—a helpful process at one level, but not if one reifies this division as if it had any final meaning. Buddhism has long insisted on the need to speak on more than one level, since ideas that are useful at one point may be hindrances at a higher one. In other words, Buddhism is far less interested in a scientific description of the world than in employing language as a means of waking up the devotees so that they can see reality directly. Zen believes in *sudden* Enlightenment; thus it denies the existence of stages of progress toward that goal, such as one finds in the Ox-herding pictures; yet those pictures are Zen classics. Faced with the alienness of Buddhism to Western tradition, one needs a bridge between the two, such as Robert Magliola's *Derrida on the Mend,* which uses deconstructive terminology to explain Buddhism and then turns around to use Buddhist metaphysics as a way of going beyond the limits of deconstruction.[28] In the present case—the problem of classifying fantasy—the relevant term is *sous rature* (under erasure), a phrase that Jacques Derrida borrowed from Martin Heidegger. A statement is made *sous rature* if the author deems it useful and at the same time self-contradictory. In summarizing my previous treatment of illuminated fantasy, I must resort to *sous rature* divisions such as the Ox-herding pictures provide.

Like the first Ox-herding picture, much illuminated fantasy portrays people who have lost their way. The ox herder is young, representing a time of life when the world seems particularly unfamiliar. Inevitably, the earlier portions of my book dealt with such an introduction into a strange universe: encountering picture/text discrepancy (the introduction), the religious history of this split (chapter 1), Blake's rebellion against growing up in a real world (chapter 2), and, particularly, fantasists' obsession with youth (chapter 3). Shunryu Suzuki well entitles one of his books *Zen Mind, Beginner's Mind.*[29] He suggests that our unprejudiced, first view of phenomena may be the most insightful and that so-called beginner's luck may result from the freshness of the novice's mind rather than pure chance. Confusion caused by the paradoxes and discrepancies of fantasy can induce such freshness and wonder. The rituals and excesses of idolatry may also have yielded such a state (although at too high a cost) and the more sophisticated fantasy of the modern era can be seen as a quest to renew the sense of wonder. In other words, the realization of being lost (the beginner's mind) is an aspect of all fantasy. It is, nevertheless, not always the dominant aspect. Indeed, as in the next stage, its opposite, didactic certainty, may dominate.

According to Suzuki, the second Ox-herding painting depicts the period when the novice has found a trace of the truth, i.e., he has just encountered the *Sutras* (Buddhist scriptures). Zen, however, is suspicious of scriptures—even of its own—for Zenists fear that the naïve may become overly fascinated with mere doctrine, keeping them from continuing in their quest. For literature, this is the stage when the author uses token fantasy as a sugar coating for his attempt to lead readers out of delusion. This token fantasy dominates in dogmatic periods (and there have certainly been many of those). People frequently flee from confusion to any security, particularly to the cheap comfort of prejudice and reified fantasies, preferably old, reassuring ones. As chapter 4 argues, the same phantasmagoric images reoccur again and again in satire's ultimately vain attempt to counter political illusion with fantasy. The latter, though, can serve as an ameliorative of specific delusions (to borrow Derrida's concept of the *pharmakon,* a word meaning both medicine and poison).[30]

In the third Ox-herding painting, the youth glimpses a reality that Zen considers too marvelous for pictures to reproduce. In his pioneer work, *The Fantastic,* Todorov defines fantasy as encounter with a seemingly supernatural event that causes the mind to hesitate momentarily, wondering whether the phenomenon is illusion or reality.[31] This is a much more narrow definition of all fantasy than common usage provides. It does, though, fairly well describe the instant when the prejudices of the second stage collapse in a new vision of what deconstuctionists call "alterity" (the irreducible difference of all phenomena from one another). My chapters 5 through 8 study the strangeness of such visionary imagery. I find, nonetheless, that alterity does not preclude grouping together images in so-called archetypal patterns as long as one realizes that these latter are merely convenient categories, not ultimate ones.

The fourth Ox-herding picture shows the capture of the beast (the youth's true self). How different, though, is ox and young man! Derrida contends that since words (mere letters and sounds) are obviously not the same as the things they name, all language about the self is inherently different from it. Thus any self we can think of is a mere fiction, and as the disorder of multiple personalities suggests, people can invent as many fictions as they like. Deconstruction goes no further. Despite criticizing Western philosophy for centering on words, Derrida sees no way out of the "prisonhouse of language." Consequently, he offers no means of transcending the narcissism described in my ninth chapter (although Zen presumes that level on level lie beyond).

In the fifth Ox-herding picture, the youth leads the beast. This level challenges one to live with a still-alien side of oneself (a common theme in comics, often involving friendship or marriage with aliens). In deconstruction, since there is no hope of determinability, life seems to be for moment-to-moment entertainment, like manipulating a pinball machine with a broken scoring mechanism. In this picture, though, the reader is advised: "Do not get the nose-string [of the ox] loose, hold it tight, and allow yourself no indulgence" (p. 361). The situation has all the seriousness, promise, and difficulty of a successful partnership.

In the sixth Ox-herding painting, the herder inexplicably demonstrates that he is "one of those who know" simply by riding skillfully, flute in hand. His gaze is no longer on this world. Comparable fantasies revel in freedom from material restraint. For instance, in the chapter "De Creatura Praetere Legem" ("Of the Creature Who is Beyond Laws") of the 1983 book *De Historia et Veritate Unicornis* ("On the History and Truth of the Unicorn"), Michael Green, the work's alleged translator (actually its author) argues that unicorns are free from laws because they embody a "union of opposites."[32] Derrida has repeatedly condemned such mysticism, considering it a crypto-logocentrism, because the idea of a union suggests a center, a point of rest and certainty outside of the ceaseless change and confusion he sees in the world.

In the seventh Ox-herding painting, by the time the herder has reached home, he has so completely identified with the ox that it no longer has a separate existence. A small group of fantasies, including Kirchner's above-mentioned story, "My Room," exemplifies this stage. Within the solipsism of this level, picture/text discrepancies may assume any form, since the protagonist's mind presumably creates whatever world it wishes. If fantasy were mere narcissism, this stage would be the ultimate one.

The eighth Ox-herding painting represents radical emptiness. Effective surrealistic illuminations attain to this level. All concepts are torn away. Picture/text differences are most radical, such as Magritte's painting of a pipe labeled, "This is not a pipe."

The ninth Ox-herding painting manifests the result of the foregoing experience (having transcended preconception); the herder need no longer concern himself with discipline but may live selflessly with nature. This is the goal of Taoism (discussed in chapter 10). Magliola distinguishes between two kinds of Zen language: (1) "logocentric" Zen (essentially the same as Taoism), the search to reach the "Source," the "Home," where opposites join, with man united to nature; and (2) "differentialist" Zen, a purely Buddhist phenomenon, rejecting the existence of any such center (p. 96).

After the ninth painting, Taoism and Zen part company.

In the tenth Ox-herding painting, the herder makes contact with society. We have never seen him do this before, so he has not really come full circle, nor is he at any center, but is, instead, fully alive in the problematic world of differences. He chats with the young, giving help that he was never shown receiving. Despite his Enlightenment, he appears not as a respectable sage but as a comic fat man, for irreverence is as common in Zen as in Western fantasy. "The dead trees come into full bloom" at his touch. He renders everyday life fantastic by his presence. This is not merely the goal of differentialist-Zen language but of some other approaches to existence as well. The Reverend Allen Whitman's *Fairy Tales and the Kingdom of God* (cited earlier) claims approximately this perspective for Christianity. In the Buddhist magazine *Loka 2* and in *Zen and Hasidism,* Rabbi Zalman Schachter laments the effects of rationalism on Judaism and urges a return to Kabalistic and other Jewish traditions that could give everyday life a touch of the fantastic and supernatural.[33] Illuminations comparable to the tenth Ox-herding painting embody insights into the miraculousness of ordinary existence and require spiritual sensitivity from any reader/viewer who intends to reconcile picture and text. Such a literature is not yet common in the West but it is perhaps incipient, considering the growth of interest in Zen language and imagery.

Doubtless, Zen itself is other than its interpretation to the Occident, but my discussion has been limited to the latter because that is what has begun to influence Anglo-American illuminations. Zen, after all, is ineffable, and dedicated Zenists are rightly suspicious of any talk about it, especially Western fascination with its paradoxes. This fascination, however, concerns us here, for it is yet another evidence of widespread longing for the fantastic—particularly for an ultimate variety—one that may in some sense be "true."

What is there in humanity that makes many people crave illuminated fantasy with its divergence of picture/text and other paradoxes? In 1981, archaeologists discovered at a site named El Juyo near Santander, Spain, a 14,000-year-old paleolithic shrine with a face split down the middle—one side a great cat, the other human.[34] Imagery of the divided self apparently goes very far back, even before there were texts. Illuminated fantasy with its division between picture and text contains a structure particularly suited to the representation of mental division. It brings together real and imaginary, prosaic time and eternal images. Well-composed fantasy helps to make the movement from one to the other palatable, but the reader/viewer must have sufficient understanding to meet the challenges of the genre, including that of intuiting overall unity in seeming chaos. Ultimately, the reader must connect the unconnectable and complete what cannot be completed by participating in fantasy as did a character described in Suzuki's *Essays in Zen Buddhism:*

Wu Tao-Tzu or Godoshi was one of the greatest painters of China, and lived in the reign of the Emperor Hsüan-tsung, of the T'ang dynasty. His last painting, according to legend, was a landscape commissioned by the Emperor for one of the walls of his palace. The artist concealed the complete work with a curtain till the Emperor's arrival, then drawing it aside exposed his vast picture. The Emperor gazed with admiration on a marvellous scene: forests, and great mountains, and clouds in immense distances of sky, and men upon the hills, and birds in flight. "Look," said the painter, "in the cave at the foot of this mountain dwells a spirit." He clapped his hands; the door at the cave's entrance flew open. "The interior is beautiful beyond words," he continued, "permit me to show the way." So saying he passed within; the gate closed after him; and before the astonished Emperor could speak or move, all had faded to white wall before his eyes, with not a trace of the artist's brush remaining. Wu Tao-Tzu was seen no more.[35]

Notes

INTRODUCTION

The introduction is an expanded version of my paper "Illuminated Science Fiction and Illuminated Fantasy" delivered at the 1983 Conference of the Southwest Popular Culture Association, October 27–29, Lubbock, Texas.

1. "Comic Books Return to Booming Status," *Lubbock Avalanche–Journal,* 21 January 1987, p. 9D.
2. Richard O'Brien, *The Golden Age of Comic Books, 1937–1945* (New York: Ballantine Books, 1977), p. 5.
3. In *Charles Dickens and George Cruikshank* (Los Angeles: William Andrews Clark Memorial Library, 1971), p. 45.
4. Roland Barthes, *Elements of Semiology,* trans. Annette Lauers and Colin Smith (London: Jonathan Cape, 1967), p. 10.
5. I Nicholas von Hoffman and Garry B Trudeau, *Tales from the Margaret Mead Taproom* (Kansas City, Mo.: Sheed and Ward, 1976), p. 116.
6. Dan Barry and Bob Fujitani, *The Amazing Adventures of Flash Gordon,* 4 vols. (New York: Grosset and Dunlap, 1977), 4:141.
7. A. E. van Vogt, "Inner Space," in *The Visual Encyclopedia of Science Fiction,* ed. Brian Ash (New York: Harmony Books, 1977), pp. 240–43.
8. Samuel Delany, *Empire: A Visual Novel* (New York: Berkley/Windhover, 1978), p. [31].
9. Kingsley Amis, *New Maps of Hell: A Survey of Science Fiction* (New York: Harcourt, Brace, 1960), p. 22.
10. Sandra Miesel, "The Mana Crisis," in Larry Niven, *The Magic Goes Away* (New York: Ace Books, 1978), p. 196.
11. Miesel, p. 199.
12. Richard Corben and Jan Strnad, *New Tales of the Arabian Nights* (New York: Simon and Schuster, 1978), p. [99]. For a study of early graphic versions of the *Nights,* see Terry Reece Hackford, "Fantastic Visions: Illustration of the Arabian Nights," in Roger C. Schlobin, ed., *The Aesthetics of Fantasy Literature and Art* (Notre Dame, Ind.: Notre Dame University Press, 1982), pp. 143–75.
13. Martin Bridgstock, "A Psychological Approach to 'Hard Science Fiction,'" *Science-Fiction Studies* 10 (March 1983): 51.
14. Liam Hudson, *Human Beings: An Introduction to the Psychology of Human Experience* (London: Jonathan Cape, 1975), pp. 134–35.

15. M. Austin, "Dream Recall and the Bias of Intellectual Ability," *Nature* 231 (1971): 59. See also Liam Hudson, *Contrary Imaginations: A Psychological Study of the Young Student* (New York: Schocken Books, 1966), p. 56. Independent studies by F. Barron, G. Welsh, and C. Mackinnon have found that "people who prefer [art] works of greater complexity are characterized by original, dissident, and eccentric personality traits, whereas those who prefer simpler works tend to be low in originality, conservative and conventional." Ellen Winner, *Invented Worlds: The Psychology of the Arts* (Cambridge, Mass.: Harvard University Press, 1982), p. 71.

16. Patients lacking a functional left-brain hemisphere manifest aphasia (impaired ability to comprehend and employ language). Most patients with a severely injured right-brain hemisphere endure visual agnosis (difficulty recognizing faces and other visual patterns) and aprodosis (difficulty perceiving and expressing emotions). Visual recognition of forms, on the one hand, and systematic verbal activities, on the other, generally occupy opposite sides of the brain. This is a suggestive fact when dealing with illuminated fantasy, where the visual and verbal have some independence from one another. First, medical researchers learned that each side of the brain can function separately in epileptics whose hemispheres were surgically severed as part of a relatively new treatment. Later, sophisticated research on "normal subjects" showed that given a task associated with one hemisphere or the other, the involved hemisphere emits "active brain waves," while the other produces an "idling rhythm." Massive evidence from such experimentation now indicates that the brain's two hemispheres examine phenomena in generally contrasting modes: for about ninety-eight percent of right-handed people and two-thirds of left-handed, the left cerebral hemisphere arranges data into systems, while the right recognizes patterns of sensations and manipulates images analogically (although growing knowledge of brain specialization is constantly refining and modifying this generalization). See, e.g., Howard Gardner, *The Shattered Mind* (New York: Alfred A. Knopf, 1975), pp. 291–349, et passim; J. E. Bogen, "Some Educational Aspects of Hemispheric Specialization," *U.C.L.A. Educator* 17 (1975): 24–32; Bob Samples, *The Metaphoric Mind* (Reading, Mass.: Addison-Wesley, 1976), p. 16, et passim; Peter J. Whitehouse, "Imagery and Verbal Encoding in Left and Right Hemisphere Damaged Patients," *Brain and Language* 14 (1981): 330; Elkhonon Goldberg and Louis D. Costa, "Hemisphere Differences in the Acquisition and Use of Descriptive Systems," *Brain and Language* 14 (1981): 144; Wendy Wapner, Suzanne Hamby, and Howard Gardner, "The Role of the Right Hemisphere in the Apprehension of Complex Linguistic Materials," *Brain and Language* 14 (1981): 15–33. Charles Hampden-Turner, *Maps of the Mind: Charts and Concepts of the Mind and Its Labyrinths* (New York: Collier, 1981), pp. 86–93, et passim; Richard M. Restak, *The Brain* (New York: Bantam Books, 1984), pp. 237–69; Jerre Levy, "Right Brain, Left Brain: Fact and Fiction," *Psychology Today* 19 (May 1985): 38–44; Doreen Kimura, "Male Brain, Female Brain: The Hidden Difference," *Psychology Today* 19 (November 1985): 144–73. Recent laboratory results even suggest that dream imagery derives from right-brain activities: Lawrence Miller, "In Search of the Unconscious," *Psychology Today* 20 (December 1986): 60–64. Some science-fiction and fantasy works have begun to make explicit use of this theory, e.g., Rich Veitch's "Abraxas and the Earthman," where one character's two cerebral hemispheres are united to promote psychic wholeness. The story was serialized in *Epic* from February 1982 to April 1983. In the 11 March 1984 episode of "Peanuts," Marcie speculates that she is a "left-brain person," Franklin a "right-brain person," and Peppermint Patty a "no-brain person."

17. As the borders between fantasy and science fiction are unstable, so there is also overlap between fantasy and non-traditional realism, as explored in Donald L. Weismann, *Language and Visual Form: The Personal Record of a Dual Creative Process* (Austin: University of Texas Press, 1968). He relates that he sought seclusion to create, for, as he quotes Saint Augustine, "*Divine things are the more clearly manifested to him who withdraws into the recesses of his heart.* And being thence warned to return to myself, I entered into my inward self . . ." (p. 19). Thus far, he resembles the narcissistic fantasists of my chapter 9. Furthermore, he decides, "that the pictures [he] would make would not illustrate the words [he] would write, but rather that both the pictures and words might conspire to illuminate the experience common to both" (pp. 13–14). His pictures are fantastic, but the text is almost completely realistic; for he wants the literal-minded reader to have some verisimilitude as a guide.

18. Charles M. Schulz, *A Smile Makes a Lousy Umbrella* (New York: Holt, Rinehart, and Winston, 1977), p. [45].

19. Gotthold Ephraim Lessing, *Laocoön*, trans. Edward Allen McCormick (New York: Bobbs-Merrill, 1962, p. 78, et passim; Ulrich Weisstein, "Literature and the Visual Arts," in

Interrelations of Literature, ed. Jean-Pierre Barricelli and Joseph Gibaldi (New York: Modern Language Association of America, 1982), p. 254. According to W. J. T. Mitchell, Lessing's Protestant desire to limit visual imagery may have caused him to exaggerate the difference between painting and poetry, for visual art actually is perceived over a period of time (albeit, usually a much shorter one than texts), *Iconology: Image, Text, Ideology* (Chicago: University of Chicago, 1986), pp. 34, 106.

20. Roger Caillois, *Au coeur du fantastique* (Paris: Gallimard, 1965); Eric S. Rabkin, *Fantastic in Literature* (Princeton, N.J.: Princeton University Press, 1976); Tzvetan Todorov, *The Fantastic in Literature,* trans. Richard Howard (Cleveland, Ohio: Case Western Reserve University, 1973). Following Caillois's use of "fantastique" (e.g., p. 171, et passim) and Todorov's employment of "fantaisie" and "fantastique," a number of other critics e.g., W[illiam] R[obert] Irwin, *The Game of the Impossible* (Chicago: University of Illinois, 1976), p. 54, distinguish between "the fantastic," in which they include all tales of marvels, and "fantasy," a smaller genre (but there is no close agreement as to what it constitutes). By "fantasy," I mean all works that feature self-contradictory elements, including myths and fairy tales (archaic fantasies whose narrators seem unaware of the contradiction), as well as modern works largely based on them. Of one of the latter, *The Wizard of Oz,* the critic Brian Attebery observes: "Baum created Oz . . . with the aid of a paradox . . . it is the United States—and it is also everything that conditions in the United States make us wish for," *The Fantasy Tradition in American Literature* (Bloomington: University of Indiana Press, 1980), p. 87. Similar paradoxes underlie the whole genre, since the fantasist has nowhere to go for imagery but to the real world; thus the reader is constantly reminded of reality, even while encountering the radically different realm of fantasy.

21. Arthur Lovejoy, *The Great Chain of Being: A Study of the History of an Idea* (Cambridge: Harvard University Press, 1936); Gaston Bachelard, *La poétique de l'espace,* 4th ed. (Paris: Presses Universitaires de France, 1964); Michel Foucault, *Les mots et les choses: Une archaeologie des sciences humaines* ([Paris]: Gallimard, 1966).

1 AROUND THE GOLDEN CALF

1. In *Addams and Evil* (New York: Random House, 1947), pp. [ii–iii].

2. Dan O'Neill, *The Collective Unconscience of Odd Bodkins* (San Francisco: Glide, 1973), p. [52]. My copy editor, Ann Harvey, suggests that I note O'Neill's punning reference to the archetypal critic Maud Bodkin, an example of the literary sophistication of some fantasy writers.

3. Howard V. Chaykin and Michael Moorcock, *The Swords of Heaven, The Flowers of Hell* (New York: H. M. Communications, 1979), p. [2].

4. Clinton R. Sanders, "Icons of the Alternate Culture: The Themes and Functions of Underground Comix" *Journal of Popular Culture,* 8 (Spring 1975): 836–52.

5. Stan Lee, *Origins of Marvel Comics* (New York: Simon and Schuster, 1974), p. [7].

6. Steven Grant et al., *The Life of Pope John II* 1 (1982): backcover.

7. E.g., a bonfire held by the First Assembly of God Church in Texas City, reported in "Church Holds 'Satanic Purge,'" *Lubbock Avalanche–Journal,* 8 May, 1982, p. 16D. A number of Christian writers have remarked the obvious, that the "Force" is not a Christian concept, most notably Frank Allnutt, *The Force of Star Wars* (Van Nuys, Calif.: Bible Voice, 1977).

8. As translated in "Prolegomenon," in *No Graven Images: Studies in Art and the Hebrew Bible,* ed. Joseph Gutmann (New York: KTAV Publishing House, 1971), pp. xiv–xv.

9. Arthur Hugh Clough, *The Poems,* ed. F. L. Mulhauser, 2d ed. (London: Oxford University Press, 1974), p. 205.

10. Martin Buber, *Jüdische Künstler* (Berlin: Jüdischer, 1903), p. 7, as translated in Gutmann, p. xiii.

11. Gutmann, p. xix.

12. Julian Jaynes, *The Origin of Consciousness in the Breakdown of the Bicameral Mind* (Boston: Houghton Mifflin, 1976), p. 311.

13. Samuel Laeuchli, *Religion and Art in Conflict: Introduction to a Cross-Disciplinary Task* (Philadelphia: Fortress Press, 1980), p. 116.

14. *Patrilogia Latina,* cxii, col. 1608, quoted in G. C. Coulton, *Art and the Reformation* (New York: Alfred A. Knopf, 1928), p. 246.

15. Barbara Tuchman, *A Distant Mirror: The Calamitous 14th Century* (New York: Alfred A Knopf, 1978), p. 236.

16. George Gordon, Lord Byron, *Selected Poetry and Prose,* ed. W. H. Auden (New York: New American Library, 1966), p. 208.

17. John Ruskin, *Works,* ed. E. T. Cook and Alexander Wedderburn (London: George Allen, 1905), 19:365.

18. W[illiam] Perkins, *Prophetica sive de sacra et unica ratione conscionandi tractatus,* Cambridge, 1592, sig. F viii *recto,* quoted and trans. in Frances A. Yates, *The Art of Memory* (Chicago: University of Chicago Press, 1966), p. 277.

19. John Phillips, *The Reformation of Images: Destruction of Art in England, 1535–1600* (Berkeley: University of California Press, [1973]), p. xii.

20. Wilbur Marshall Urban, *Language and Reality: The Philosophy of Language and the Principles of Symbolism* (New York: Macmillan, 1951), pp. 584–85. For the application of this idea to Blake, see Leopold Damrosch, Jr., *Symbol and Truth in Blake's Myth* (Princeton, N.J.: Princeton University Press, 1980), pp. 174–75.

21. All parenthetical references to Chaucer are to F N. Robinson, ed., *The Works of Geoffrey Chaucer,* 2d ed. (Boston: Houghton Mifflin, 1957). For more detailed treatment, see James Whitlark, "Chaucer and the Pagan Gods," *Annuale Mediaevale* 18 (1977): 65–75.

22. In Melvin Macye Cammack, *John Wyclif and the English Bible* (New York: American Tract Society, 1938), p. 74.

23. Roger Sherman Loomis, *A Mirror of Chaucer's World* (Princeton, N.J.: Princeton University Press, 1965), p. 53.

24. André Malraux, *The Metamorphosis of the Gods,* trans. Stuart Gilbert (Garden City, N.Y.: Doubleday, 1960), p. 372.

25. Rosemary Jackson, *Fantasy: The Literature of Subversion* (New York: Methuen, 1981), p. 66.

26. James Wolfe, "Three Congregations," in *The New Religious Consciousness,* ed. Charles Y. Glock and Charles N. Bellah (Berkeley: University of California, 1976), p. 232.

27. Humphrey Palmer, *Analogy: A Study of Qualification and Argument in Theology* (London: Macmillan, 1973), p. 106.

28. Jean Hagstrum, *The Sister Arts: The Tradition of Literary Pictorialism and English Poetry From Dryden to Gray* (Chicago: University of Chicago Press, 1958), p. 10.

29. Ibid., pp. 103, 113, et passim.

30. W. J. T. Mitchell, *Blake's Composite Art: A Study of the Illuminated Poetry* (Princeton, N.J.: Princeton University Press, 1978), pp. 14–24, et passim.

2 BLAKE: VISIONARY AGAINST THE COMMONPLACE

This chapter is an expanded version of my paper, "The Divided Mind in Blake: Songs of Innocence and Experience," delivered at the 1983 Conference on the Fantastic in the Arts, March 24–27, Boca Raton, Florida.

1. William Blake, *Songs of Innocence and of Experience,* annotated by Geoffrey Keynes (New York: Oxford University Press, 1977), p. 46. Unless otherwise specified, references to *Songs* are to this edition, and (unless otherwise indicated) references to his other works are to *Complete Poetry and Prose of William Blake,* ed. David V Erdman, rev. ed. (Berkeley and Los Angeles: University of California Press, 1982).

2. Jack Lindsay, *William Blake: His Life and Work* (London: Constable, 1978), p. 3.

3. Mitchell, *Iconology,* p. 43.

4. A[braham] M[arie] Hammacher, *Phantoms of the Imagination: Fantastic Art and Literature From Blake to Dali* (New York: Harry N. Abrams, 1981), p. 32.

5. George Wingfield Digby, *Symbol and Image in William Blake* (Oxford: Clarendon Press, 1957), p. 19.

6. According to Clayton Koelb, texts that are deliberately incredible derive their unbelievable elements from play with their own language. *The Incredulous Reader: Literature and the Function of Disbelief* (London: Cornell University, 1984), p. 44. Thus, Blake's visual fantasy sometimes grows from the same roots as verbal fantasy.

7. Mitchell, *Composite,* p. 33.

8. *Jerusalem* 69:42 in *Complete Poetry and Prose,* p. 223; S. Foster Damon, *A Blake Dictionary* (New York: E. P. Dutton, 1971), p. 281.

9. C. N. Manlove, *The Impulse of Fantasy Literature* (Kent, Ohio: Kent State University,

1983), p. ix. Manlove's position here shows his deepened understanding since his earlier, more critical study *Modern Fantasy* (Cambridge: Cambridge University Press, 1975). There the desire to "contemplate things for themselves" is deemed a "temptation" to which some fantasists inordinately succumb (p. 259).

    10. *The Illuminated Blake,* annotated by David V. Erdman (Garden City, N.Y.: Doubleday, 1974), p. 55.

    11. Harold Bloom, *Blake's Apocalypse: A Study in Poetic Argument* (Garden City, N.Y.: Doubleday, 1963), pp. 137, 147.

    12. Complete Poetry and Prose, p. 600, discussed in Bloom, p. 38.

    13. Poetry and Prose of William Blake, ed. G. L. Keynes (Oxford: Oxford University Press, 1966), p. 372.

    14. Damon, *Blake Dictionary,* pp. 264–65.

    15. *Illuminated Blake,* p. 143.

    16. Lindsay, pp. 158–61.

    17. *The Complete Graphic Works of William Blake,* ed. David Bindman ([New York]: Thames and Hudson, 1978), plate 110.

    18. S. Foster Damon, *William Blake* (Gloucester, Mass.: Peter Smith, 1958), pp. 237–38.

    19. Frederic Raphael and Kenneth McLeish, *The List of Books* (New York: Harmony Books, 1981), p. 127.

3 PICTURE BOOKS FOR THE ETERNAL CHILD

    The Carroll section in this chapter derives from my paper "Lewis Carroll's Nightmare of Disorder" delivered at the 1984 Conference on the Fantastic in the Arts, March 22–25, Boca Raton, Florida.

    1. William Wordsworth, *Poetical Works* (London: Oxford University Press, 1966), p. 460.

    2. *The Complete Graphic Works of William Blake,* ed. David Bindman ([New York]: Thames and Hudson, 1978), plates 115–32. Stephen Prickett, *Victorian Fantasy* (Hassocks, Sussex, U. K.: Harvester, 1979), pp. xv–xvi.

    3. Quoted in John Aquino, *Fantasy in Literature* (Washington, D.C.: National Education Association, 1977), p. 10.

    4. In Ursula K. Le Guin, *The Language of the Night: Essays on Fantasy and Science Fiction,* ed. Susan Wood (New York: G. P. Putnam's Sons, 1979), p. 39.

    5. Attebery, pp. vii, et passim.

    6. Thomas Byrom, *Nonsense and Wonder* (New York: E. P. Dutton, 1977), p. 120.

    7. Edward Lear, *Later Letters,* ed. [Constance] Strachey (New York: Duffield and Co., 1911), pp. 231–32.

    8. *The Complete Illustrated Works of Lewis Carroll* (New York: Avenel Books, 1982), p. 85. All references to Carroll's works are to this edition.

    9. Nina Demurova, "Toward a Definition of Alice's Genre: The Folktale and Fairy-Tale Connections," in Edward Guiliano, ed., *Lewis Carroll: A Celebration* (New York: Clarkson N. Potter, 1982), pp. 75–86.

    10. Vladimir Propp, *Morfologia skaski* [1928], 2d ed. (Moscow: Nanka, 1969; trans. Laurence Scott, under the title *Morphology of the Folktale,* 2d ed., Austin: University of Texas Press, 1968).

    11. Jeffrey Stern, "Lewis Carroll the Pre-Raphaelite: Fainting in Coils," in Guiliano, pp. 166–71.

    12. Julia Whitsitt, "'To See Clearly': Perspective in Pre-Raphaelite Poetry and Painting," *The Journal of Pre-Raphaelite Studies* 3 (May 1983): 69–79. In "The Child's Relations with Others," trans. W. Cobb, in *The Primacy of Perception,* ed. J. M. Edie (Evanston, Ill.: Northwestern University, 1964), p. 152, Maurice Merleau-Ponty presents clinical evidence that very young children lack the ability to comprehend perspective in drawings because such comprehension requires "the idea that [the child] sees [things] from a single point of view instead of living in them."

    13. George P. Landow, "And the World Became Strange: Realms of Literary Fantasy," *Georgia Review* 33 (Spring 1979): 11.

    14. Henry James, *Autobiography,* ed. Frederick Dupee (New York: Criterion Books, [1956]), p. 169, quoted in J. Hillis Miller, *Charles Dickens and George Cruikshank* (Los Angeles: William Andrews Clark Memorial Library, 1971), p. 44.

    15. In Charles Dickens, *The Christmas Books,* vol. 1 (New York: Penguin Books, 1971), p. 68.

16. Edmund Wilson, "Dickens: The Two Scrooges," in *The Wound and the Bow: Seven Studies in Literature* (New York: Oxford University Press, 1947), p. 64.

17. *Rudyard Kipling, The Collected Works.* (New York: AMS Press, 1970), 12:18.

18. Aubrey Beardsley, *The Story of Venus and Tannhäuser or Under the Hill* (New York: St. Martin's Press, 1974); Aldous Huxley, *Brave New World* (1932; reprint New York: Harper and Row, 1972), pp. 100, et passim.

19. Joseph R. Dunlap, *The Book That Never Was* (New York: Oriole Editions, 1971), pp. 39–40, et passim.

20. Edward Dunsany, *The Book of Wonder* (New York: Boni and Liveright, 1918), p. 56; Paul W. Skeeters, *Sidney H. Sime: Master of Fantasy* (Pasadena, Calif.: Ward Ritchie Press, 1978), pp. 8–18, 62.

21. Edward Dunsany, *Patches of Sunlight* (New York: Reynal and Hitchcock, [1938]), pp. 19–25. See also Skeeters, p. 9.

22. J. M. Barrie, *The Novels, Tales and Sketches* (New York: Charles Scribner's Sons, 1911), 12:220.

23. Roger Lancelyn Green, *Fifty Years of Peter Pan* (London: Peter Davies, 1954), p. 39.

24. Michael DeLarrabeiti, *The Borribles* (New York: Macmillan, 1978) and *The Borribles Go for Broke* (New York: Ace Books, 1981).

25. J. R. R. Tolkien, *Tree and Leaf* (Boston: Houghton Mifflin, 1964), pp. 10, 37.

26. Transcribed in Paul F. Ford, *Companion to Narnia* (San Francisco: Harper and Row, 1980), pp. xxii–xxiii. Tolkien objected to the Narnia stories because of their inconsistencies, including mingled mythologies. Humphrey Carpenter, *The Inklings* (New York: Ballantine, 1978), pp. 245–47.

27. Transcribed in Jeanette Anderson Bakke, *The Lion and the Lamb and the Children: Christian Childhood Education Through "The Chronicles of Narnia,"* Ph.D. diss., University of Minnesota, 1975 (Ann Arbor, Mich.: University Microfilms, 76-4021), quoted in Ford, *Companion* p. xxii.

28. C. S. Lewis, *Of Other Worlds,* ed. Walter Hooper (New York: Harcourt Brace Jovanovich, 1966), p. 27.

29. Charles Platt, ed., *Dream Makers, II* (New York: Berkley, 1983), p. 100.

30. *Voorloper* ([New York]: Ace Books, 1980), p. 18.

31. Barbara Young, *This Man from Lebanon: A Study of Kahlil Gibran* (New York: Alfred A Knopf, 1945), p. 22.

32. Kahlil Gibran, *The Prophet* (New York: Alfred A. Knopf, 1923), p. 17.

33. Young, p. 19.

34. Interview with Richard Bach, *Psychic* (October 1974); Russell Targ and Harold E. Puthoff, *Mind-Reach: Scientists Look at Psychic Ability* (New York: Dell, 1977), pp. xxiii–xxv, 90. As Bach alleges in *Psychic* magazine, the former work was inspired by his hearing a mysterious voice calling out the title; the latter seems to be partly related to ESP experiments he underwent in 1974, from which he drew conclusions similar to the basic message of *Illusions*: " . . . we are limited by the world only because we believe that we are limited by it."

35. Susan Chitty, *The Beast and the Monk: A Life of Charles Kingsley* (London: Hodder and Stoughton, 1974), unnumbered picture following p. 62.

36. Paul Ford, ed., *The New England Primer,* Classics in Education, no. 13 ([N.p.]: Columbia University, 1962), p. 27. Among the non-English language illuminated rhyming alphabets, one of the most notable is *Naturgeschichtliches Alphabet* by the famous nineteenth-century writer and cartoonist Wilhelm Busch. The modern critic Wolfgang Kayser notes its "humorous" use of picture/text "discrepancy," *Das Groteske: seine Gestaltung in Malerei und Dichtung* (Oldenburg: Gerhard Stalling Verlag, 1957; trans. by Ulrich Weisstein, under the title *The Grotesque in Art and Literature,* Bloomington: Indiana University Press, 1963), p. 118.

37. Edward Gorey, *Amphigorey* (New York: G. P. Putnam's Sons, 1972), p. [127]. Parenthetical references to Gorey's works are to this collection or to *Amphigorey Too* (New York: G.P. Putnam's Sons, 1975).

38. *Master Snickup's Cloak* (New York: Harper and Row, 1979), p. [27].

39. James Bogan and Fred Goss, eds., *Sparks of Fire: Blake in a New Age* (Richmond, Calif.: North Atlantic Books, 1982), p. 40.

40. Nancy Willard, "The Tiger asks Blake for a Bedtime Story," *A Visit to William Blake's Inn: Poems for Innocent and Experienced Travellers* (New York: Harcourt Brace Jovanovich, 1981), p. 40.

41. Denis Gifford, *The International Book of Comics* (New York: Crescent, 1984), p. 22.

42. Brian Ash, ed., *The Visual Encyclopedia of Science Fiction* (New York: Harmony Books, 1977), p. 322.

43. Samuel Daniel, *The Complete Works,* ed. Alexander Grossart (London: Hazell, Watson, and Viney, 1885), 3:320.

44. Stephen King, *Creepshow* (New York: Plume, 1982); Gifford, p. 184.

45. Frederic Wertham, *The Seduction of the Innocent* (New York: Rinehart, [1954]).

46. "Comics Code Rejects Daredevil Story," *The Comics Journal* (Summer 1980), p. 8.

47. Ariel Dorfman and Armand Mattelart, *How to Read Donald Duck,* trans. David Kunzle (New York: International General, 1975).

4   ENDURING ELEMENTS OF POLITICAL FANTASY

This chapter is an expanded version of my paper "Religious Motifs in Modern Visual Satire" delivered at the 1983 Conference of the Science Fiction Research Association, June 10–11, Midland, Michigan.

1. John Geipel, *The Cartoon* (South Brunswick, N.J.: A. S. Barnes, 1972), p. 24.

2. Northrop Frye, *Anatomy of Criticism* (Princeton, N.J.: Princeton University Press, 1957), p. 224.

3. Bevis Hillier, *Cartoons and Caricatures* (London: Studio Vista, 1970), p. 12.

4. Robert Philippe, *Political Graphics: Art as a Weapon* (Milan: Arnoldo Mondadori Editore, 1980), p. 25.

5. David Kunzle, *The Early Comic Strip,* vol. 1 of *History of the Comic Strip* (Berkeley: University of California Press, 1973), 71, 404–17; Ronald Paulson, ed., *Hogarth's Graphic Works,* rev. ed. (New Haven: Yale University Press, 1970), 2: catalogue no. 202.

6. T. Durwood, interview with David Levine, *Crimner's,* Spring 1976, p. 7.

7. Both pamphlets are included in [William Hone], *A Treat for Every One. . . .* (London: J. Stokes, 1820), [not consecutively paginated].

8. E.g., "Ceylon," *The Christian Observer* 15 (1816): 68.

9. [Ron Tyler], *The Image of America in Caricature and Cartoon* (Fort Worth, Tex.: Amos Carter Museum of Western Art, 1975), p. 43.

10. Ibid., p. 50.

11. J. Chal Vinson, *Thomas Nast, Political Cartoonist* (Athens: University of Georgia Press, 1967), p. 19.

12. Ibid., p. 1.

13. Paul Conrad, *Pro and Conrad* (San Rafael, Calif.: Neff-Kane, 1979), p. 42.

14. John Osborne, *The Fifth Year of the Nixon Watch* (New York: Liveright, 1974), p. 75.

15. Thomas Nast St. Hill, *Thomas Nast: Cartoons and Illustrations* (New York: Dover, 1974), plate 55.

16. Hamlin Hill, ed., *Mark Twain's Letters to His Publishers, 1867–1894* (Berkeley and Los Angeles: University of California Press, 1967), pp. 253–54.

17. Letter [to L. E. Parkhurst] quoted in Cyril Clemens, "Unpublished Letters to Dan Beard," *Mark Twain Quarterly* 7, no. 2 (1945): 22.

18. Henry Nash Smith, *Mark Twain's Fable of Progress: Political and Economic Ideas in "A Connecticut Yankee"* (New Brunswick, N.J.: Rutgers University Press [1964]), pp. 79–81.

19. Edward Sorel, *Superpen* (New York: Random House, 1978), p. 40.

20. *Pro and Conrad,* p. 13.

21. Ibid., p. 97.

22. Ibid., p. 80.

23. Paul Conrad, *The King and Us,* ed. Les Guthman (Los Angeles: Clymer, 1974), p. 111.

24. As Dr. Dale Davis of Texas Tech University remarked to me in conversation, the democratic desire to see God as lower and closer to mankind may have found metaphoric expression in the description of God as "Ground of Being" in some theology.

25. *Pro and Conrad,* p. 95.

26. Bob Abel, ed., *American Cartoon Album 1955–1966* (New York: Dodd, Mead, 1974), p. 96.

27. Carmine Peppe, ed., *New Yorker Album 1955–1965: Fortieth Anniversary* (New York: Harper and Row, 1965), p. [6].

28. Mike Peters, *The Nixon Chronicles* (Dayton, Ohio: Lorenz Press, 1976), p. 150.

29. Peters, p. 69.

30. Tony Auth, *Behind the Lines* (Boston: Houghton Mifflin, 1977), p. [102].

31. Pat Oliphant, *Four More Years* (New York: Simon and Schuster, 1973), p. 70.

32. Edward Sorel, *Making the World Safe for Hypocrisy* (Chicago: Swallow Press, 1972), p. 42.

33. Peters, p. 137.

34. Ibid., p. 48.

35. *Making the World Safe for Hypocrisy,* p. 4.

36. Herbert Block, *Herblock Special Report* (New York: Norton, 1974), p. [122].

37. *The King and Us,* p. 203.

38. *Superpen,* p. 12.

39. *The King and Us,* p. 197.

40. *Superpen,* p. 22.

41. Block, p. 186.

42. Kurt Vonnegut, "In a Manner that Must Shame God Himself," *Wampeters, Foma, and Granfalloons: (Opinions)* (New York: Dell, 1976), p. 192. In November 1983, Vonnegut told me that "Trueblood" was actually a fictional portrait of a real Roman Catholic prelate.

43. E.g., a cartoon by Hans Moser in John Bailey, ed., *Great Cartoons of the World,* 7th ser. (New York: Crown, 1973), p. [102]. Similarly, beginning in 1953, the Franciscan Fred McCarthy (who eventually left that order) drew the comic strip *Brother Juniper,* the title character of which also had a "stained-glass windshield." Richard Marschall, "Brother Juniper," *The World Encyclopedia of Cartoons,* ed. Maurice Horn (New York: Chelsea House, 1980), p. 142.

5 ILLUMINATING THE CLASSICS

1. Hubert H. Crawford, *Crawford's Encyclopedia of Comic Books* (Middle Village, N.Y.: Jonathan David, 1978), pp. 206–7.

2. David Leon Higdon, *Time and English Fiction* (Totowa, N.J.: Rowman and Littlefield, 1977), pp. 1–14, et passim.

3. Daryl Sharp, *The Secret Raven: Conflict and Transformation in the Life of Franz Kafka* (Toronto: Inner City Books, 1980), p. 53.

4. Franz Kunn, ed., *On Kafka: Semi-Centenary Perspectives* (London: Paul Elek, 1976), p. 120.

5. For the relation of these parables to what Kafka called his "long study" of Taoism, see James Whitlark, "Kafka and the Taoist Sages," *Journal of the Kafka Society of America* 8 (June/December 1984): 28–34.

6. Dave Morice, *Poetry Comics: A Cartooniverse of Poems* (New York: Simon and Schuster, 1982), p. 7.

7. William Shakespeare, *Macbeth: The Folio Edition,* illuminated by Von (New York: Workman, 1982).

8. John Livingston Lowes, *The Road to Xanadu* (Constable and Co., 1927; reprint, London: Pan Books, 1978), pp. 359–62.

6 CINEMATIC MAGIC

1. Admittedly, the study of artificial intelligence is in its infancy with some experts' speculating that mechanical brains may eventually simulate all characteristics of organic ones—the basic argument of Douglas Hofstadter, *Gödel, Escher, Bach* (New York: Vintage Books, 1979), pp. 710–13, et passim.

2. Alain Silver, *The Samurai Film* (Woodstock, N.Y.: The Overlook Press, 1983), p. 185.

3. C. G. Jung, *The Archetypes and the Collective Unconscious,* trans. R. F. C. Hull, Bollingen Ser. no. 20 (Princeton, N.J.: Princeton University Press, 1959), p. 38.

7 LEGENDS OF THE TAROT

1. Richard Cavendish, *The Tarot* (New York: Harper and Row, 1975), p. 15.

2. T. S. Eliot, *The Complete Poems and Plays 1909–1950* (New York: Harcourt, Brace and World, 1952), p. 38.

3. Eden Gray, *A Complete Guide to the Tarot* (New York: Bantam, 1970), p. 5. "The inner meaning" is difficult to determine, since there are so many conflicting accounts; therefore, Bill Butler has compiled a variorum of interpretations according to fourteen divergent authorities (including himself) and twelve different decks, *Dictionary of the Tarot* (New York: Schocken, 1975).

4. Cavendish, p. 15. The most convincing speculation about the Tarot's origin is Gertrude Moakley's argument that the cards stem from the imagery of Renaissance parades, *The Tarot Cards* (New York: New York Public Library, 1966), pp. 43–59.

5. Cavendish, p. 164.

6. Arthur Edward Waite, *The Pictorial Key to the Tarot* (London: W. Rider, 1911; reprint, Blauvelt, N.Y.: Rudolf Steiner, 1971), p. 152.

7. Carl B. Yoke, *Roger Zelazny,* Starmont Reader's Guide, no. 2 (West Linn, Ore.: Starmont House, 1979), pp. 80–91; Roger Zelazny, *The Illustrated Zelazny* (New York: Ace Books, 1978), pp. 65–80.

8. Italo Calvino, *The Castle of Crossed Destinies,* trans. William Weaver (New York: Harcourt Brace Jovanovich, 1976), p. 3; *Il castello dei destini incrociati* (Turin, Italy: Einaudi, 1973), p. 3.

9. Cavendish, p. 163.

8   ARCHETYPAL ARCANA: A CATALOGUE OF IMAGERY

1. Cavendish, p. 66.

2. P. Craig Russell and Patrick C. Mason, *Parsifal* (Hayward, Calif.: Star Reach, 1978), p. 32.

3. Jessie Weston, *From Ritual to Romance* (Garden City, N.Y.: Doubleday, 1957), pp. 77–79, et passim.

4. Paul Radin, *The Trickster: A Study in Amerindian Mythology* (New York: Philosophical Library, 1956), p. 3, et passim.

5. C. G. Jung, "On the Psychology of the Trickster Figure," trans. R. F. C. Hull, in Radin, p. 196.

6. Gray, p. 14.

7. Dick O'Donnell, "It's Magic," in *The Comic-Book Book,* ed. Don Thompson and Dick Lupoff (Carlstadt, N.J.: Rainbow Books, 1977), pp. 145–72.

8. Cavendish, p. 71.

9. John Phillip Peecher, ed., *The Making of Star Wars: Return of the Jedi* (New York: Ballantine Books, 1983), p. 114.

10. Ibid., p. 229.

11. In Mike Friedrich, ed., *Star Reach: Greatest Hits* (Berkeley, Calif.: Star Reach, 1979), [not consecutively paginated].

12. Virginia Adams, "Mommy and I Are One," *Psychology Today* 16 (May 1982): 24–36.

13. Charles M Schulz, *You're My Hero, Charlie Brown!* (Greenwich, Conn.: Fawcett, 1950), p. [92].

14. Jung, *Archetypes,* p. 22.

15. Vernard Eller, *The Mad Morality or the Ten Commandments Revisited* (New York: New American Library, 1970).

16. In *Extrapolation* 24 (Spring 1983): 33–46.

17. Leland E. Hinsie and Robert Jean Campbell, *Psychiatric Dictionary,* 4th ed. (New York: Oxford University Press, 1970), p. 763.

18. Ana-Maria Rizzuto, *The Birth of the Living God: A Psychoanalytic Study* (Chicago: University of Chicago Press, 1979), p. 192, et passim.

19. David Oliphant and M Barbara O'Brien, *Solarman: The Beginning* (West Haven, Conn.: Pendulum Press, 1979), p. 14, et passim.

20. Mike and Nancy Samuels, *Seeing with the Mind's Eye: The History, Techniques and Uses of Visualization* (New York: Random House/Bookworks, 1975), p. 109.

21. Richard W Lewis, *American Adam* (Chicago: University of Chicago Press, 1955), pp. 1–10, et passim. Berger presents a less extreme form of this innocence theme throughout his *The Comic-Stripped American* (New York: Walker, 1973).

22. What Mircea Eliade calls "in ille tempore" in his *Myth and Reality,* trans. Willard R. Trask (New York: Harper and Row, 1963), p. 140.

9 NARCISSUS AND THE THEORY OF THE DOUBLE

This chapter is an expanded version of my papers "Alice as Narcissus: *Through the Looking-Glass*," delivered at the Conference on Narcissim (The World as Mirror), June 4–6, 1983, Oxford, Ohio; and "Superheroes as Dream Doubles," delivered at the Conference on the Fantastic in the Arts, March 18–21, 1981, Boca Raton, Fla.

1. Marie Coleman Nelson, ed., *The Narcissistic Condition: A Fact of Our Lives and Times* (New York: Human Sciences Press, 1977), pp. 14–15, et passim; Christopher Lasch, *The Culture of Narcissism* (New York: Norton, 1979), pp. 150–51, et passim.
2. Jackson, pp. 88–91, et passim.
3. Jacques Lacan, *The Language of the Self: The Function of Language in Psychoanalysis*, trans., with notes and commentary by Anthony Wilden (Baltimore, Md.: Johns Hopkins University Press, 1968), p. 172, et passim.
4. Quoted in Peter Homans, *Jung in Context: Modernity and the Making of a Psychology* (Chicago: University of Chicago Press, 1979), ɔp. 70–71, n. 6. Homans praises Jung and Freud for the insights they gained from their own narcissism.
5. Lou Andreas-Salomé, "The Dual Orientation of Narcissism," *Imago* 31 (1962): 1–30.
6. Allen Whitman, *Fairy Tales and the Kingdom of God* (Pecos, N.M.: Dove, 1983), p. 18.
7. *The Archetypes and the Collective Unconscious*, p. 22, et passim. The symptomology of narcissism itself (as described by Kohut) resembles the symptoms (hypochondria, etc.) associated by Jungians with domination by the *puer* (child) archetype. See Sharp, p. 53.
8. Lacan, p. 172, et passim.
9. In Nelson, pp. 213–47.
10. Dodgson, p. 90.
11. Dodgson, p. 85.
12. Derek Hudson, *Lewis Carroll: An Iḻustrated Biography* (New York: Clarkson N. Potter, 1977), pp. 242–43.
13. Heinz Kohut, *The Analysis of the Self* (New York: International Universities Press, 1971), p. 9, et passim.
14. Joseph Mileck, *Hermann Hesse: Life and Art* (Berkeley and Los Angeles: University of California Press, 1978), pp. 67, 99–109.
15. Theodore Ziolkowski, ed. and introd., *Pictor's Metamorphoses* by Hermann Hesse, trans. Rida Lesser (New York: Farrar, Straus and Giroux, 1981), p. xx.
16. Ibid.
17. Robert Rogers, *The Double in Literature* (Detroit, Mich.: Wayne State University Press, 1970), p. vii.
18. Jakob Grimm, *Teutonic Mythology*, trans. James Steven Stallybrass, 4 vols. (New York: Dover, 1965), 4: 1571; E. Tonnelat, "Teutonic Mythology," *New Larousse Encyclopedia of Mythology*, trans. Richard Aldington and Delano Ames (London: Hamlyn, 1959), p. 277.
19. Wilhelm Heinrich Wackenroder, *Werke und Briefe* (Heidelberg: Lambert Schneider, 1967), pp. 197–202; Marianne Thalmann, *The Romantic Fairy Tale* (Ann Arbor: University of Michigan, 1964), pp. 1–10.
20. *Selected Writings of E. T. A. Hoffmann*, ed. and trans. Leonard J. Kent and Elizabeth C. Knight (Chicago: University of Chicago, 1969), p. 315; E. T. A. Hoffmann, *Letze Erzählungen* in *Poetisch Werke* (Berlin: Walter De Gruyter, 1962), p. 58.
21. E.g., Lee, p. 5; "Bullpen Bulletins," *Star Wars*, no. 13 (1978), p. 30; *Thor* 1 (Oct. 1980): [48].
22. Jules Feiffer, ed., *The Great Comic Book Heroes* (New York: Dial Press, 1965), pp. 1–17, et passim.
23. Rogers, pp. 9–10, et passim.
24. Chris Claremont, *The Man-Thing* 2 (July 1981): 22.
25. Lawrence Kayton, "The Relationship of the Vampire Legend to Schizophrenia," *Journal of Youth and Adolescence* 1 (1972): 311.
26. Donald F. Glut, "Frankenstein meets the Comics," in *The Comic-Book Book*, pp. 89–117.
27. Mary Shelley, *The Annotated Frankenstein*, ed. Leonard Wolf (New York: Clarkson N. Potter, 1977), pp. 29, 324.
28. Michael L. Fleischer, *The Great Superman Book*, The Encyclopedia of Comic Book Heroes, no. 3 (New York: Warner, 1978), pp. 17–24.

29. Lee, *Origins of Marvel Comics,* back cover.

30. Chris Claremont, "The Wildfire Express," *Spider-Woman* 1 (Jan. 1981): 14.

31. Jack C. Harris, et al., *Secrets of the Legion of Super-Heroes* 1 (Feb. 1981): 15.

32. David Moench, et al., "The Blind God's Tears," *The Fantastic Four* 1 (Dec. 1980): 28.

33. Gerry Conway, et al., "Whatever Happened to the Golden Age Atom?" *Superman and Black Canary* 4 (Feb. 1981): 3. DC Comics has subsequently revised its "multiverse" (multiple universes).

34. Peter Gillis, "What If Dr. Strange Had Been a Disciple of Dormammu?" *What If* 1 (Dec. 1979): 1.

35. Bill Flanagan, et al., "What if . . . Spiderman's Clone Had Survived?" *What If* 1 (Dec. 1981): 1–31.

36. A[lfred] E[rnest] Crawley, "Doubles," *Encyclopaedia of Religion and Ethics,* vol. 3 (New York: Charles Scribner's Sons, 1951), p. 858.

37. Claire Gilbert, *Nerval's Double* ([N.p.]: University of Mississippi Romance Monographs, 1979), p. 40, et passim.

38. T. E. Apter, *Fantasy Literature: An Approach to Reality* (Bloomington: University of Indiana Press, 1982), pp. 130–51.

10　THE YIN AND YANG OF TAOISM

1. *Chuang-Tzu, The Sayings* (Hong Kong: Grand Cultural Service, 1973), p. 28.

2. Ibid., p. 2.

3. Kuang-Ming Wu, *Chuang-Tzu: World Philosopher at Play* (New York: Crossroad, 1982), p. 43.

4. In *The Translation of Art: Essays on Chinese Painting and Poetry,* ed. James Watt (Hong Kong: Chinese University of Hong Kong, 1976), p. 86.

5. Kai Wang, *The Tao of Painting: A Study of the Ritual Disposition of Painting* Bollingen Ser., no. 49 (New York: Pantheon Books, 1956), p. 92.

6. François Cheng, *Chinese Poetic Writing,* trans. Donald A Riggs and Jerome P Seaton (Bloomington: Indiana University Press, 1982), p. 34.

7. Barbara Bucknall, *Ursula K. Le Guin* (New York: Frederick Ungar, 1981), p. 31.

8. In *The Language of the Night: Essays on Fantasy and Science Fiction,* ed. Susan Wood (New York: G. P. Putnam's Sons, 1979), p. 169.

9. Bucknall, p. 68.

10. Ibid., p. 62.

11. Ursula K. Le Guin, *A Wizard of Earthsea* (New York: Bantam Books, 1968).

12. A. C. Graham, trans. and with an explanation, *Chuang-Tzu: The Seven Inner Chapters and Other Writings from the Book of Chuang-Tzu* (London: George Allen and Unwin, 1981), p. 26.

13. Richard Wilhelm, German trans. and explanation, *The Secret of the Golden Flower,* trans. from the German Cary Baynes (New York: Causeway, 1975), p. 73.

14. Chi-yu Wu, "A Study of Han-shan," *T'oung Pao,* 45 (1957): 412.

15. Bucknall, p. 38.

16. Arthur Waley, *The Way and Its Power: A Study of the Tao Te Ching and Its Place in Chinese Thought* (London: George Allen and Unwin, 1934), pp. 56, 151.

17. Bucknall, pp. 48–49.

18. Jean Shinoda Bolen, *The Tao of Psychology: Synchronicity and the Self* (New York: Harper and Row, 1979), p. 6, et passim.

19. Quoted in R. L. Wing, trans., *The Illustrated I Ching* (Garden City, N.Y.: Doubleday, 1982), p. 9.

20. Howard Zimmerman, "Ed. Notes," *Comics Scene* 1 (Jan. 1982): 66.

21. Quoted in Benjamin Hoff, *The Tao of Pooh* (New York: Dutton, 1982), pp. 141–42.

22. Anthony C. Yu, trans., *The Journey to the West,* by Wu Ch'eng-en, vol. 1 (Chicago: University of Chicago Press, 1977), pp. 36–37.

23. Ibid., p. 29; Jaroslav Prusek, "The Creative Methods of Chinese Medieval Story-Tellers," in his *Chinese History and Literature* (Dordrecht, Holland: Reidel, 1970), pp. 386, 393.

24. Cary F Baynes, English trans. and intro., "Introduction," in *The Secret of the Golden Flower,* p. xii.

11 ZEN AND THE ULTIMATE ILLUMINATION

1. Hofstadter, pp. 231–32.

2. Yasuichi Awakawa, *Zen Painting*, trans. John Bester (Tokyo: Kodansha, 1970), pp. 36–37.

3. Quoted in Bruno Ernst, *The Magic Mirror of M. C. Escher* (New York: Ballantine Books, 1976), p. 82.

4. Quoted in Hofstadter, p. 387.

5. Quoted in Uwe M Schneede, *René Magritte*, trans. W. Walter Jaffe (London: Barron's, 1982), p. 44.

6. Schneede, p. 13.

7. Stewart W. Holmes and Chimyo Horioka, *Zen Art for Meditation* (Tokyo: Charles E. Tuttle, 1973), pp. 22–27.

8. Thomas Hoover, *The Zen Experience* (New York: New American Library, 1980), p. 10, et passim; David J. Kalupahana, *Buddhist Philosophy: A Historical Analysis* (Honolulu: University Press of Hawaii, 1976), p. 172.

9. Philip B. Yampolsky, trans., *The Platform Sutra of the Sixth Patriarch* (New York: Columbia University Press, 1967), p. 130.

10. Ibid., p. 132.

11. Max Ernst, *The Hundred Headless Woman* (New York: George Braziller, 1981), pp. 154–55.

12. Ioanna Salajan, *Zen Comics* (Tokyo: Charles E. Tuttle, 1974), p. [89].

13. Hugo Munsterberg, *Zen and Oriental Art* (Tokyo: Charles E. Tuttle, 1965), pp. 31, 35.

14. Daisetz Teitaro Suzuki, *Essays in Zen Buddhism* (3d ser.), ed. Christmas Humphreys (1953; reprint, New York: Samuel Weiser, 1970), p. 353.

15. Anne Bancroft, *Zen: Direct Pointing to Reality* ([New York]: Thames and Hudson, 1979), p. 72.

16. Awakawa, pp. 140–41.

17. Bancroft, p. 5.

18. Daisetz Teitaro Suzuki, *Essays in Zen Buddhism* (lst ser.) (London: Luzac and Co., 1927), p. 306.

19. Thomas Merton, *Zen and the Birds of Appetite* (New York; New Directions, 1968), pp. 54–55.

20. Frederick Franck, *EveryOne: The Timeless Myth of "Everyman" Reborn* (Garden City, N.Y.: Doubleday, 1978), p. 153.

21. Frederick Franck, *The Zen of Seeing: Seeing/Drawing as Meditation* (New York: Alfred A. Knopf, 1973).

22. Paul Reps, *Zen Telegrams: 79 Picture Poems* (Rutland, Vt.: Charles E. Tuttle, 1959), p. 56.

23. Paul Siudzinski, *Sumi-e: A Meditation in Ink* (New York: Drake, 1978), p. ix.

24. *Essays in Zen Buddhism* (1st ser.), pp. 347–67, 409–11.

25. R. H. Blyth, trans., *Mumonkan,* Zen and Zen Classics, no. 4 (Tokyo: Hokoseido Press, 1966), p. 323.

26. Toshimitsu Hasumi, *Zen in Japanese Art,* trans. John Petrie (New York: Philosophical Library, 1962), p. 83.

27. Todorov, p. 33; Han-liang Chang, "Towards a Structural Generic Theory of T'ang Ch'uen-chi," in *Chinese-Western Comparative Literature Theory and Strategy,* ed. John J. Deeney (Hong Kong: Chinese University Press, 1980), pp. 25–59.

28. Robert Magliola, *Derrida on the Mend* (West Lafayette, Ind.: Purdue University Press, 1984), pp. 176–87, et passim.

29. Shunryu Suzuki, *Zen Mind, Beginner's Mind* (New York: Weatherhill, 1970).

30. Jacques Derrida, *Dissemination,* trans. Barbara Johnson (Chicago: University of Chicago Press, 1981), pp. 69–197.

31. Todorov, pp. 25–26.

32. Michael Green, *De Historia et Veritate Unicornis* (Philadelphia: Running Press, 1983), pp. 50–51.

33. Zalman Schachter, "Torah and Dharma," *Loka 2: A Journal From Naropa Institute,* ed. Rick Fields (Garden City, N.Y.: Doubleday Solidus Anchor, 1976), pp. 93–98; "Some Gurus not Inimical to Judaism," *Zen and Hasidism,* ed. Harold Heifetz (Wheaton, Ill.: Theosophical Publishing House, 1978), pp. 135–37.

34. "Ancient Religious Shrine Discovered in Spain," *Lubbock Avalanche–Journal*, 28 Nov. 1981, p. 12B.

35. Daisetz Teitaro Suzuki, *Essays in Zen Buddhism* (lst ser.), pp. 292–93.

Works Cited

Abel, Bob, ed., *American Cartoon Album 1955–1966*. New York: Dodd, Mead, 1974.

Adams, Virginia. "Mommy and I Are One." *Psychology Today* 16 (May 1982): 24–36.

Addams, Charles. *Addams and Evil*. Introduction by Wolcott Gibbs. New York: Random House, 1947.

Allnutt, Frank. *The Force of Star Wars*. Van Nuys, Calif.: Bible Voice, 1977.

Amis, Kingsley. *New Maps of Hell: A Survey of Science Fiction*. New York: Harcourt, Brace, 1960.

"Ancient Religious Shrine Discovered in Spain," *Lubbock Avalanche–Journal*, 28 Nov. 1981, p. 12B.

Andreas–Salomé, Lou. "The Dual Orientation of Narcissism." *Imago* 31 (1962): 1–30.

Anthony, Piers [Piers Anthony Dillingham Jacob]. *Faith of Tarot*. New York: Berkley, 1983.

———. *God of Tarot*. New York: Berkley, 1983.

———. *Vision of Tarot*. New York: Berkley, 1983.

Apter, T. E. *Fantasy Literature: An Approach to Reality*. Bloomington: University of Indiana Press, 1982.

Aquino, John. *Fantasy in Literature*. Washington, D.C.: National Education Association, 1977.

Ash, Brian, ed. *The Visual Encyclopedia of Science Fiction*. New York: Harmony Books, 1977.

Attebery, Brian. *The Fantasy Tradition in American Literature: From Irving to Le Guin*. Bloomington: University of Indiana Press, 1980.

Austin, M. "Dream Recall and the Bias of Intellectual Ability." *Nature* 231 (1971): 59.

Auth, Tony. *Behind the Lines*. Boston: Houghton Mifflin, 1977.

Awakawa, Yasuichi. *Zen Painting*. Translated by John Bester. Tokyo: Kodansha, 1970.

Bach, Richard. *Illusions: The Adventures of a Reluctant Messiah*. [New York]: Delacorte Press, 1977.

———. *Jonathan Livingston Seagull*. [New York]: Macmillan, [1970].

Bachelard, Gaston, *La poétique de l'espace*. 4th ed. Paris: Presses Universitaires de France, 1964.

Bailey, John, ed. *Great Cartoons of the World*. 7th ser. New York: Crown, 1973.

Bancroft, Anne. *Zen: Direct Pointing to Reality*. [New York]: Thames and Hudson, 1979.

Barrie, J. M. *The Novels, Tales and Sketches*. 12 vols. New York: Charles Scribner's Sons, 1901–11.

Barry, Dan, and Bob Fujitani. *The Amazing Adventures of Flash Gordon*. 4 vols. New York: Grosset and Dunlap, 1977.

Barthes, Roland. *Elements of Semiology*. Translated by Annette Lauers and Colin Smith. London: Jonathan Cape, 1967.

Beardsley, Aubrey. *The Story of Venus and Tannhäuser or Under the Hill*. New York: St. Martin's Press, 1974.

Berger, Arthur Asa. *The Comic-Stripped American*. New York: Walker, 1973.

Blake, William. *The Complete Graphic Works of William Blake*. Edited by David Bindman. [New York]: Thames and Hudson, 1978.

———. *Complete Poetry and Prose of William Blake*. Edited by David V. Erdman. Rev. ed. Berkeley: University of California Press, 1982.

———. *The Illuminated Blake*. Annotated by David V. Erdman. Garden City, N.Y.: Doubleday, 1974.

———. *Poetry and Prose of William Blake*. Edited by G. L. Keynes. Oxford: Oxford University Press, 1966.

———. *Songs of Innocence and of Experience*. Annotated by Geoffrey Keynes. New York: Oxford University Press, 1977.

Block, Herbert. *Herblock Special Report*. New York: Norton, 1974.

Bloom, Harold. *Blake's Apocalypse: A Study in Poetic Argument*. Garden City, N.Y.: Doubleday, 1963.

Blyth, R. H., trans. *Mumonkan*. Zen and Zen Classics, No. 4. Tokyo: Hokoseido Press, 1966.

Bodkin, Maud. *Archetypal Patterns in Poetry: Psychological Studies of Imagination*. London: Oxford University, 1934.

Bogan, James, and Fred Goss, eds. *Sparks of Fire: Blake in a New Age*. Richmond, Calif.: North Atlantic Books, 1982.

Bogen, J. E. "Some Educational Aspects of Hemispheric Specialization." *U.C.L.A. Educator* 17 (1975): 24–32.

Bolen, Jean Shinoda. *The Tao of Psychology: Synchronicity and the Self*. New York: Harper and Row, 1979.

Bridgstock, Martin. "A Psychological Approach to 'Hard Science Fiction.'" *Science-Fiction Studies*, 10 (March 1983): 51.

Buber, Martin. *Jüdische Künstler*. Berlin: Jüdischer, 1903.

Bucknall, Barbara. *Ursula K. Le Guin*. New York: Frederick Ungar, 1981.

Butler, Bill. *Dictionary of the Tarot*. New York: Schocken, 1975.

Byrom, Thomas. *Nonsense and Wonder*. New York: Dutton, 1977.

Byron, George Gordon, Lord. *Selected Poetry and Prose*. Edited by W. H. Auden. New York: New American Library, 1966.

Caillois, Roger. *Au coeur du fantastique*. Paris: Gallimard, 1965.

Calvino, Italo. *Il Castello dei destini incrociati*. Turin, Italy: Einaudi, 1973; *The Castle of Crossed Destinies*. Translated by William Weaver. New York: Harcourt Brace, 1976.

Cammack, Melvin Macye. *John Wyclif and the English Bible*. New York: American Tract Society, 1938.

Carpenter, Humphrey. *The Inklings*. New York: Ballantine, 1978.

Cavendish, Richard. *The Tarot*. New York: Harper and Row, 1975.

"Ceylon." *The Christian Observer*, 15 (1816): 68.

Chaucer, Geoffrey, *The Works of Geoffrey Chaucer*. Edited by F. N. Robinson. 2d ed. Boston: Houghton Mifflin, 1957.

Chaykin, Howard V., and Michael Moorcock. *The Swords of Heaven, The Flowers of Hell*. New York: H. M. Communications, 1979.

Cheng, François. *Chinese Poetic Writing*. Translated by Donald A. Riggs and Jerome P. Seaton. Bloomington: University of Indiana Press, 1982.

Chitty, Susan. *The Beast and the Monk: A Life of Charles Kingsley*. London: Hodder and Stoughton, 1974.

Chuang-Tzu. *The Sayings*. Hong Kong: Grand Cultural Service, 1973.

Clemens, Cyril. "Unpublished Letters to Dan Beard." *Mark Twain Quarterly* 7, no. 2 (1945): 22.

Clemens, Samuel Longhorne. *A Connecticut Yankee in King Arthur's Court*. Ed. Bernard L. Stein. Berkeley: University of California Press, 1979.

Clough, Arthur Hugh. *The Poems*. Edited by F. L. Mulhauser. 2d ed. London: Oxford University Press, 1974.

Comenius, Johann Amos. *Orbis Sensualium Pictus*. Sydney, Australia: Sydney University Press, 1967.

"Comic Books Return to Booming Status." *Lubbock Avalanche–Journal*. January 1987, p. 9D.

"Comics Code Rejects Daredevil Story." *The Comics Journal* (Summer 1980), p. 8.

Conrad, Paul. *The King and Us*. Edited by Les Guthman. Los Angeles: Clymer, 1974.

———. *Pro and Conrad*. San Rafael, Calif.: Neff-Kane, 1979.

Corben, Richard, and Jan Strnad. *New Tales of the Arabian Nights*. New York: Simon and Schuster, 1978.

Coulton, G. C. *Art and the Reformation*. New York: Alfred A. Knopf, 1928.

Crawford, Hubert H. *Crawford's Encyclopaedia of Comic Books*. Middle Village, N.Y.: Jonathan David, 1978.

Crawley, A[lfred] E[rnest]. "Doubles." *Encyclopaedia of Religion and Ethics.* Vol. 3 New York: Charles Scribner's Sons, 1951.

Dali, Salvador, illuminator. *Salvador Dali's Tarot,* by Rachel Pollack, Salem, N.H.: Salem House, 1985.

Damon, S. Foster. *A Blake Dictionary.* New York: E. P. Dutton, 1971.

———. *William Blake.* Gloucester, Mass.: Peter Smith, 1958.

Damrosch, Leopold, Jr. *Symbols and Truth in Blake's Myth.* Princeton, N.J.: Princeton University Press, 1980.

Daniel, Samuel. *The Complete Works.* Edited by Alexander Grossart. 3 vols. London: Hazell, Watson and Viney, 1885.

Deeney, John J. *Chinese-Western Comparative Literature Theory and Strategy.* Hong Kong: Chinese University Press, 1980.

Delany, Samuel. *Empire: A Visual Novel.* New York: Berkley/Windover, 1978.

DeLarrabeiti, Michael. *The Borribles.* New York: Macmillan, 1978.

———. *The Borribles Go for Broke.* New York: Ace Books, 1981.

Derrida, Jacques. *Dissemination.* Translated by Barbara Johnson. Chicago: University of Chicago, 1981.

Dickens, Charles. *The Christmas Books.* 2 vols. New York: Penguin Books, 1971.

Digby, George Wingfield. *Symbol and Image in William Blake.* Oxford: Clarendon Press, 1957.

Dodgson, Charles. *The Complete Illustrated Works of Lewis Carroll.* New York: Avenel Books, 1982.

Dorfman, Ariel, and Armand Mattelart. *How to Read Donald Duck.* Translated by David Kunzle. New York: International General, 1975.

Dunlap, Joseph R. *The Book That Never Was.* New York: Oriole Editions, 1971.

Dunsany, Edward. *The Book of Wonder* New York: Boni and Liveright, 1918.

———. *Patches of Sunlight.* New York: Reynal and Hitchcock [1938].

Durwood, T. Interview with David Levine. *Crimner's,* Spring 1976.

Eliade, Mircea. *Myth and Reality.* Translated by Willard R Trask. New York: Harper and Row, 1963.

Eliot, T. S. *The Complete Poems and Plays 1909–1950.* New York: Harcourt, Brace and World, 1952.

Eller, Vernard. *The Mad Morality or the Ten Commandments Revisited.* New York: New American Library, 1970.

Ernst, Bruno. *The Magic Mirror of M. C. Escher.* New York: Ballantine Books, 1976.

Ernst, Max. *The Hundred Headless Woman.* New York: George Braziller, 1981.

Feiffer, Jules, ed. *The Great Comic Book Heroes.* New York: Dial Press, 1965.

Fleischer, Michael L. *The Great Superman Book.* The Encyclopedia of Comic Book Heroes, no. 3. New York: Warner, 1978.

Ford, Paul, ed. *The New England Primer.* Classics in Education. No. 13. [N.p.]: Columbia University, 1962.

Ford, Paul F. *Companion to Narnia.* San Francisco: Harper and Row, 1980.

Foucault, Michel. *Les mots et les choses: Une archaeologie des sciences humaines.* [Paris]: Gallimard, 1966.

Franck, Frederick. *EveryOne: The Timeless Myth of "Everyman" Reborn.* Garden City, N.Y.: Doubleday, 1978.

———. *The Zen of Seeing: Seeing/Drawing as Meditation.* New York: Alfred A. Knopf, 1973.

Friedrich, Mike, ed. *Star Reach: Greatest Hits.* Berkeley, Calif.: Star Reach, 1979.

Frye, Northrop. *Anatomy of Criticism.* Princeton, N.J.: Princeton University Press, 1957.

Gardner, Howard. *The Shattered Mind.* New York: Aifred A. Knopf, 1975.

Geipel, John. *The Cartoon.* South Brunswick, N.J.: A. S. Barnes, 1972.

Gibran, Kahlil. *The Prophet.* New York: Alfred A. Knopf, 1923.

———. *Spirits Rebellious.* Translated by Anthony Rizcallah Ferris and edited by Martin L. Wolf. New York: Philosophical Library [1947].

Gifford, Denis. *The International Book of Comics.* New York: Crescent, 1984.

Gilbert, Claire. *Nerval's Double: A Structural Study.* [N.p.]: University of Mississippi Romance Monographs, 1979.

Goldberg, Elkhonon, and Louis D. Costa. "Hemisphere Differences in the Acquisition and Use of Descriptive Systems." *Brain and Language* 14 (1981): 144–73.

Gorey, Edward. *Amphigorey.* New York: G. P. Putnam's Sons, 1972.

———. *Amphigorey Too.* New York: G. P. Putnam's Sons, 1975.

Graham, A. C., translated by and with an explanation. *Chuang-Tzu: The Seven Inner Chapters and Other Writings from the Book of Chuang-Tzu.* London: George Allen and Unwin, 1981.

Gray, Eden. *A Complete Guide to the Tarot.* New York: Bantam, 1970.

Green, Michael. *De Historia et Veritate Unicornis.* Philadelphia: Running Press, 1983.

Green, Roger Lancelyn. *Fifty Years of Peter Pan.* London: Peter Davies, 1954.

Grimm, Jakob. *Teutonic Mythology.* Translated by James Steven Stallybrass. 4 vols. New York: Dover, 1965.

Guiliano, Edward, ed. *Lewis Carroll: A Celebration.* New York: Clarkson N. Potter, 1982.

———, ed. *Lewis Carroll Observed.* New York: Clarkson N. Potter, 1976.

Gutmann, Joseph, ed. *No Graven Images: Studies in Art and the Hebrew Bible.* New York: KTAV Publishing House, 1971.

Hagstrum, Jean. *The Sister Arts: The Tradition of Literary Pictorialism and English Poetry from Dryden to Gray.* Chicago: University of Chicago Press, 1958.

Hammacher, A[braham] M[arie]. *Phantoms of the Imagination: Fantastic Art and Literature from Blake to Dali.* New York: Harry N. Abrams, 1981.

Hampden-Turner, Charles. *Maps of the Mind: Charts and Concepts of the Mind and Its Labyrinths.* New York: Collier, 1981.

Hasumi, Toshimitsu. *Zen in Japanese Art.* Translated by John Petrie. New York: Philosophical Library, 1962.

Heifetz, Harold, ed. *Zen and Hasidism*. Wheaton, Ill.: Theosophical Publishing House, 1978.

Hesse, Hermann. *Pictor's Metamorphoses*. Translated by Rika Lesser and edited with an introduction by Theodore Ziolkowski. New York: Farrar, Straus and Giroux, 1981.

Higdon, David Leon. *Time and English Fiction*. Totowa, N.J.: Rowman and Littlefield, 1977.

Hill, Hamlin, ed. *Mark Twain's Letters to His Publishers, 1867–1894*. Berkeley and Los Angeles: University of California Press, 1967.

Hillier, Bevis. *Cartoons and Caricatures*. London: Studio Vista, 1970.

Hinsie, Leland E., and Robert Jean Campbell. *Psychiatric Dictionary*. 4th ed. New York: Oxford University Press, 1970.

Hoff, Benjamin. *The Tao of Pooh*. New York: Dutton, 1982.

Hoffmann, E. T. A. *Letze Erzählungen* in *Poetisch Werke*. Berlin: Walter De Gruyter, 1962.

———. *Selected Writings*. Edited and translated by Leonard J. Kent and Elizabeth C. Knight. Chicago: University of Chicago, 1969.

Hofstadter, Douglas. *Gödel, Escher, Bach*. New York: Vintage Books, 1979.

Holmes, Stewart W., and Chimyo Horioka. *Zen Art for Meditation*. Tokyo: Charles E. Tuttle, 1973.

Homans, Peter. *Jung in Context: Modernity and the Making of a Psychology*. Chicago: University of Chicago Press, 1979.

[Hone, William]. *A Treat for Every One. . . .* London: J. Stokes, 1820.

Hoover, Thomas. *The Zen Experience*. New York: New American Library, 1980.

Horn, Maurice, ed. *The World Encyclopedia of Cartoons*. New York: Chelsea House, 1980.

Hudson, Derek. *Lewis Carroll: An Illustrated Biography*. New York: Clarkson N. Potter, 1977.

Hudson, Liam. *Contrary Imaginations: A Psychological Study of the Young Student*. New York: Schocken Books, 1966.

———. *Human Beings: An Introduction to the Psychology of Human Experience*. London: Jonathan Cape, 1975.

Huxley, Aldous. *Brave New World*. 1932; reprint. New York: Harper and Row, 1972.

Irwin, W[illiam] R[obert]. *The Game of the Impossible: A Rhetoric of Fantasy*. Chicago: University of Illinois, 1976.

Jackson, Rosemary. *Fantasy: The Literature of Subversion*. New York: Methuen, 1981.

James, Henry. *Autobiography*. Edited by Frederick Dupee. New York: Criterion Books, [1956].

Jaynes, Julian. *The Origin of Consciousness in the Breakdown of the Bicameral Mind*. Boston: Houghton Mifflin, 1976.

Jung, C. G. *The Archetypes and the Collective Unconscious*. Translated by R. F. C. Hull. Bollingen Ser. No. 20. Princeton, N.J.: Princeton University Press, 1959.

Kafka, Franz. *Der Prozess, Roman*. Edited by Max Brod. New York: S. Fischer Verlag, [1953].

Kalupahana, David J. *Buddhist Philosophy: A Historical Analysis.* Honolulu: University Press of Hawaii, 1976.

Kayser, Wolfgang. *Das Groteske: seine Gestaltung in Malerei und Dichtung.* Oldenburg: Gerhard Stalling, Verlag, 1957. Translated by Ulrich Weisstein, under the title *The Grotesque in Art and Literature.* Bloomington: Indiana University Press, 1963.

Kayton, Lawrence. "The Relationship of the Vampire Legend to Schizophrenia." *Journal of Youth and Adolescence* 1 (1972): 311.

Kent, Leonard J., and Elizabeth C. Knight, eds. and trans. *Selected Writings of E. T. A. Hoffmann.* Chicago: University of Chicago, 1969.

Kimura, Doreen. "Male Brain, Female Brain: The Hidden Difference." *Psychology Today* 19 (November 1985): 144–73.

King, Stephen. *Creepshow.* New York: Plume, 1982.

Kingsley, Charles. *The Water-Babies: A Fairy Tale for a Land-Baby [sic].* London: Macmillan, 1863.

Kipling, Rudyard. *The Collected Works.* 28 vols. New York: AMS Press, 1970.

Koelb, Clayton. *The Incredulous Reader: Literature and the Function of Disbelief.* London: Cornell University, 1984.

Kohut, Heinz. *The Analysis of the Self.* New York: International Universities Press, 1971.

Kunn, Franz, ed. *On Kafka: Semi-Centenary Perspectives.* London: Paul Elek, 1976.

Kunzle, David. *History of the Comic Strip.* 2 vols. Berkeley and Los Angeles: University of California Press, 1973.

Lacan, Jacques. *The Language of the Self: The Function of Language in Psychoanalysis.* Translated with notes and commentary by Anthony Wilden. Baltimore, Md.: Johns Hopkins University Press, 1968.

Landow, George P. "And the World Became Strange: Realms of Literary Fantasy." *Georgia Review* 33 (Spring 1979): 7–42.

Laeuchli, Samuel. *Religion and Art in Conflict: Introduction to a Cross-Disciplinary Task.* Philadelphia: Fortress Press, 1980.

Lasch, Christopher. *The Culture of Narcissism.* New York: Norton, 1979.

Lear, Edward. *Later Letters.* Edited by [Constance] Strachey. New York: Duffield and Co., 1911.

Lee, Stan. *Origins of Marvel Comics.* New York: Simon and Schuster, 1974.

Le Guin, Ursula K. *The Language of the Night: Essays on Fantasy and Science Fiction.* Edited by Susan Wood. New York: G. P. Putnam's Sons, 1979.

———. *A Wizard of Earthsea.* New York: Bantam Books, 1968.

Lessing, Gotthold Ephraim. *Laocoön: An Essay on the Limits of Painting and Poetry.* Translated by Edward Allen McCormick. New York: Bobbs-Merrill, 1962.

Levy, Jerre. "Right Brain, Left Brain: Fact and Fiction." *Psychology Today* 19 (May 1985): 38–44.

Lewis, C. S. *The Lion, the Witch and the Wardrobe: A Story for Children.* New York: Macmillan [1950].

———. *Of Other Worlds.* Edited by Walter Hooper. New York: Harcourt Brace Jovanovich, 1966.

Lewis, Richard W. *American Adam*. Chicago: University of Chicago Press, 1955.

Lindsay, Jack. *William Blake: His Life and Work*. London: Constable, 1978.

Loomis, Roger Sherman. *A Mirror of Chaucer's World*. Princeton, N.J.: Princeton University Press, 1965.

Lovejoy, Arthur. *The Great Chain of Being: A Study of the History of an Idea*. Cambridge, Mass.: Harvard University Press, 1936.

Lowes, John Livingston. *The Road to Xanadu: A Study in the Ways of the Imagination*. Constable and Co., 1927. Reprint. London: Pan Books, 1978.

Lynn, Elizabeth A. *The Dancers of Arun*. New York: Berkley, 1983.

———. *The Watchtower*. New York: Berkley, 1982.

Magliola, Robert. *Derrida on the Mend*. West Lafayette, Ind.: Purdue University Press, 1984.

Malraux, André. *The Metamorphosis of the Gods*. Translated by Stuart Gilbert. Garden City, N.Y.: Doubleday, 1960.

Manlove, C. N. *The Impulse of Fantasy Literature*. Kent, Ohio: Kent State University, 1983.

———. *Modern Fantasy*. Cambridge: Cambridge University Press, 1975.

Merleau-Ponty, Maurice. "The Child's Relations with Others." Translated by W. Cobb. In *The Primacy of Perception*. Edited by J. M. Edie. Evanston, Ill.: Northwestern University, 1964.

Merton, Thomas. *Zen and the Birds of Appetite*. New York: New Directions, 1968.

Mileck, Joseph. *Hermann Hesse: Life and Art*. Berkeley and Los Angeles: University of California Press, 1978.

Miller, J. Hillis. *Charles Dickens and George Cruikshank*. Los Angeles: William Andrews Clark Memorial Library, 1971.

Miller, Lawrence. "In Search of the Unconscious," *Psychology Today* 20 (December 1986): 60–64.

Mitchell: W. J. T. *Blake's Composite Art: A Study of the Illuminated Poetry*. Princeton, N.J.: Princeton University Press, 1978.

———. *Iconology: Image, Text, Ideology*. Chicago: University of Chicago Press, 1986.

Moakley, Gertrude. *The Tarot Cards*. New York: New York Public Library, 1966.

Morice, Dave. *Poetry Comics: A Cartooniverse of Poems*. New York: Simon and Schuster, 1982.

Morris, William. *The Collected Works*. 24 vols. London: Longmans, Green and Co., 1910–15.

Munsterberg, Hugo. *Zen and Oriental Art*. Tokyo: Charles E. Tuttle, 1965.

Nelson, Marie Coleman, ed. *The Narcissistic Condition: A Fact of Our Lives and Times*. New York: Human Sciences Press, 1977.

Niven, Larry. *The Magic Goes Away*. Afterword by Sandra Miesel. New York: Ace Books, 1978.

Norton, Andre. *Voorloper*. [New York]: Ace Books, 1980.

O'Brien, Richard. *The Golden Age of Comic Books, 1937–1945*. New York: Ballantine Books, 1977.

Oliphant, David, and M. Barbara O'Brien. *Solarman: The Beginning.* West Haven, Conn.: Pendulum Press, 1979.

Oliphant, Pat. *Four More Years.* New York: Simon and Schuster, 1973.

O'Neill, Dan. *The Collective Unconscience of Odd Bodkins.* San Francisco: Glide, 1973.

Osborne, John. *The Fifth Year of the Nixon Watch.* New York: Liveright, 1974.

Palmer, Humphrey. *Analogy: A Study of Qualification and Argument in Theology.* London: Macmillan, 1973.

Palumbo, Donald. "Adam Warlock: Marvel Comics' Cosmic Christ Figure." *Extrapolation* 24 (Spring 1983): 33–46.

Paulson, Ronald, ed. *Hogarth's Graphic Works.* Rev. ed. 2 vols. New Haven, Conn.: Yale University Press, 1970.

Peecher, John Phillip, ed. *The Making of Star Wars: Return of the Jedi.* New York: Ballantine Books, 1983.

Peppe, Carmine, ed. *New Yorker Album 1955–1965: Fortieth Anniversary.* New York: Harper and Row, 1965.

Perkins, W[illiam]. *Prophetica sive de sacra et unica ratione conscionandi tractatus.* Cambridge, 1592.

Peters, Mike. *The Nixon Chronicles.* Dayton, Ohio: Lorenz Press, 1976.

Philippe, Robert. *Political Graphics: Art as a Weapon.* Milan: Arnoldo Mondardori Editore, 1980.

Phillips, John. *The Reformation of Images: Destruction of Art in England, 1535–1600.* Berkeley and Los Angeles: University of California Press, [1973].

Pini, Wendy and Richard. *ElfQuest: Book I.* Edited by Kay Reynolds. Virginia Beach, Va.: Donning, 1981.

Platt, Charles, ed. *Dream Makers, II.* New York: Berkley, 1983.

Prickett, Stephen. *Victorian Fantasy.* Hassocks, Sussex, U. K.: Harvester, 1979.

Propp, Vladimir. *Morfológia Skaski* [1928]. 2d ed. Moscow: Nanka, 1969. Translated by Laurence Scott, under the title *Morphology of the Folktale.* 2d ed. Austin: University of Texas Press, 1968.

Prusek, Jaroslav. *Chinese History and Literature.* Dordrecht, Holland: Reidel, 1970.

Rabkin, Eric S. *Fantastic in Literature.* Princeton, N.J.: Princeton University Press, 1976.

Radin, Paul. *The Trickster: A Study in Amerindian Mythology.* New York: Philosophical Library, 1956.

Raphael, Frederic, and Kenneth McLeish. *The List of Books.* New York: Harmony Books, 1981.

Reps, Paul. *Zen Telegrams: 79 Picture Poems.* Rutland, Vt.: Charles E. Tuttle, 1959.

Restak, Richard M. *The Brain.* New York: Bantam Books, 1984.

Rizzuto, Ana-Maria. *The Birth of the Living God: A Psychoanalytic Study.* Chicago: Chicago University Press, 1979.

Rogers, Robert. *The Double in Literature.* Detroit, Mich.: Wayne State University Press, 1970.

Ruskin, John. *Works.* Edited by E. T. Cook and Alexander Wedderburn. 39 vols. London: George Allen, 1903–12.

Russell, P. Craig, and Patrick C. Mason. *Parsifal.* Hayward, Calif.: Star Reach, 1978.

St. Hill, Thomas Nast. *Thomas Nast: Cartoons and Illustrations.* New York: Dover, 1974.

Salajan, Ioanna. *Zen Comics.* Tokyo: Charles E. Tuttle, 1974.

Samples, Bob. *The Metaphoric Mind.* Reading, Mass.: Addison-Wesley, 1976.

Samuels, Mike and Nancy. *Seeing with the Mind's Eye: The History, Techniques and Uses of Visualization.* New York: Random House/Bookworks, 1975.

Sanders, Clinton R. "Icons of the Alternate Culture: The Themes and Functions of Underground Comix." *Journal of Popular Culture,* 8 (Spring 1975): 836–52.

Schachter, Zalman. "Torah and Dharma." *Loka 2: A Journal From Naropa Institute.* Edited by Rick Fields. Garden City, N.Y.: Doubleday/Anchor, 1976.

Schlobin, Roger C., ed. *The Aesthetics of Fantasy Literature and Art.* Notre Dame, Ind.: Notre Dame University Press, 1982.

Schneede, Uwe M. *René Magritte.* Translated by W. Walter Jaffe. London: Barron's, 1982.

Schulz, Charles M. *A Smile Makes a Lousy Umbrella.* New York: Holt, Rinehart and Winston, 1977.

———. *You're My Hero, Charlie Brown!* Greenwich, Conn.: Fawcett, 1950.

Shakespeare, William. *Macbeth: The Folio Edition.* Illuminated by Von. New York: Workman, 1982.

Sharp, Daryl. *The Secret Raven: Conflict and Transformation in the Life of Franz Kafka.* Toronto: Inner City Books, 1980.

Shelley, Mary. *The Annotated Frankenstein.* Edited by Leonard Wolf. New York: Clarkson N. Potter, 1977.

Silver, Alain. *The Samurai Film.* Woodstock. N.Y.: The Overlook Press, 1983.

Siudzinski, Paul. *Sumi-e: A Meditation in Ink.* New York: Drake, 1978.

Skeeters, Paul W. *Sidney H. Sime: Master of Fantasy.* Pasadena, Calif.: Ward Ritchie Press, 1978.

Smith, Henry Nash. *Mark Twain's Fable of Progress: Political and Economic Ideas in "A Connecticut Yankee."* New Brunswick, N.J.: Rutgers University Press, [1964].

Sorel, Edward. *Making the World Safe for Hypocrisy.* Chicago: Swallow Press, 1972.

———. *Superpen.* New York: Random House, 1978.

Strachey, [Constance]. ed. *Later Letters of Edward Lear.* New York: Duffield and Co., 1911.

Suzuki, Daisetz Teitaro. *Essays in Zen Buddhism.* 1st ser., London: Luzac and Co., 1927.

———. *Essays in Zen Buddhism.* 3d ser., Edited by Christmas Humphreys, 1953; reprint, New York: Samuel Weiser, 1970.

Suzuki, Shunryu. *Zen Mind, Beginner's Mind.* New York: Weatherhill, 1970.

Targ, Russell, and Harold E. Puthoff. *Mind-Reach: Scientists Look at Psychic Ability.* New York: Dell, 1977.

Thackeray, William Makepeace. *The Rose and the Ring.* 1855. Reprint. New York: Brentano's, 1954.

Thalmann, Marianne. *The Romantic Fairy Tale.* Ann Arbor: University of Michigan, 1964.

Theroux, Alexander. *Master Snickup's Cloak.* Illuminated by Brian Froud. New York: Harper and Row, 1979.

Thompson, Don, and Dick Lupoff. *The Comic-Book Book.* Carlstad, N.J.: Rainbow Books, 1977.

Todorov, Tzvetan. *The Fantastic in Literature: A Structural Approach to Literary Genre.* Translated by Richard Howard. Cleveland, Ohio: Case Western Reserve University, 1973.

Tolkien, J. R. R. *The Father Christmas Letters.* Edited by Baillie Tolkien. Boston: Houghton Mifflin, 1976.

———. *The Hobbit: or, There and Back Again.* Boston: Houghton, Mifflin, [1966].

———. *The Lord of the Rings.* 3 vols. 2d ed., rev. Boston: Houghton Mifflin, 1965.

———. *Tree and Leaf.* Boston: Houghton Mifflin, 1964.

Tonnelat, E. "Teutonic Mythology." *New Larousse Encyclopedia of Mythology.* Translated by Richard Aldington and Delano Amos. London: Hamlyn, 1959.

Tuchman, Barbara. *A Distant Mirror: The Calamitous 14th Century.* New York: Alfred A. Knopf, 1978.

Tyler, Ron. *The Image of America in Caricature and Cartoon.* Fort Worth, Tex.: Amos Carter Museum of Western Art, 1975.

Urban, Wilbur Marshall. *Language and Reality: The Philosophy of Language and the Principles of Symbolism.* London: George Allen and Unwin, [1951].

Vinson, J. Chal. *Thomas Nast, Political Cartoonist.* Athens: University of Georgia Press, 1967.

Von Hoffman, I. Nicholas, and Garry B. Trudeau. *Tales from the Margaret Mead Taproom.* Kansas City, Mo.: Sheed and Ward, 1976.

Vonnegut, Kurt. "In a Manner that Must Shame God Himself." *Wampeters, Foma, and Granfalloons: (Opinions).* New York: Dell, 1976.

Wackenroder, Wilhelm Heinrich. *Werke und Briefe.* Heidelberg: Lambert Schneider, 1967.

Waite, Arthur Edward. *The Pictorial Key to the Tarot.* London: W. Rider, 1911. Reprint. Blauvelt, N.Y.: Rudolf Steiner, 1971.

Waley, Arthur. *The Way and Its Power: A Study of the Tao Te Ching and Its Place in Chinese Thought.* London: George Allen and Unwin, 1934.

Wang Kai. *The Tao of Painting: A Study of the Ritual Disposition of Chinese Painting.* Bollingen Ser. No. 49. New York: Pantheon Books, 1956.

Wapner, Wendy, Suzanne Hamby, and Howard Gardner. "The Role of the Right Hemisphere in the Apprehension of Complex Linguistic Materials." *Brain and Language* 14 (1981): 15–33.

Watt, James, ed. *The Translation of Art: Essays on Chinese Painting and Poetry.* Hong Kong: Chinese University of Hong Kong, 1976.

Weismann, Donald L. *Language and Visual Form: The Personal Record of a Dual*

Creative Process. Austin: University of Texas Press, 1968.

Weisstein, Ulrich. "Literature and the Visual Arts." In *Interrelations of Literature,* edited by Jean-Pierre Barricelli and Joseph Gibaldi. New York: Modern Language Association of America, 1982.

Wertham, Frederic. *The Seduction of the Innocent.* New York: Rinehart, [1954].

Weston, Jessie. *From Ritual to Romance.* Garden City, N.Y.: Doubleday, 1957.

Whitehouse, Peter J. "Imagery and Verbal Encoding in Left and Right Hemisphere Damaged Patients." *Brain and Language* 14 (1981): 330.

Whitlark, James. "Chaucer and the Pagan Gods." *Annuale Mediaevale* 18 (1977): 65–75.

———. "Kafka and the Taoist Sages." *Journal of the Kafka Society of America* 8 (June/December 1984): 28–34.

———. "Superheroes as Dream Doubles." *Aspects of Fantasy: Selected Essays from the Second International Conference on the Fantastic in Literature and Film.* Edited by William Coyle. Contributions to the Study of Science Fiction and Fantasy, No. 19. Westport, Conn.: Greenwood Press, 1986.

Whitman, Allen. *Fairy Tales and the Kingdom of God.* Pecos, N.M.: Dove, 1983.

Whitsitt, Julia. "'To See Clearly': Perspective in Pre-Raphaelite Poetry and Painting." *The Journal of Pre-Raphaelite Studies* 3 (May 1983): 69–79.

Wilhelm, Richard, German trans. and explanation. *The Secret of the Golden Flower: A Chinese Book of Life.* Translated from the German and introduction by Cary Baynes with commentary by C. G. Jung. New York: Causeway, 1975.

Willard, Nancy. *A Visit to William Blake's Inn: Poems for Innocent and Experienced Travellers.* New York: Harcourt Brace Jovanovich, 1981.

Williams, Charles. *The Greater Trumps.* New York: Noonday Press, 1950.

Wilson, Edmund. *The Wound and the Bow: Seven Studies in Literature.* New York: Oxford University Press, 1947.

Wing, R. L., trans. *The Illustrated I Ching.* Garden City, N.Y.: Doubleday, 1982.

Winner, Ellen. *Invented Worlds: The Psychology of the Arts.* Cambridge: Harvard University Press, 1982.

Wolfe, James. "Three Congregations." In *The New Religious Consciousness,* edited by Charles Y. Glock and Charles N. Bellah. Berkeley: University of California, 1976.

Wollstonecraft, Mary. *Original Stories from Real Life; with Conversations, Calculated to Regulate the Affections, and Form the Mind to Truth and Goodness.* London: J. Johnson, 1791.

———. *A Vindication of the Rights of Woman: With Strictures on Political and Moral Subjects.* London: J. Johnson, 1792.

Wordsworth, William. *Poetical Works.* London: Oxford University Press, 1966.

Wu, Chi-yu. "A Study of Han-shan." *T'oung Pao* 45 (1957): 412.

Wu, Kuang-Ming. *Chuang-Tzu: World Philosopher at Play.* New York: Crossroad, 1982.

Yampolsky, Philip B., trans. *The Platform Sutra of the Sixth Patriarch.* New York: Columbia University Press, 1967.

Yates, Frances A. *The Art of Memory.* Chicago: University of Chicago Press, 1966.

Yoke, Carl B. *Roger Zelazny.* Starmont Reader's Guide, no. 2. West Linn, Ore.: Starmont House, 1979.

Young, Barbara. *This Man from Lebanon: A Study of Kahlil Gibran.* New York: Alfred A. Knopf, 1945.

Yu, Anthony C., trans. *The Journey to the West,* By Wu Ch'eng-en. Vol. 1. Chicago: University of Chicago Press, 1977.

Zelazny, Roger. *The Illustrated Zelazny.* New York: Ace Books, 1978.

Index

235